THE PHILOSOPHICAL FOUNDATIONS OF EXTRATERRITORIAL PUNISHMENT

The Philosophical Foundations of Extraterritorial Punishment

ALEJANDRO CHEHTMAN

OXFORD
UNIVERSITY PRESS

OXFORD
UNIVERSITY PRESS

Great Clarendon Street, Oxford, OX2 6DP,
United Kingdom

Oxford University Press is a department of the University of Oxford.
It furthers the University's objective of excellence in research, scholarship,
and education by publishing worldwide. Oxford is a registered trade mark of
Oxford University Press in the UK and in certain other countries

First published 2010

Published in the United States of America by Oxford University Press
198 Madison Avenue, New York, NY 10016, United States of America

British Library Cataloguing in Publication Data
Data available

Library of Congress Control Number: 2010041919

ISBN 978-0-19-960340-4

For Vero and Nico

Acknowledgements

This book is based on my PhD dissertation, 'The Morality of Extraterritorial Punishment', which was defended at the LSE in March 2009. During my time as a PhD student, I received several research studentships from the Law Department at LSE, as well as the Harold G Fox Education Fund Scholarship (2006–7 and 2007–8) and the Karten Scholarship (2007–8). Parts of Chapters 3, 4, and 6 have appeared in Alejandro Chehtman, 'The Extraterritorial Scope of the Right to Punish', *Law and Philosophy* 29 (2010), 127–57 and Alejandro Chehtman, 'Citizenship v. Territory: Explaining the Scope of the Criminal Law', *New Crim L Rev* 13/1 (2010), 427–48. I would like to thank these journals and Presses for allowing me to draw upon this work. I am also grateful to Ruth Mackenzie and Philippe Sands, for their unfailing support while working as a Research Associate at the Centre for International Courts and Tribunals (UCL) over the last two years. John Louth, Merel Alstein, Ela Kotkowska, and Joy Ruskin-Tompkins at OUP have been truly fantastic.

I have presented several parts of this book before different audiences. I am grateful to participants at the LSE Criminal Law and Social Theory Seminar, the LSE Forum for Legal and Political Theory, the Political Theory PhD Seminar at the Department of Government (LSE), the Brave New World Conference at Manchester University, the ALSP Conference at Keele University, the Law and Philosophy Conference at Stirling University, the Annual Post-Graduate Colloquium on International Law at SOAS, the Society for Applied Philosophy Annual Conference in Manchester, the UK IVR Conference at the University of Edinburgh, the War Crimes Conference at the IALS, the LSE Symposium on Citizenship and Criminalization, the Research Seminar at the Universidad Torcuato di Tella, and the Criminal Law Seminar at the Faculty of Law of the University of Buenos Aires. In particular, I would like to thank Markus Dubber, Antony Duff, Katrin Flikschuh, Mathew Kramer, Bernd Krehoff, Andrew Lang, Alan Norrie, Tom Poole, Peter Ramsay, Massimo Renzo, Eduardo Rivera López, Paul Roberts, Horacio Spector, and Hillel Steiner for helpful comments and criticisms. I benefited from a detailed discussion with Christopher Greenwood on the argument of Chapter 3, and from several conversations with Fabricio Guariglia, Ana Messuti, Daniel Pastor, and, specially, Marcelo Sancinetti.

Many colleagues and friends read previous drafts of different chapters (sometimes, more than once), and provided detailed feedback. I am indebted to Chris Bennett, Alasdair Cochrane, Alfonso Donoso, Marcelo Ferrante, Charles Garraway, Manuel Iturralde, Gabriela Jugo, Nico Krisch, Larry May, Udoka Nwosu, and John Upton for the many ways in which they have improved this book. Niki Lacey and Robert Cryer examined the thesis and provided me with a challenging, though wholly enjoyable viva experience. Their written reports and the advice they gave me were invaluable to start working on the manuscript for this book. The three anonymous reviewers for OUP (two of whom are no longer *that* anonymous) have made constructive and pertinent suggestions which helped me tie up several loose ends.

My greatest intellectual debt, however, is to my PhD supervisors. I have been immensely fortunate to work with Cecile Fabre, Gerry Simpson, and Mike Redmayne at the vibrant LSE. This book owes an enormous deal to their generosity, wit, and rigour. They all read every chapter several times, providing detailed—sometimes demolishing, but always insightful—criticism as the arguments developed. Working with them has been not only intellectually stimulating, but also extraordinary fun.

Finally, I wish to thank my parents for their support. They have even read, silently and persistently, several chapters of this book. Vero has been there for me all the way. She is responsible, in one way or another, for a great deal of the happiness I have enjoyed in the last ten years. She has also contributed with a superb image for the cover. Nico came to our life two years ago, only to make it brighter and fuller. He's been patient and accommodating. I am afraid that any weaknesses or logical flaws that may remain in the argument can no longer be blamed on sleep deprivation.

Contents

Table of Cases

List of Abbreviations

AJIL	American Journal of International Law
BYIL	British Year Book of International Law
ECtHR	European Court of Human Rights
EJIL	European Journal of International Law
ICC	International Criminal Curt
ICJ	International Court of Justice
ICLQ	International and Comparative Law Quarterly
ICTR	International Criminal Tribunal for Rwanda
ICTY	International Criminal Tribunal for Yugoslavia
IHT	Iraqi High Tribunal
ILM	International Legal Materials
LQR	Law Quarterly Review
Max Planck UNYB	Max Planck Yearbook of United Nations Law
OJLS	Oxford Journal of Legal Studies
PCIJ	Permanent Court of International Justice
SC	Security Council
UKHL	UK House of Lords

Introduction

1. The Morality of Extraterritorial Punishment

Why should a Spanish court take jurisdiction over an American lawyer accused of facilitating torture in Guantanamo Bay? What empowers a London magistrate to sign an arrest warrant for a former Chilean dictator? Can it be legitimate or morally defensible for an Israeli court to try a former Nazi whose crimes occurred outside Israel and indeed prior to the establishment of Israel? This book provides a philosophical assessment of the underlying normative and conceptual issues that concern extraterritorial punishment as regulated under international law.

Extraterritoriality is deeply entrenched in the modern practice of legal punishment. States often claim the right to punish certain offences provided for under their own domestic laws even when they are committed outside their territorial boundaries. Many of them, for instance, claim the right to punish certain offences committed abroad by or against their own nationals, or certain crimes such as the counterfeiting of their currency, espionage, or treason. Furthermore, since the end of the Second World War, but especially since the end of the Cold War there have been important developments in the practice of extraterritorial punishment for crimes provided under international law. Many individuals have been prosecuted in different parts of the world for crimes against humanity, war crimes, genocide, and so on before domestic, international, or 'hybrid' tribunals which were often located outside the territorial boundaries or institutional structure of the state in which the offences had been perpetrated. Paradigmatic examples of this trend, and of the palpable difficulties it creates, are the current proceedings against Omar Al-Bashir, standing President of Sudan, before the International Criminal Court in The Hague, and the extradition proceedings against former Chilean dictator Augusto Pinochet in the UK. Finally, the issue of extraterritorial punishment is also relevant in the light of the emergence of new forms of globalized crime. The US currently holds several hundred people detained in Guantanamo and other foreign prisons. A crucial underlying claim in this situation is that the US has the right to punish these individuals even if the overwhelming majority of the acts for which they would be prosecuted have been committed outside US territory. Several of the normative claims made in this context have been applied, *mutatis mutandis*, to other phenomena such as transnational organized crime, including drug-trafficking, cybercrime, trafficking in human beings, and so on.

The legal regime governing this practice is covered in every textbook on Public International Law.[1] This book provides a different type of enquiry on the rules

[1] See eg Ian Brownlie, *Principles of Public International Law* (Oxford: Oxford University Press, 2008), Part VI. There are also other texts examining the issue of extraterritorial criminal jurisdiction from both an international and a domestic law perspective, such as Michael Hirst, *Jurisdiction*

governing extraterritorial criminal jurisdiction. It builds a philosophical argument that enables us critically to assess this legal framework, and identify which of its basic tenets can be consistently defended at the bar of justice. It is therefore neither a black-letter law analysis of the principles that are currently in force as a matter of law, nor an abstract normative account which purports to come up with an entirely innovative set of principles that should regulate the practice of extraterritorial punishment. This work is therefore inscribed in contemporary debates regarding the philosophy of international law, the justification for legal punishment, and the requirements and limits of global justice.

The topic of extraterritorial punishment certainly has a salient moral dimension. Extraterritorial prosecutions for war crimes are often accompanied by a great deal of moral enthusiasm. Many have cheered the detention of Augusto Pinochet in London, the prosecution of Charles Taylor by the Special Court of Sierra Leone, or the establishment of an International Criminal Court as a triumph of justice. Advocates of these developments are strongly committed to enlarging the reach of this 'accountability project'. Yet, this process has also been the object of controversy. Besides the fear of abusive prosecutions and unfair trials, there are other more fundamental objections. It is argued that such trials are a form of victor's justice, of moral or cultural imperialism, and of 'show trials'. Interestingly, much of what is at issue in these controversies concerns the legitimacy of extraterritorial prosecutions as a matter of right, not merely as a matter of international or even domestic law.

The search for the philosophical foundations of a particular institution can sometimes be subject to conflation or misinterpretation. The purpose of this book is not to present a set of views which claim validity across all time and space; rather, it is to provide a specific argument aimed at tackling certain issues arising from contemporary circumstances. Nor does this book present an account of what counts as a moral foundation; such an enquiry is obviously beyond the scope of the possibilities here. In David Rodin's words, its purpose is mainly to 'transform our pre-reflective moral responses into a [more] systematic whole'.[2] That is, its aim is to subject our technical understandings and moral intuitions of the practice of extraterritorial punishment to careful critical scrutiny under the light of more basic or fundamental normative considerations, so as to develop a more consistent and coherent whole. The building blocks of such examination will be moral considerations, philosophical analysis, and principles of international and criminal law as they currently stand. This book, thereby, draws heavily both on thought experiments and actual cases to illustrate or test its conceptual or normative claims.

Despite its eminently theoretical focus, this account builds on existing factual circumstances and widely endorsed legal rules and practices. That is, it takes as a given that the world is divided into territorially defined states with their own political organization and a more or less permanent population. It also acknowledges

and the Ambit of the Criminal Law (Oxford: Oxford University Press, 2003) and Cedric Ryngaert, *Jurisdiction in International Law* (Oxford: Oxford University Press, 2008).

[2] David Rodin, *War & Self-Defense* (Oxford: Oxford University Press, 2003), 8.

the existence of international criminal tribunals and other forms of supranational arrangements, and seeks to examine their actual legal framework. There are good reasons to address the empirical context in which a normative or philosophical argument is made. Even though normative claims and factual conditions belong to different levels of discourse, they are not entirely unrelated. Factual conditions usually constitute an exogenous limitation that links any normative argument to a certain state of affairs. More importantly, perhaps, they also raise normative questions. The question of extraterritorial punishment would have little relevance under other types of institutional arrangements, such as a world state, or ancient modes of political organization.[3] At the same time, however, this approach needs to stand apart from these factual conditions by looking at the normative principles on the basis of which they can be justified.

Accordingly, to conduct this enquiry we shall proceed by the method of 'reflective equilibrium' or 'coherence model' between fundamental moral considerations and the relevant legal framework.[4] That is, we will start with a set of moral principles that may be considered reliable. These are neither simple moral intuitions, nor mere personal preferences. They are normative claims which will be argued in some detail. On the basis of these principles, we shall assess the basic rules governing extraterritorial punishment under international and domestic criminal law. It is likely that some principles have such normative force that they will force us to revise certain standard legal practices; but it is also likely that some established legal rules are seen as so fundamental as to count against certain of these principles. The coherence method entails going back and forth between the basic principles and the established set of rules and practices until we reach a perfect fit between basic reliable principles and morally justified legal rules, namely, a point of 'reflective equilibrium'. This method presupposes that readers will

> be willing to modify or relinquish some of their beliefs if they could be shown that by so doing, they would strengthen the support for others that are more fundamental, and increase internal coherence generally.[5]

This book argues that a philosophical account of extraterritorial punishment both sheds new light on, and challenges, some widely held positions regarding the way in which the scope of the right to punish is currently regulated as a matter of international law. Connecting the existing legal framework regulating extraterritoriality to the normative justification for legal punishment forces us to question our 'received' knowledge regarding the appropriate regulation of this important right held by states. The proposed account also confronts the current leading philosophical justifications for legal punishment with extraterritoriality,

[3] See, eg, Shalom Kassan, 'Extraterritorial Jurisdiction in the Ancient World', AJIL 29/2 (1935), 237–47.

[4] See John Rawls, *A Theory of Justice* (Cambridge, MA: Belknap Press of Harvard University Press, 1999) and Norman Daniels, 'Wide Reflective Equilibrium and Theory Acceptance in Ethics', *J of Philosophy* 75/5 (1979). For applications of this method in criminal law theory see Joel Feinberg, *The Moral Limits of the Criminal Law*, vol 1, *Harm to Others* (Oxford: Oxford University Press, 1984); this is also similar to the methodology in Antony Duff et al, *The Trial on Trial*, vol 3, *Towards a Normative Theory of the Criminal Trial* (Oxford: Hart, 2007).

[5] Feinberg, *Harm to Others*, 18.

an important problem that has remained largely underexplored. It will be argued, for instance, that both standard retributive and deterrence-based accounts have serious difficulties in tackling the issue of extraterritoriality, by obscuring rather than illuminating the rationality of the rules that regulate this area as a matter of law. These issues are of growing importance in the context of globalization, and the initial consolidation of a system of international criminal law.

This book will defend five interrelated propositions.

1. For a given body A to have the right to punish a certain individual (O) someone's interest must be sufficiently important to warrant conferring upon A (in particular) that right, *and* A must be able to claim the authority to do so.
2. In order to explain the *extraterritorial* scope of this right we need to look at the interest that explains conferring upon that given body the right to mete out legal punishment to O.
3. A state's right to punish is justified mainly by reference to the collective interest that individuals in that state have in there being a system of criminal rules prohibiting murder, rape, theft, etc in force.
4. The scope of states' right to punish is primarily territorial, but it can be legitimately exercised extraterritorially over domestic offences perpetrated against sovereignty, security, or important governmental functions of the state.
5. There are certain offences, namely international crimes, which warrant conferring upon individual states generally the right to punish O irrespective of where the alleged crime was committed, or the nationality of either the offender or the victim.

These propositions are largely consistent with the existing framework regulating extraterritoriality under international law. They provide a rationale for distinguishing domestic from international crimes, and account for the distinct rules or principles regarding the extraterritorial scope of the right of individual states and other international bodies to punish their perpetrators. To that extent, the normative account advocated in the book can claim a significant explanatory force as to the moral defensibility of this institutional arrangement.

At the same time, however, this book also challenges some of the widely held conceptions and rules regarding the scope of the right to punish both as a matter of law and as a matter of normative argument. In this respect, it puts forward four rather controversial propositions. First, it claims that the leading normative justifications for legal punishment are generally ill-suited to deal with the issue of extraterritoriality. This is because either they lead to problematic restrictions to the territorial application of a state's domestic criminal laws (such as the inability of a state to punish offences committed on its territory by foreigners); or they collapse the distinction between domestic and international crimes by advocating broad principles of extraterritorial jurisdiction for both. Secondly, this book submits that some of the legal rules or principles currently in force governing the extraterritorial application of states' domestic criminal laws are ultimately illegitimate at the bar of justice. In particular, it argues against the right that states have to punish an offender based on the fact that either she or the victim is a national of that state. Thirdly, it argues that as a matter of normative argument, the International Criminal Court should have a broader jurisdictional scope than is currently provided under article 12 of the Rome Statute. And finally, this book suggests that although a convincing account of authority is necessary to provide a complete justification for the right to punish, the extraterritorial scope of this right is unrelated to the considerations on which this authority is explained. The authority of any given court, it will be argued, depends ultimately on the defendant receiving a fair trial and the verdict being credibly based on reliable evidence.

Before presenting the structure of the book, the specific normative question at the centre of this enquiry should be isolated further from other, closely related issues. Ultimately, any justification for legal punishment needs to make an argument of the following sort: 'A is morally justified in punishing an offender (O) on the grounds of C, D, etc' where A is a certain individual or body that metes out punishment to O, and C, D, etc are the reasons that justify inflicting this punishment. Jeffrie Murphy has suggested that providing a full account of that claim involves answering at least five interrelated, albeit distinct questions.[6] First, one needs to provide an adequate theory of criminalization, that is, of the sort of behaviours that can be the object of criminal sanctions, and distinguish criminal punishment from, for instance, torts or liability for damages. Secondly, one needs to explain the moral justification for legal punishment, namely, 'how a certain conduct which is clearly morally wrong when considered in isolation ... can be morally justified all things considered'.[7] Thirdly, one needs to explain why a particular body (eg, the state) would be legitimately entitled to perform this task. Fourthly, one would need to provide an adequate theory of criminal liability, that is, a set of rules governing, inter alia, justifications, excuses, and other defences. And finally, one would need an account of the appropriate punishments.

Arguably, not every one of these questions is relevant to the case for extraterritoriality. This does not mean that they are entirely unrelated but rather that a plausible argument on the specific issue of extraterritoriality need not sort out all of them in full. For example, examining the rules that should govern individual criminal liability in the international sphere is certainly beyond the scope of this work. On similar grounds, this book will not provide either an account of what makes certain conduct criminal or the appropriate punishments that should be available (ie, sentencing rules). In sum, it will concentrate only on the specific considerations on which *the extraterritorial scope* of the right to punish rests which, it will be argued, concern the justification for a particular body A holding the right to mete out legal punishment to a particular offender.

[6] Jeffrie Murphy, 'Does Kant Have a Theory of Punishment?', *Columbia L Rev* 87 (1987), 509–32.

[7] Ibid, 510.

2. A Brief Overview

Let me now briefly summarize the structure of this book. Chapter 1 clarifies the moral methodology and advocates using a rights-based approach to address the topic at hand. That is, it assumes that the issue of extraterritorial criminal jurisdiction can be adequately explored by considering whether and under what conditions we will confer upon a particular body (or bodies) the right to punish a particular offender. This approach has two direct sources. On the one hand, it builds upon Wesley Hohfeld's classic distinction between different types of rights, and suggests that the right to punish is essentially a normative power. On the other hand, it draws heavily on a plausible version of the interest theory of rights. This rights-based approach concedes, however, that in order to confer upon a particular state or tribunal the right to punish an offender, it does not suffice to identify a particular interest as sufficiently important to be protected by a right; we must also account for that specific body having the authority to exercise that right. Distinguishing these two arguments is crucial for the purposes of providing an analytically sound account of extraterritorial punishment, as will be argued throughout the book. Chapter 1 is also concerned with explaining the specific moral challenge presented by extraterritoriality. This normative challenge is closely associated with the principle of state sovereignty, and with the normative argument on which it rests. The book endorses a broad cosmopolitan position and advances an account of state sovereignty based on the interest of individuals living or belonging to a particular state. Under this particular framework, the main normative challenge is the fact that states enjoy a right to self-government which entails a prima facie (ie, defeasible) immunity against extraterritorial bodies enforcing criminal prohibitions on its territory.

Chapter 2 presents a justification for the power to punish based on the interest of individuals in a given state having in force a system of rules prohibiting murder, rape, and so on. This argument rests on a jurisprudential point about the existence of a legal system, and on a normative point about the way in which criminal law systems can contribute to the well-being of individuals living under them. Moreover, this justification arguably has two important advantages over most of its prominent rivals available in the literature. First, it allows us to account for the fact that the right to punish is a Hohfeldian power, and not simply a liberty to inflict suffering upon the offender. Secondly, it can accommodate the fact that both states and international criminal tribunals claim the power to punish an innocent individual (by mistake), while at the same time retaining the core intuition that it would be wrong (ie, impermissible) for them to do so.

Chapter 3 critically examines the principles that ground extraterritorial criminal jurisdiction over domestic offences under international law. It argues that the reasons that account for a state holding the power to punish advocated in Chapter 2 explain it having jurisdiction over any offence committed on its territory and over offences committed abroad against its sovereignty, security, or important governmental functions (principle of protection). It suggests, however, that these reasons are incompatible with the widely held principles according to which states claim extraterritorial jurisdiction over an offence on the basis of the nationality of either the offender (nationality principle) or the victim (principle of passive personality). Finally, this chapter argues that overall this general framework is more convincing that one that would result from some of the most influential justifications for legal punishment available in the literature.

The next part of the book is concerned with international criminal law. Chapter 4 presents a jurisdictional theory of international crimes. It argues that the defining feature of the concept of an international crime is that it warrants conferring upon at least some extraterritorial authority the power to punish perpetrators. It critically examines the leading arguments available in the literature and submits that they ultimately fail to account for the specific jurisdictional regime of international crimes mainly because they are entirely unrelated to the reasons that initially justify meting out legal punishment to offenders. By contrast, the argument provided in Chapter 2 allows us to explain precisely this normative implication for standard cases of international crimes. Chapter 4 also examines certain cases of war crimes to assess the explanatory potential of the view here endorsed.

Chapter 5 provides a fresh look at the issues of international and universal jurisdiction, that is, at the theoretical explanation for the scope of the jurisdiction of the International Criminal Court and the proposition that *every* state should have the right to punish an offender for an international crime. It challenges the standard position that seeks to explain the territorial scope of the Court's jurisdiction by reference to state consent or delegation of powers and rejects arguments for universal jurisdiction based, for example, on the pursuit of peace, and the interests of humanity as such. By contrast, it offers an alternative account based on the interests of individuals worldwide in the legal prohibitions of war crimes, crimes against humanity, etc being in force. It also examines and rejects some of the pressing charges against universal jurisdiction, such as that it criminalizes political decision-making, that it would be liable to political hijacking, or that it is ultimately an expensive taste for western elites.

The final chapter provides a theory of legitimate authority to try offenders. It applies Joseph Raz's service conception of authority to the question of what conditions a given body should meet in order to claim, itself, the power to punish an offender. This approach will enable us to conduct a philosophical examination of certain charges often raised against extraterritorial prosecutions, such as 'show trials', victor's justice, 'clean hands', *tu quoque*, and trials *in absentia* or against defendants who have been abducted abroad. It ultimately argues that although some of these considerations might undermine a particular state holding the authority to punish a given offender, they are all unrelated to the fact that it purports to punish an offender extraterritorially. In other words, although the argument for a given body's authority is necessary in order to provide a complete justification for that body holding the power to punish an offender, it is conceptually and normatively mistaken to consider these obstacles as objections to extraterritoriality.

1

Rights, Individuals, and States

1. A Rights-Based Account

This enquiry is about the right to punish offenders for crimes committed extraterritorially. This question refers to the rights that states and other international bodies generally claim at the bar of justice. Accordingly, any answer would need to clarify a number of important issues, namely, what sort of thing is a right? Why does it carry normative weight, and how much weight does it carry? And most importantly perhaps, what has to be the case for us validly to claim that X has the right to φ? These questions suggest that the language of rights can play an important role in arguing about legal punishment and its extraterritorial application. Accordingly, this book provides a rights-based account of the normative foundations of extraterritorial criminal jurisdiction.

Right-based theories may be favoured by normative, epistemological, and purely practical considerations. From a normative perspective, they are usually deontological theories. To that extent they are free from the deep difficulties raised against justifications grounded on a teleological or consequentialist structure (goal-based theories).[1] As a result of its rising popularity among contemporary philosophers and legal theorists, the language of rights has also acquired a great deal of clarity and insight. This means, from an epistemological standpoint, that the source and significance of the moral weight attached to rights can be explicated convincingly. We can make explicit to a significant extent what rights are, what it means to have a right, and what the case for a particular right is. Finally, rights discourse has become extremely influential in national and international politics, as well as in moral and legal philosophy. As we see every day, actors characteristically frame their demands in terms of rights, whether that be the right to life, the right to privacy, the right to social welfare, the right to private property, etc. This inflationary trend has cast some doubts regarding the emancipatory potential of rights discourse,[2] but it has certainly not undermined their established popularity. Rights, in short, provide a common and compelling language in which competing arguments are framed.

[1] For some of the well-known criticisms see eg Bernard Willams's *A Critique of Utilitarianism* in J J C Smart and Bernard Williams, *Utilitarianism: For and Against* (London: Cambridge University Press, 1973), 108–18.

[2] See Costas Douzinas, *The End of Human Rights: Critical Legal Thought at the Turn of the Century* (Oxford: Hart, 2000); David Kennedy, *The Dark Sides of Virtue* (Princeton: Princeton University Press, 2004).

This initial assumption about the place of rights in normative theory, however, must be made thinner and more plausible in the light of the existing literature. First, using a rights-based approach does not amount to claiming that morality in general is exclusively rights-based. There are some convincing objections against the latter claim, which I need not consider here.[3] Secondly, for a given theory to be rights-based, rights need not necessarily figure in its first premise. Some rights will be based on some more fundamental right or sets of rights. For instance, the specific right to write a political pamphlet is normally grounded on the right to freedom of speech. But not all rights are necessarily valued for rights-related reasons. Some basic or ultimate rights will usually be grounded on considerations that are, themselves, not framed in the language of rights. To illustrate, in Dworkin's theory of rights the fundamental right to be treated with equal concern and respect is not grounded on a more fundamental right but on human beings' dignity or their political equality.[4] Similarly, other rights, such as the right of individuals to criticize their government, are usually considered important wholly or primarily as the instrument of social goods. Thus, right-statements work as some kind of middle-level reasons which help us to tackle difficult philosophical issues. They 'belong to the ground level of practical thought in which we use simple-to-apply rules'.[5]

Rights-based theories may also be resisted in terms of their fit to an enquiry about the criminal law. Someone may object, for instance, that the view that the criminal law is rights-based is analytically unwarranted. Although rules and rights are usually related to one another in many normative contexts, this is only a somewhat recent, contingent association.[6] Rules and normative systems in general have functioned without being construed in terms of rights throughout most of human history.[7] More importantly, the criminal law is usually described exclusively in terms of duties and liabilities rather than rights. Its statutes describe conduct such as murder, assault, robbery, and so on, and prescribe or attach certain penalties to those who commit them. There is, many would argue, something artificial in arguing that the legal rule which penalizes the intentional killing of another person is basically stating that individuals have a (legal) right to life.[8]

Admittedly, the criminal law is best described in terms of duties and liabilities. However, these concepts can, themselves, be normatively *justified* in terms of rights, or so I shall argue below. The legal duty not to kill someone is arguably best justified by reference to the right of that person not to be killed. Similarly, A's liability to have punishment inflicted upon her for murdering B can be normatively explained

[3] See, eg, Joseph Raz, *The Morality of Freedom* (Oxford: Oxford University Press, 1988), ch 8.

[4] Dworkin, *Taking Rights Seriously* (The Impression, London, Duckworth, 1994), 198.

[5] Joseph Raz, *Ethics in the Public Domain: Essays in the Morality of Law and Politics* (Oxford: Clarendon Press, 1994), 48.

[6] See Richard Tuck, *Natural Rights Theories: Their Origin and Development* (Cambridge: Cambridge University Press, 1979).

[7] The most famous example of this is the Ten Commandments' *Thou shalt not kill*, which says nothing about anyone having a right to life.

[8] Hart in his classic *Legal Rights* claims that expounding the criminal law in terms of rights would be confusing and even redundant (H L A Hart, *Essays on Bentham* (Oxford: Oxford University Press, 1982), 186 and esp 192).

by reference to the state's right to punish offenders. It is that right that needs to be accounted for. Simply put, then, the conceptual and normative apparatus that the language of moral rights provide is not only adequately suited to tackle the issue at hand; it also clarifies to a significant extent the specific questions that we need to address, and the kind of answer we need to provide.

This chapter is therefore set to do two things. First, it will advance a particular account of moral rights, and explain how this theoretical framework applies both to individuals and states (or other artificial persons). Secondly, it will clarify the particular kind of case this book needs to make against the background of individual's basic rights, and states' rights to territorial integrity and political sovereignty over their own affairs.

2. An Account of Moral Rights

Rights have become pervasive and fundamental features of practical thought in law, morality, and politics. In virtue of this, it may be assumed that they, themselves, need no justification but rather that they call for an explanation.[9] Regardless of whether conceived as trumps,[10] side-constraints,[11] valid claims,[12] or exclusionary or pre-emptive reasons,[13] rights have significant normative force. That is, right-claims account for the strength of particular normative statements. The following pages do not provide an original account of what rights are. Rather, they concentrate on what I consider the most plausible account available in the literature. But first, a point of terminology is in order. Unless specified otherwise, this book is not about legal rights. As suggested above, the subject of our enquiry is not what legal rights and duties individuals and states have under current international or domestic law, but rather what legal rights and duties they should have at the bar of justice. The way in which this question will be answered is by recourse to an explanation of what moral rights they have.[14] Throughout, the standard assumption is made that legal and moral rights have the same structure.[15]

[9] See Raz at the beginning of Personal Well-being in his *The Morality of Freedom*. Against this, Scanlon, 'Rights, Goals and Fairness' in Jeremy Waldron (ed), *Theories of Rights* (Oxford: Oxford University Press, 1984), 137 and Cécile Fabre, *Social Rights under the Constitution: Government and the Decent Life* (Oxford: Oxford University Press, 2000), 15.

[10] Dworkin, *Taking Rights Seriously*; Waldron, *Theories of Rights*.

[11] Robert Nozick, *Anarchy, State, and Utopia* (Oxford: Blackwell, 1974).

[12] Joel Feinberg, 'The Nature and Value of Rights', reprinted in his *Rights, Justice and the Bounds of Liberty* (Princeton: Princeton University Press, 1980), 143–55.

[13] See Raz, *The Morality of Freedom*, 195–6. On this, see below. For criticism of Raz's position on this matter, see N E Simmonds's *Rights at the Cutting Edge* in Matthew H Kramer, N E Simmonds, and Hillel Steiner, *A Debate over Rights* (Oxford: Oxford University Press, 1998), 204.

[14] Moral rights must be distinguished from the much more controversial concept of 'natural rights'. Regardless of the specific content of natural rights, the main conceptual difference between them is that natural rights normally claim an 'ontological status' (Hart in Waldron, *Theories of Rights*, 78) that, to my knowledge, has never been successfully established.

[15] Fabre, *Social Rights under the Constitution*, 114; Peter Jones, *Rights* (London: Macmillan, 1994), 47–8 and Raz, *Ethics in the Public Domain*, 238.

2.1 The conceptual analysis of rights

Wesley Hohfeld's classical analysis of types of legal rights, as well as its application *mutatis mutandis* to moral rights, remains in its essential features substantially unchallenged.[16] Hohfeld argued that the proposition 'A has a right to φ' distinguishes four distinct types of jural relations or incidents, namely,

Claim-right	Liberty	Power	Immunity
↕	↕	↕	↕
Duty	No-right	Liability	Disability[17]

To say that A has a claim-right means that she is owed a duty by other(s). For instance, my right to personal safety means, among other things, holding everyone to a duty not to attack me physically. To have a liberty-right, by contrast, is to be free from a duty to act (or refrain from acting) in a certain way.[18] Take Hart's famous example: under English law, I am at liberty to look over my garden fence at my neighbour meaning that I have no legal duty not to do that. This, of course, does not entail that my neighbour is under a duty to allow himself to be looked at. He could certainly build a taller wall or plant a tree. A power can be defined as the ability to change one or more of these jural relations (liberties, claims, powers, or immunities). Examples of powers include the right to vote, to make contracts, to marry, and crucially for our purposes, the right to punish. Conversely, someone is said to possess an immunity when someone else lacks precisely this ability. Under public international law heads of state and other high-ranking officials are generally considered immune from the jurisdiction of the domestic courts of other states. This means that, at least while they are in office, they are not liable to being punished by a foreign state.

Rights are characteristically formed by more than one of these jural relations.[19] Most rights are 'molecular' rights in that they comprise several of these incidents. The right to vote, for example, is composed by a normative power, but also by a liberty (in that A is not under a duty not to vote), and arguably also a claim-right against others interfering with this act. This book will make specific reference to particular incidents when appropriate. By contrast, when using the term 'right' it will normally refer to the 'molecular' right composed by all the relevant incidents.

[16] Wesley Hohfeld, *Fundamental Legal Conceptions* (New Haven: Yale University Press, 1919). For recent accounts on rights that draw heavily on him, Kramer et al, *A Debate over Rights*; Leif Wenar, 'The Nature of Rights', *Philosophy and Public Affairs* 33/3 (2005); David Rodin, *War & Self-Defense* (Oxford: Clarendon Press, 2003); and Cécile Fabre, *Whose Body Is It Anyway?: Justice and the Integrity of the Person* (New York: Oxford University Press, 2006), ch 1. For some dispute, see L W Sumner, *The Moral Foundation of Rights* (Oxford: Clarendon Press, 1987).

[17] I modify Hohfeld's terminology in line with the most usual expressions in current use for each of these positions.

[18] Hart, *Essays on Bentham*, 166–7. Saying that B has no duty to φ is logically identical to saying that A has no right that B φs. At least a duty derived from that right. To that extent, the jural position that contradicts a liberty is termed a 'no-right'. No-right stands for no-claim-right.

[19] See, characteristically, Wenar, 'The Nature of Rights'.

Three distinctions are in order here. First, these four jural relations can be plausibly divided into two levels, the first one covering claim-rights and liberties and the second one, powers and immunities. While first order relations concern the deontic modalities, that is, they determine whether a particular action is permissible, impermissible, or obligatory, second order relations determine the possibility or impossibility of a change in someone's moral situation, namely alethic modalities.[20] To claim that A is under a duty not to deprive B of her freedom of movement means that it is impermissible (wrong) for her to do so. By contrast, to say that A is under a disability to vote does not (necessarily) mean that it would be wrong or impermissible for her to do so. Rather, the implication would be that her vote would be null and void, that is, of no legal (or moral) effect. This book is about the extraterritorial scope of a particular power: the power to punish. In this respect, this distinction accounts for the specific implications of claiming that a court C acted *ultra vires* or lacked the power to punish a particular offender.

Secondly, and related, to say that A has the power to φ does not necessarily mean that she is at liberty to do so. Typically, Amy may have the power to sell a good G she knows was stolen to Bert, even if she would be under a duty not to do so. She would be criminally liable for her act, and liable to pay compensation to the original owner, but the legal effects of the sale would stand. There is, hence, some degree of normative independence between the different levels. This is not to claim, however, that there are certain situations in which the wrong involved in transferring or modifying certain rights is such that it precludes the transference or modification itself.[21] Indeed, individuals generally lack the power to vote for a neo-Nazi or genocidal party in general elections.

Finally, a crucial feature of Hohfeld's analysis of rights is that rights are essentially a relational concept. Put differently, rights capture a normative relation between A, the right-holder, and B a certain (potentially identifiable) individual who is bound to respect that right. For instance, when Amy lends Bob her complete DVD collection of *Seinfeld*, Bob is under a duty towards Amy in particular to return it. If this is true, however, we need to make sense of a particular distinction usually made in the literature. Some rights are said to be held *in personam* while others are said to be *in rem*. This means that while the former are held against a specific individual or group, others are said to be held against humanity at large. An example of the former is Amy's right that Bob returns her *Seinfeld* collection. An example of the latter is X's claim-right not to be tortured. Rights *in rem* may seem to undermine this relational aspect of rights. However, they do nothing of the kind. Rights *in rem* should be understood as a shortcut for a significant amount of bilateral jural relationships between A and several potentially identifiable duty-bearers. The fact that we need not identify them all at once does not mean that we cannot do so. In sum, the concept of rights *in rem* is simply another way in which rights talk simplifies our normative thinking.

[20] Rodin, *War & Self-Defense*, 21.

[21] Fabre, *Whose Body Is It Anyway?*, 26. From a non-Hohfeldian perspective see Jeremy Waldron, 'A Right to Do Wrong', *Ethics* 92/1 (1981), 21–39.

2.2 The interest-will theories debate: identifying the right-holder

In the contemporary literature on rights, there are two main general theories that purportedly explain the nature of rights, that is, the choice or will theory and the interest theory of rights. The debate between them has been described as a 'stand-off'.[22] This debate is prominent enough not to merit a full description here. Both theories presuppose that rights confer some sort of benefit to the right-holder. The specific point of contention is the 'directionality of duties', that is, it has to do with identifying the right-holder to whom the relevant duty is owed.[23]

The will theory claims that having a right means having a 'legally respected choice'.[24] Thus, the essential feature of a right is that the right-holder is able to control the performance of the duty that is owed to her. She may waive or extinguish the duty or leave it in existence; after breach, she may leave it 'unenforced' or may 'enforce' it, for example by suing for compensation; and she may in turn waive or extinguish the obligation to pay compensation.[25]

There are at least three fundamental shortcomings to this theory. First, it leads (explicitly and inevitably) to the implausible claim that, inter alia, babies, children, and the severely mentally ill cannot be right-holders. After all, they do not have this legally protected choice themselves. This may not be fatal, as some of its proponents argue,[26] but it certainly seems to be inconsistent with the general understanding of rights in moral, legal, and political discourse.

Secondly, the will theory of rights finds it difficult to accommodate rights over which we have no control regarding their disposition, such as the right not to be tortured. Under almost every system of criminal law, victims of torture lack both the power to waive someone else's duty not to commit any such act, and they even lack the power to waive the enforcement of their rights by the state. Hillel Steiner has attempted to rescue the will theory by suggesting that under the criminal law the will theory vests rights in state officials.[27] But certainly it seems odd, to say the least, to suggest that the holder of the right that I am not tortured is a state official. Steiner finds this implication unproblematic. Yet, because the issue at stake is precisely the 'directionality of duties', it goes against our basic understanding of what it is to hold a right not to be tortured to claim that this right lies with the state and not with the individual.

This claim takes us to the third difficulty with the will theory of rights. In short, it fails to capture why rights are so important in moral and legal discourse, namely,

[22] H Steiner, 'Working Rights', in Kramer et al, *A Debate over Rights*. For an illustration of some of the tensions underlying the debate between these two theories, see Horacio Spector, 'Value Pluralism and the Two Concepts of Rights', *San Diego L Rev* 46/4 (2009), 819–38.

[23] Matthew H Kramer and Hillel Steiner, 'Theories of Rights: Is There a Third Way?', OJLS 27/2 (2007), 298.

[24] Hart, *Essays on Bentham*, 190. On this, see also Jones, *Rights* (London: Macmillan, 1994), 32–6 and Sumner, *The Moral Foundation of Rights* (Oxford: Clarendon Press, 1987).

[25] Hart, *Essays on Bentham*, 184.

[26] See, eg, Carl Wellman, 'The Growth of Children's Rights', *Archiv für Rechts und Sozialphilosophie* 70/4 (1984), 441–53.

[27] H Steiner, 'Working Rights', in Kramer et al, *A Debate over Rights*, 250.

that someone is *harmed* if her right is not respected. In particular, what seems to be harmed is an interest of hers.[28] To illustrate: not all rights can be explained as protections to their holders' title to control the performance of a duty. If Charles beats up Debbie very badly on the street, leaving her permanently injured, it would be clear that Charles has violated Debbie's right to her physical integrity. Now, arguably, the main reason for this concerns the pain she endured and the permanent injury she suffered, not the fact that Charles did not ask for her consent. It is therefore Debbie's interest in being free from this kind of pain and in not being injured permanently, not (merely) her title to control the performance of Charles's duty that her right protects.

The interest theory, by contrast, explains the 'directionality of duties' by reference to whose interest would be affected by the violation of the duty or would be protected by that right.[29] It therefore has no trouble explaining that children and the mentally ill have rights, or why the right not to be tortured lies with each individual and not with a state official. This account, however, is not without difficulties. A standard objection against this conception of rights is that it is unable to accommodate third-party beneficiary cases.[30] Suppose Amy hires Bert to look after her aged mother (Mary) in her absence. Normally, we would say that Amy has a right against Bert that he will look after Mary. But this seems to contradict the fact that it is Mary who has the most pressing interest in Bert fulfilling his duty. This objection is designed to make two different, albeit concurrent, points. First, that the interest theory is unable to explain the distribution of rights in this simple case; and secondly, that the choice theory explains the situation cogently. After all, it would be up to Amy and not Mary to demand the fulfilment of Bert's duty, its enforcement by the state, or eventually to extinguish it.

This objection, however, seems to miss an important feature of any plausible version of the interest theory, namely, that not every interest qualifies as an appropriate basis for the attribution of a right. If the interest of Mary were of the kind that should be protected by a right, this would make the agreement between Amy and Bert morally (and legally) superfluous. By implication, not only Bert would be under a duty to look after Mary in Amy's absence, but also other people in a similar position, such as Demian, Erin, and Florence would be similarly duty-bound. Put differently, this example does not cast doubt on the 'directionality' aspect of the interest theory; rather it shows that it needs further refinement as to which kinds of interests are in fact protected by rights. Just as Mary's interest in being looked after would not do, nor would Amy's interest in having some free time to go to see the new Woody Allen movie suffice to explain Bert's duty in particular to look after her mother.

[28] For this way of understanding rights see Dworkin, *Taking Rights Seriously*, 198 and Fabre, *Social Rights under the Constitution*, 15.

[29] For standard formulations of the interest theory, see Raz, *The Morality of Freedom*; Matthew Kramer's 'Rights Without Trimmings' in Kramer et al, *A Debate over Rights*; and Neil MacCormick, 'Rights in Legislation' in P M S Hacker and Joseph Raz, *Law, Morality and Society* (Oxford: Clarendon Press, 1977).

[30] Hart, *Essays on Bentham*, 187–8.

In sum, it is suggested that the best way to identify the right-holder is arguably to look at whose interest is being protected by the relevant right, and what that interest is. However, interests can do more than simply help us to identify the right-holder. They can, in fact, help us to answer the question of what must be the case for X to have a right *vis-à-vis* Y.

2.3 Assigning moral rights: identifying the relevant interest

Joseph Raz has influentially argued that

> X has a right if and only if X can have rights, and other things being equal, an aspect of X's well-being (his interests) is a sufficient reason for holding some other person(s) to be under a duty.[31]

Let us assume here that this method for assigning rights can be applied, *mutatis mutandis*, to all Hohfeldian incidents, namely, that interests explain not only claims, but also liberties, powers, and immunities. X would have a right if she has an interest which is sufficiently important to hold some other person(s) to be under a duty, a no-right, a liability or a disability, respectively.

It may be appropriate to note that under Raz's definition, rights do not simply correlate with duties, liabilities, etc; they ground them.[32] Rights then are considerations that operate at the level of the justification of a given institution, policy, or decision. They are considerations concerning the reasons on which governments or other people should, or should not, act. To illustrate, the right to be free from physical assault does not simply protect a sphere of personal liberty from being violated. It works as a reason to prohibit other people infringing this sphere by, for example, attacking me on the street. This is important because it shows that the explanation of who has a right, precedes the determination of who owes the person a duty and what the content of that duty is.[33]

Moreover, the notion of interest can help us to account for where the normative force that rights have in moral argument comes from. The interest theory of rights advocated here relies on the insight claimed generally by consequentialists that it matters morally whether someone's life goes well or badly for them. Interests, under this approach, connect the concept of rights to individuals' well-being. Individuals' well-being is, therefore, the fundamental consideration on which the rights-based argument provided in this book will ultimately stand. Raz argues that rights should be understood as reasons of peremptory force. That is, rights are not simply considerations of a particularly weighty sort that should be subsumed in a broader overall calculus; rights *end* that particular argument by telling us what is to be done. We should not construe this proposition as suggesting that,

[31] Raz, *The Morality of Freedom*, 166.

[32] In short, it is submitted here that both these propositions are true. Logical correlativity and normative implication are not mutually exclusive and can perfectly be coextensive. For an illustration, see Rowan Cruft, 'Rights: Beyond Interest Theory and Will Theory?', *Law and Philosophy* 23/4 (2004), 370.

[33] Raz, *The Morality of Freedom*, 184–5 and Alasdair Cochrane, 'Moral Obligations to Non-Humans' (PhD LSE, 2007), 78.

by establishing the existence of a right we have reached the end of our enquiry about what is to be done.[34] As it will be clear throughout this book, much more argument is needed in order to examine who is the bearer of the relevant right, what is its content, its scope, and exactly who is under the relevant duty, liability, etc. Rather, the proposition that rights have peremptory force means that they work as constraints on the maximization of well-being, and allow us to accommodate the key deontological insistence on the value and separateness of individuals.

Admittedly, the peremptory force of rights might create a difficulty if considered under the light of another well-extended feature of rights discourse, namely, the fact that rights tend to conflict. If we follow the interest theory of rights, conflicts of rights seem inevitable. For instance, Amy might have an interest in expressing her views that might be sufficiently important to be protected by a right. However, Bert might also have an interest in not being insulted publicly which would also warrant conferring upon him a right. Provided Amy desires publicly to insult Bert their rights would clearly be in conflict. This would seem inconsistent with Raz's claim that rights have peremptory force. Yet this is not the case for two reasons. From the point of view of terminology, we can rescue this general understanding of rights by simply suggesting that interests of the relevant type only give rise to prima facie rights. Prima facie rights exist outside particular circumstances. However, once we have examined the concrete situation we may assign one of the parties a right. Although prima facie rights can conflict, once a right is assigned in the specific case, that right works as a peremptory reason. From a normative perspective, interests can help us to tackle conflicts of rights. In this particular situation it would seem that Bert's interest in not being insulted publicly outweighs Amy's interest in being able to do so. Accordingly, we could consistently argue that although Amy has a prima facie right to freedom of speech generally, she lacks the right to insult Bert in these particular circumstances.

A further central aspect of Raz's version of the interest theory is that it provides a plausible criterion by which moral rights are to be assigned, a neglected question in some of the most influential accounts of rights.[35] His definition stipulates that someone has a right not merely if she is an intended beneficiary of a duty, but only if her interest is *a sufficient reason* for holding another person under a duty, liability, etc. Three issues become immediately relevant here. In order properly to grasp the relationship that rights capture between those who hold them and those against whom they are held we need, first, to examine more closely what kind of things interests are. As Fabre suggests, there are two mistakes we can make with regard to the concept of interest: we may define interests exclusively by what their holder wants; or we may define them as things that contribute to her good, irrespective of what she wants.[36] If we make the former mistake, we would be committing ourselves to the implausible view that a drug addict has a right that we supply him with heroin; if we make the latter mistake, we might end up forcing terminally

[34] N E Simmonds, 'Rights at the Cutting Edge' in Kramer et al, *A Debate over Rights*, 204.

[35] See, eg, Hart's criticisms of Nozick and Dworkin in H L A Hart, 'Between Utility and Rights', *Columbia L Rev* 79/5 (1979).

[36] Fabre, *Whose Body Is It Anyway?*, 17.

ill people to follow painful, though life-extending, medical treatments. A more plausible conception of interest would rely on generally making X the final judge about her own good, though it would have to admit that in certain situations she would not be in a position to make that judgement.

Secondly, whether A has a right to φ does not merely depend on the importance that φ has for her. The fact that I have an interest in watching Lionel Messi play for Barcelona FC generally does not mean that someone is under a duty to provide me with tickets for a match. This is because watching a football game is arguably not sufficiently important to hold anyone under a duty to provide anyone else with tickets. This consideration helps us to sort out the problem of third-party beneficiaries outlined above. Indeed, it would hardly be the case that Mary's (Amy's mother) interest in being looked after while Amy is absent is a sufficient reason to hold Bert, who is not related to her, under a duty to do so. This explains why Mary herself lacks that right against Bert. By contrast, the interest that Amy and Bert may have in her being able to contract his services as caretaker for her mother might, all things considered, justify the allocation of a right to do so. Sometimes the interest of the right-holder is precisely in having the power to transfer a duty, or transfer some subsidiary rights.[37] Much more moral argument is needed in order to make this case. Yet the point here is simply to suggest that in order to assign Amy the right to φ we need to identify an interest which is sufficiently important to hold someone else under the relevant duty, liability, etc towards her.

Finally, and crucially, this interest need not be an interest of A's. Take the following standard example mentioned above: under most legal systems A holds, in certain situations, the power to sell some good G to C, a bona fide buyer, that she has stolen from B. In other words, if C did not know that the good was stolen, the transference of property rights over G would be perfectly valid. It would, of course, be wrong for A to do that, that is, she would not be under a liberty to do so; but this is beside the point. What matters for us here is that if A holds herself that normative power, it would clearly not be because *she* has an interest in selling G. That interest can hardly warrant the protection of a right. If there is some interest that explains this particular power, it has to be the interest of individuals in that society (and buyers in particular) in commercial transactions on certain goods being easy and relatively secure.[38]

This point can help us to solve a well-known challenge to the interest theory of rights. Peter Jones among many others has argued that the interest theory is unable to explain powers invested in particular offices.[39] The argument goes: we normally say that a judge J has the legal power to sentence criminal offenders;

[37] Joseph Raz, 'On Respect, Authority, and Neutrality: A Response', *Ethics* 120/2 (2010), 291.

[38] Other standard examples that illustrate this proposition are a parent's right to bring a claim in court on behalf of an infant, and journalists' right to freedom of expression. These rights are ultimately explained by reference to the interest of the infant or to the public interest, respectively (see Feinberg, 'The Nature and Value of Rights', 164; and Raz, *The Morality of Freedom*, 179).

[39] Jones, *Rights*, 31–2. See also Wenar, 'The Nature of Rights', 242. For a different response to this conceptual difficulty see N MacCormick, 'Rights Claims and Remedies' in M A Stewart, *Law, Morality, and Rights* (Dordrecht: Reidel, 1983), 165–7.

however, it is unclear how his holding that right stems from an interest she may have in doing so. One could say that she would probably have an interest in holding that power because she receives a salary for doing so and that is her job. But no-one would accept that this interest is a sufficient reason for holding some other person to be under a liability to have her right to, for example, liberty modified by J.

This objection fails, however, because it conflates J's rights in her individual capacity with the rights that belong to the public office she holds, that is, to the state. It is not individual J who has the power to sentence criminal offenders but rather it is any person occupying her office. Indeed, once she finishes work, hangs up her robe, and goes home, J lacks the normative power to punish the thief who tries to steal her purse on the tube. There seems to be no other way of explaining how these rights are transferred from judge J to judge Z when, for instance, J goes on holiday, or is on leave due to illness and Z decides an urgent pending case. Once J is back at work it would be awkward for her to say that *her* rights have been infringed by Z. The only plausible way of explaining the situation is by saying that these powers belong to the state, and that they are assigned to a particular office rather than to a particular person. Of course some individual must occupy that office, but this hardly entails that the powers are her own. If we consider that power as belonging to the state (as an artificial person) then the interest that explains that power is probably not the individual interest of the office-holder, but a collective interest in the state having that legal power.

We need not examine this claim any further here. But it may be worth pointing to a specific feature of the justification for this kind of power that will be of significant importance later in the book. In some cases, it is not enough for X to have the power to φ, that an interest of X's would be served by the conferral of that power; X must also have the authority to φ.[40] Let me illustrate this distinction. Suppose A needs drug D to fight her illness and B, who is an advanced student of medicine, knows about this illness and knows that drug D would be appropriate. Although B would arguably be justified in prescribing D to A, he would not have the normative power to do so. This is not because A lacks the relevant interest in getting the drug, or B lacks the relevant interest in prescribing it for her, but rather because B lacks the authority to do so. Similarly, it might well be, for instance, that the state in which a particular offence was committed—that is, the territorial state—would be justified in punishing the offender. This only means that someone has a relevant interest in the territorial state punishing this offender that is sufficiently important to be protected by a power. However, we may refuse to assign to that state (in particular) such power because that state would decide whether she should be punished on the basis of a confession extracted by torture. That is, although this state would be justified in punishing this offender, it would arguably lack the authority to do so.[41]

[40] Joseph Raz, *Practical Reason and Norms* (Oxford: Oxford University Press, 1999), 101.

[41] A full account of the authority to punish is provided in Chapter 6 below.

2.4 Who can have rights: individual interests and the state

A final point is in order. Under the version of the interest theory of rights endorsed here, X would have a right if and only if X is the kind of entity that can have interests. It would seem clear that human beings are the kind of beings that can have interests, and that some of these interests are sufficiently important to be protected by rights. It is also quite uncontroversial that states and international institutions (as well as corporations) are also the type of entities that can have rights. Raz makes this point explicitly when he argues that X is capable of having rights if and only if either his well-being is of ultimate value or he is an 'artificial person'.[42] This point, however, should not be conflated with the point about whose interest explains the rights that states have.[43] Irrespective of whether states have rights as a result of their being of ultimate or merely of derivative or instrumental value, the fact is that the claim that they can have rights hardly needs any defence in light of the current literature. What kind of rights states have and why they do so is the topic of the next section.

3. The Normative Challenges of an Account of Extraterritorial Punishment

To clarify the type of case this book needs to make, it is necessary to identify the specific normative challenges that the issue of extraterritoriality raises. As suggested above, the account of extraterritorial punishment that will be advocated here relies on the proposition that the extraterritorial scope of a state's power to punish a given offender is largely determined by the reasons that justify it holding this power in the first place. Accordingly, the answer to the question about the relevant challenges lies with a significant feature of the concept of normative justification, namely, with the question regarding to whom we have to justify the power of a particular body to mete out legal punishment to a particular offender. Standard accounts of legal punishment have been concerned with justifying this power *vis-à-vis* the offender. The account developed here will address a particularly demanding variation of this traditional problem, namely, the need to justify to the offender being under a liability to be punished by an *extraterritorial body.*

Yet extraterritorial punishment has also been considered inconsistent with, or at least problematic under, the light of the principle of state sovereignty.[44] The world is divided into political entities with an exclusive right to regulate the conduct

[42] Raz, *The Morality of Freedom*, 166.

[43] For the time being it is not necessary to take sides with either the corporate or the collective theory of group rights. On this debate see below.

[44] See, eg, Andrew Altman and Christopher Heath Wellman, *A Liberal Theory of International Justice* (Oxford: Oxford University Press, 2009), 76; Larry May, *Crimes against Humanity. A Normative Account* (Cambridge: Cambridge University Press, 2005), Introduction; Geoff Gilbert, 'Crimes sans Frontières: Jurisdictional Problems in English Law', *BYIL* 63 (1992), 416; and Walter Wheeler Cook, 'The Application of the Criminal Law of a Country to Acts Committed by Foreigners Outside the Jurisdiction', *West Virginia LQ* XL/4 (1934), 303–4.

of individuals within their territorial borders. A crucial normative difficulty with extraterritorial criminal jurisdiction is, then, that it is not claimed exclusively on the high seas, or Antarctica for that matter, but rather on the territory of another sovereign state. In Brownlie's words, 'the sufficiency of grounds for jurisdiction is an issue normally considered relative to the rights of other states and not [only] as a question of basic competence'.[45] Analytically, the classical doctrine of state sovereignty can be conceptualized in terms of three basic propositions. A sovereign state is, first of all, a 'political authority which recognizes no superior', that is, that claims supreme law-making and enforcement authority over a certain territory.[46] Sovereignty also entails the 'claim [of every state] to be politically and juridically independent'.[47] Finally, not only can each state claim independence from any political superior for itself, but each must also recognize the validity of the same claim by all the others.[48]

This traditional account of state sovereignty as a defining element of the constitutional doctrine of the laws of nations would seem to bar the exercise of extraterritorial criminal jurisdiction entirely, unless authorized by the territorial state. International law, however, seems to allow for the exercise of extraterritorial jurisdiction under certain circumstances, irrespective of any explicit authorization.[49] Thus, if we are to explain the precise normative challenge that the principle of state sovereignty presents for an account of extraterritorial punishment, we need to provide a more nuanced explanation of the normative argument underpinning this legal principle.

There have been three main traditions of political and philosophical thought that have tried to make sense of the concept of state sovereignty. For the sake of simplicity, we may distinguish them under the names of Realists, Social Liberals, and Cosmopolitans.[50] This book advocates a standard version of the cosmopolitan position. Its main purpose is to explain how this position accounts for certain specific rights that states hold, and which raise normative challenges for the justification of extraterritorial punishment. But before going into this, let me

[45] Ian Brownlie, *Principles of Public International Law* (Oxford: Oxford University Press, 2008), 299.

[46] Martin Wight, *Systems of States* (Swansea: Leicester University Press, 1977), 23 and 129; Charles Beitz, *Political Theory and International Relations* (Princeton: Princeton University Press, 1979); and Caney, *Justice Beyond Borders*, 150. See also Art I of the Montevideo Convention on Rights and Duties of States (signed 26 December 1933), and Brownlie, *Principles of Public International Law*, 105 and ff.

[47] Wight, *Systems of States*, 130. See also, Francis Harry Hinsley, *Sovereignty* (Cambridge: Cambridge University Press, 1966), which is still arguably the standard text on this issue.

[48] Wight, *Systems of States*, 23.

[49] These circumstances will be examined in Chapters 3 and 4 below.

[50] I follow here Charles Beitz in the Afterword to his *Political Theory and International Relations*, 214–15. See also David Held, 'Law of States, Law of Peoples', *Legal Theory* 8/2 (2002), 1–44 and Caney, *Justice Beyond Borders* (although he adds to this threefold distinction the Nationalists). They have received, however, different names in the literature. Hedley Bull calls them Machiavellians (or Hobbesians), Grotians, and Kantians (see his introduction to Martin Wight, *International Theory: The Three Traditions* (London: Leicester University Press, 1991). Martin Wight refers to them as Realists, Rationalists, and Revolutionists (id).

briefly clarify why I will set aside the claims of Realists and Social Liberals for the purposes of this book.

Realists' and Social Liberals' arguments usually share at least two important features: they are both state-centric and they portray international society as a state-of-nature situation between (generally self-interested) state actors.[51] Accordingly, they base their positions on a two-level argument. First, they assume that states in the international sphere are analogous to individuals in the interpersonal realm (this position is usually referred to as the domestic analogy). The second step, however, is different for each of them. Realists use the philosophical apparatus of a Hobbesian state of nature, namely, they claim that sovereigns are in a state of war of every sovereign against every sovereign.[52] Social Liberals, by contrast, describe it more in Lockean terms. They acknowledge the existence of international moral norms or a 'law of nature that obliges every one', but they are concerned with the lack of centralized enforcement.[53] Ultimately, Social Liberals build their normative argument on both individuals' and states' claims to negative liberty, by which they mean the right to non-intervention or non-interference in their internal affairs.[54]

Regardless of other considerations, it may be argued that these two positions share a common weakness. Namely, they rely too heavily on the domestic analogy. States are portrayed in the international arena as artificial persons and they are recognized as having roughly the same capacities and rights that individuals would have in a similar state-of-nature situation. Hence, both the Realists and Social Liberals consider states as the ultimate units of moral concern for the purposes of any discussion on principles of international justice. Jeff McMahan has plausibly suggested that this domestic analogy has somewhat lost much of its appeal as a heuristic device for thinking about the moral relations among states in light of recent events.[55] With conflicts *within* states becoming the norm rather than the exception, it has become clear that states' violations of the human rights of their citizens have become a major source of concern. To put it more broadly, unlike individuals, states are formed by a multiplicity of persons and groups who are to be considered distinct from the state, and who are themselves units of moral concern.

[51] This is true of many of the classical scholars of international theory or international law. Among them are the works by Hobbes, Locke, Wolff, de Vattel, and Puffendorf.

[52] Thomas Hobbes, *Leviathan* (Indianapolis: Hackett, 1994), 76. Standardly, Hans Morgenthau argued that there is 'a profound and neglected truth hidden in Hobbes's extreme dictum that the state creates morality as well as law, and that there is neither morality nor law outside the state' (quoted in Gerry Simpson, 'The Guises of Sovereignty' in Thakur and Sampford (eds), *The End of Westphalia* (Tokyo: United Nations University Press, 2006) 11).

[53] John Locke, *Two Treatises of Government* (Cambridge: Cambridge University Press, 1988) II, ch VI.

[54] Beitz, *Political Theory and International Relations*, 69–70. I follow him in his distinction between negative—justifying the right to non-intervention—and positive autonomy—that explains the right to self-determination (ibid, 92–3). While the former requires only that states do not interfere in any way in the internal affairs of other states, eg by punishing offences committed in their territory, the latter 'requires that the internal authority of international order be changed and might support intervention by third parties in a group's struggle for independence from foreign rule' (ibid). Only the former notion is needed to justify state sovereignty along the lines described above.

[55] Jeff McMahan, 'Aggression and Punishment' in Larry May (ed), *War: Essays in Political Philosophy* (Cambridge: Cambridge University Press, 2008), 73.

Moreover, states also lack the unity of consciousness that characterizes individuals, and are not organic wholes with the integrity attached to persons *qua* persons.[56] As Peter Jones puts it

> When an individual sacrifices one of his desires for the sake of another of his desires, the individual who sacrifices is also the individual who gains. When a society sacrifices the good of some individuals for the good of other individuals, the losers are not identical with the gainers.[57]

Thus, while the first case is generally unproblematic, the second one can often be morally unacceptable. This point has implications for the second step of each of these arguments.

In the case of Realists, the Hobbesian state-of-nature argument standardly grounds an absolute right to self-preservation. This is not meant only as an empirical or explanatory thesis but also as a normative one.

> The necessity (or 'duty') to follow the national interest is dictated by a rational appreciation of the fact that other states will do the same, using force when necessary, in a manner unrestrained by a consideration of the interests of other actors or of the international community.[58]

The corollary of this is that 'every Common-wealth, (not every man) has an absolute Libertie, to doe what it shall judge ... most conducing to their benefit'.[59]

A first difficulty with this position lies with the notion of national or better state interest and how best to define it. As argued above, a plausible conception of interests can be defined neither on purely objective (eg, 'physical survival, autonomy, and economic well-being')[60] nor on purely subjective grounds. Realists do not provide a solution to this difficulty.[61] It has been argued here that, with certain restrictions, interests must generally be defined by those who hold them. But ultimately this position obscures rather than clarifies the challenge that sovereignty poses for extraterritorial punishment. If states are morally entitled to pursue their national interest and each one of them is the relevant judge as to what that interest is, there seem to be no moral grounds on which they can oppose or criticize the extraterritorial application of other states' domestic criminal law or of international criminal laws on their territory. Thus, regardless of its explanatory power in terms of how states actually behave, the realist position is simply unable to account for the normative challenge that state sovereignty presents *vis-à-vis* the justification for extraterritorial punishment.

Besides, one may readily argue that many of the empirical premises on which the Hobbesian interpersonal state-of-nature argument rests, are simply inaccurate when applied at the inter-state level. Namely, that individuals are the only actors in interpersonal relations, that they are relatively equal in power, that they are entirely independent of each other, and that they cannot have reliable expectations

[56] Beitz, *Political Theory and International Relations*, 81.
[57] Jones, *Rights*, 63.
[58] Beitz, *Political Theory and International Relations*, 28.
[59] Hobbes, *Leviathan*, 149.
[60] Alexander Wendt, *Social Theory of International Politics* (Cambridge: Cambridge University Press, 1999), 235–7.
[61] Caney, *Justice Beyond Borders*, 8–9.

of reciprocal compliance. All these features which seem relatively accurate in interpersonal relationships are much more controversial as plausible empirical descriptions applicable to states in the international society.[62] In the international sphere we see beside states, international institutions such as the United Nations, the International Monetary Fund, the World Trade Organization, the International Court of Justice, non-state actors and organizations such as NGOs, corporations, etc, and certainly a growing concern with individuals. States are obviously unequal in power, and they are increasingly interdependent as a consequence of globalization. Finally, to a significant extent and partly because of their interdependence and their acknowledgement of other actors they can to a significant extent have reliable expectations of reciprocal compliance in a large number of areas. This, in short, seems to undermine the normative implications of the argument, that is, that we ought to recognize in states the kind of unfettered liberties which this argument would grant individuals in that state-of-nature situation.

A similar objection may be raised against the Social Liberals' second step of the argument. Individual liberty is generally considered of moral value because we assume that each individual is in a better position than anyone else to decide what is good for her. This explains the individual right to non-interference in a state-of-nature situation. States, so the argument goes, may also claim a right to non-intervention on the ground that they are also in a better position to decide what is good for them. So far, so simple. However, as previously argued, states differ from individuals in that they are formed by independent units which are themselves of ultimate moral concern. An absolute principle of state sovereignty *qua* negative liberty (non-intervention) would thus be problematic precisely because it would allow unlimited conflict with the right to the negative liberty of individuals in that state. This is of particular relevance in a world, such as our own, in which a number of states persist in carrying out mass atrocities against sections of their own populations. To put it boldly, it is precisely because individuals must be respected as sources of moral concern that we should not allow states to claim a right to non-interference analogous to that which individuals hold in a Lockean state-of-nature situation or in a Millian type of civil society.[63]

These considerations have led many scholars to deny that the principle of sovereignty is of any moral worth. In some recent work, sovereignty seems to be one of the major threats to the accomplishment of certain goals that are deemed of great value such as the protection of human rights.[64] According to this point of view, the principle of state sovereignty necessarily contains the 'unfortunate implication of providing legitimacy for the national repression of citizens, or at least impunity for tyrants'.[65] However, this conclusion is unwarranted. This line

[62] See Beitz, *Political Theory and International Relations*, 36. For an instructive discussion about the inaccuracy of these empirical assumptions see id, 37–50.

[63] Ibid, 81. See also McMahan, 'Aggression and Punishment', 72.

[64] See, eg, Antonio Cassese, *International Law in a Divided World* (Oxford: Clarendon Press, 1986), 148 and Geoffrey Robertson, *Crimes against Humanity* (London: Allen Lane, 1999).

[65] Martti Koskenniemi, 'The Future of Statehood', *Harvard International LJ* 32/2 (1991), 397.

of argument seems to overlook the fact that sovereignty has also been praised for its emancipatory potential and its status as a bulwark against imperialism.[66] State sovereignty is therefore not simply an anachronistic political concept with a long history on its back and a bunch of unpresentable moral credentials. The principle of state sovereignty can not only be made compatible with the fundamental rights of individuals; it can also be *justified* by reference to their own status as ultimate units of moral concern.

To provide such an account we may draw on two complementary sources. On the one hand, we can rely on a standard version of the cosmopolitan position. Cosmopolitanism can be succinctly defined by three basic propositions: (a) individuals are the ultimate units of moral concern; (b) this status of ultimate unit of moral concern is attached to every single human being; and (c) this special status has global force, that is, individuals are ultimate units of moral concern for everyone, not only their fellow nationals, co-religionists, etc.[67] So defined, cosmopolitanism is not necessarily committed to advocating global institutions. We should not conflate this set of basic moral tenets (moral cosmopolitanism) with the issue of its proper institutionalization (institutional cosmopolitanism).[68]

On the other hand, this account will draw on the conceptual analysis of rights elaborated above. That is, to clarify the normative challenge that the principle of state sovereignty creates for an account of extraterritorial punishment it is necessary to identify not only the rights entailed by this principle, but also the specific Hohfeldian incidents that characterize each of them. This type of analysis will provide our account with a great deal of clarity and precision. As suggested, each of these incidents must be explained by reference to a particular interest. This leads us to an important analytical point. Most if not all the rights associated with the principle of state sovereignty will be conceived as group rights. Now, there are two conceptions of group rights in the literature, collective and corporate rights. While the former are based only on a joint interest in a good that justifies the imposition of duties, liabilities, etc upon others, and takes individuals as the ultimate units of moral concern,[69] corporate rights are based on the attribution of moral standing to a group that is somehow separate from, and not wholly reducible to, the moral

[66] Frédéric Mégret, 'The Politics of International Criminal Justice', *EJIL* 13/5 (2002).

[67] Thomas Pogge, 'Cosmopolitanism and Sovereignty' in Chris Brown (ed), *Political Restructuring in Europe: Ethical Perspectives* (London: Routledge, 1994), 89–90.

[68] For this distinction see Charles Beitz, 'Cosmopolitan Liberalism and the States System', in ibid, 124–6.

[69] Peter Jones, 'Group Rights and Group Oppression', *J of Political Philosophy* 7/4 (1999) quoting Joseph Raz who, in turn, argues that, in order to be a collective right, the following conditions must be met:

> First, it exists because an aspect of the interest of human beings justifies holding some person(s) to be subject to a duty. Second, the interests in question are the interests of individuals as members of a group in a public good and the right is a right to that public good because it serves their interest as members of the group. Thirdly, the interest of no single member of that group in that public good is sufficiently by itself to justify holding another person to be subject to a duty. (Raz, *The Morality of Freedom*, 208.).

standing of the individuals who constitute the group.[70] The argument advocated here for assigning certain rights to states is based on the collective conception of group rights. This conception is not only compatible with the cosmopolitan moral position endorsed above, but it also avoids the shortcomings of both the Realist and Social Liberal positions, or so it will be argued below.

Of the many cosmopolitan arguments underpinning the principle of state sovereignty available in the literature, I shall examine here only two.[71] The first is ultimately based on its capacity to provide individuals with physical protection. The second rests on the concept of self-determination or, more precisely, self-government. Each of them can be translated into the language of rights, and they are both ultimately based on the well-being of individuals. Together they explain some of the core features of the principle of state sovereignty without necessarily falling into any of the flaws considered above. Yet each of them accounts for different Hohfeldian incidents. The argument based on physical security only entails states holding a claim-right to territorial integrity. By contrast, the argument based on self-government will account for states' power to dictate legal rules and, crucially, to their holding an immunity against extraterritorial authorities dictating legal rules on their territory. It is this latter argument that ultimately constitutes the relevant normative challenge that a justification for extraterritorial punishment must meet.

Let me turn, first, to the argument based on physical security. Larry May, for instance, develops his account of crimes against humanity mainly against this particular argument. He argues that

> One of the most common arguments in favor of sovereignty ... is that [s]tates do a reasonably good job of protecting the well-being and freedom of individual subjects.[72]

This position suggests that

> The moral purpose of the modern state [lies on] the augmentation of individuals' purposes and potentialities, in the cultivation of a social, economic and political order that enables individuals to engage in the self-directed pursuit of their 'interests'.[73]

This, of course, is grounded on the assumption that it is only within a territorially defined state that individuals can enjoy sufficient physical security to act autonomously and achieve a significant amount of well-being. In Antonio Cassese's words,

> Today it could be maintained with greater truthfulness that without the protection of a State human beings are likely to endure more suffering and hardship than what is likely to be their lot in the normal course of events.[74]

[70] Jones, 'Group Rights and Group Oppression', 362–3.

[71] For a summary of different varieties of cosmopolitanism, see Caney, *Justice Beyond Borders*, ch 5.

[72] May, *Crimes against Humanity*, 10.

[73] Christian Reus-Smit, *The Moral Purpose of the State* (Princeton: Princeton University Press, 1999), 123.

[74] Antonio Cassese, *International Law* (Oxford: Oxford University Press, 2001), 4.

This proposition holds, admittedly, as long as there is no world sovereign. As Grotius argued, state sovereignty is important largely because there is no world state that would protect individuals from attacks by enemy and competing groups.

A plausible version of the physical security argument goes as follows:

1. Individuals' well-being is of moral worth.
2. Individuals can only enjoy a decent amount of well-being when they have some degree of physical security.
3. In the absence of a world state, states provide individuals with a significant level of physical security.
4. States can only provide this security when they are granted a right to territorial integrity.
5. Thus, this joint interest shared by individuals in a given state is sufficiently important to warrant conferring upon that state a prima facie right to territorial integrity.

It is worth examining the precise implications of this argument. The right to territorial integrity is a right that only states can claim. This right is based on an argument of an instrumental kind, that is, it is morally justified on the basis of individuals' well-being. As a result of this, it is not an absolute right; it is valuable only insofar as it provides individuals with a significant amount of physical security and contributes, thereby, to their well-being. The problem with this argument for an account of extraterritorial punishment, however, is that it does not capture the real normative difficulty that state sovereignty creates for the power to punish an offender extraterritorially. It provides only a justification for a first order claim-right held by states against other extraterritorial bodies physically intervening on their territory. This is all a state needs to be granted in order to supply individuals with the amount of security that is assumed in point 3, and this claim-right is entirely compatible with any form of extraterritorial punishment. To put it in the language of international law, this account explains why states cannot exercise their executive criminal jurisdiction, not their legislative or adjudicative jurisdiction over crimes committed abroad.[75] Indeed, it is widely accepted that when an extraterritorial state wants lawfully to prosecute a particular offender for an offence she committed abroad (on the territory of S2), it has to request her extradition and request S2's assistance for any investigatory activities on S2's territory. Accordingly, the physical security argument does not ultimately explain what the problem with extraterritorial law-making and adjudication would be if the prosecuting state avoids sending its security forces to enforce a particular decision without S2's consent.

Self-government constitutes the other standard justification for the cluster of rights arising from the principle of state sovereignty.[76] Its value, it has been

[75] See, eg, Michael Akehurst, 'Jurisdiction in International Law', *BYIL* 46 (1972–1973), 145–257.

[76] There are two different questions related to the right to self-determination or self-government that need not be conflated. One of them concerns who has the right to make certain decisions on public matters. A related, although different (and possibly prior), question is who has the right to

suggested, is the value of entrusting political power over a group and its members to the group itself.[77] This proposition already has an important limit built into it: not every decision is subject to this cluster of rights, but only public or political matters. It is beyond the scope of this enquiry to examine this limitation in any detail; it should suffice to note that this consideration allows for the important liberal intuition that there are certain private matters which neither the state nor any other political authority should hold the power to regulate. An obvious example would be the choice of sexual partners. In any event, insofar as this book does not specifically deal with issues of criminalization, that is, of which specific conduct can be the subject of criminal prohibition, this aspect is largely unproblematic for the account of extraterritoriality that will be advocated here. Criminal wrongdoing, at least when it refers to standard cases such as murder, rape, or crimes against humanity, is uncontroversially considered a public matter.

A convincing explanation of the value of the right to self-government goes as follows:[78]

1. Individuals' well-being is of moral worth.
2. Membership of certain encompassing groups, such as nations, has a profound and far reaching influence on individuals' lives.
3. To some significant extent, the well-being of these individuals depends on the prosperity and self-respect of the group to which they belong.
4. The prosperity and self-respect of the group is aided by, or it might be impossible to secure without, the group enjoying political sovereignty over its own affairs.
5. Thus, the enjoyment of political sovereignty by the group is an important aspect of the individual well-being of its members and, as such, sufficiently important to warrant the protection of a prima facie right.[79]

As it stands, this argument has at least three important implications. First, it is directly related to the question of political authority. It answers the question, 'who has the right to decide?' Secondly, self-government accounts for the main features

answer that first question. The answers to these questions may overlap; however, the justification for both answers would be different. For our purposes here, only the first question is relevant. The literature on secession, the field in which this general right has been more extensively discussed, is concerned with the second question. Finally, neither of these questions should be conflated with the issue of title to *a specific* area of territory, such as the conflicting claims of Israelis and Palestinians (see Tamar Meisels, *Territorial Rights* (Dordrecht: Springer, 2005)). For present purposes, the issue in point is the general right held by states to legislate on a given area of land without interference from other states or extraterritorial bodies.

[77] Joseph Raz and Avishai Margalit, 'National Self-Determination' in Raz, *Ethics in the Public Domain*, 126.

[78] I follow Raz and Margalit's core argument as stated in ibid. For a similar conception of the collective right to self-government see Brian Barry, *Culture & Equality* (Oxford: Polity Press, 2001), 117.

[79] Admittedly, this moral defence of the principle of self-government holds only insofar as the relevant group is not morally obnoxious. This objection, however, is not particularly problematic for us here since we are not defending this or that particular state's right to self-government, but rather states generally holding this entitlement prima facie as a matter of principle.

of the principle of state sovereignty as a Hohfeldian power to dictate legal rules which are binding on a given territory. Namely, it is an explanation of the basis of its jurisdictional competence. But at the same time, the interest that individuals in a given state have in enjoying political sovereignty over their own affairs explains why states also hold a prima facie immunity against extraterritorial authorities dictating criminal legal rules which are binding on their territory. That is, it explains the fact that criminal rules dictated by Turkey are in principle invalid in the territory of South Africa.

Finally, this argument contains two interrelated qualifications. The right to self-government as advocated here is a collective, not a corporate, right; it is based on the joint interest of individuals in the territorial state not on the interest of that state itself. Unlike corporate rights, collective rights need not stand on the controversial assumption that states bear rights because they have themselves a particular moral standing. This lack of autonomous moral standing entails that collective rights, unlike other conceptions of group rights, are not liable to the charge of allowing the moral standing of the state to displace that of individuals and sub-groups who fall within the state's compass.[80] As a result, they do not generally pose a serious threat to the rights of individuals belonging to the state.

Secondly, this argument also stands on instrumental grounds. The power and immunity that the right to self-government contains have no intrinsic value. They are valuable only insofar as they contribute to the well-being of the members of that group. This right is neither absolute nor unconditional. It is limited both by the interests of non-members and by the interests of members other than their interests as members (eg, their fundamental individual interests, or their interests as members of other relevant groups).[81] This means both that states hold a prima facie immunity against extraterritorial bodies dictating criminal laws on their territory, and that this immunity can be overcome. It can be overcome if it is the case that a large enough number of individuals have a sufficiently important interest to confer upon that extraterritorial body the power to do so, and if this interest is sufficiently important to outweigh the interest on which this immunity is based. Interestingly, this also means that the territorial state's immunity can equally be overridden on the basis of some fundamental interest of the individuals in the particular state where the events have taken place, namely, the territorial state.[82]

To conclude, the Hohfeldian power to self-government that individuals hold collectively within a state accounts for the specific normative challenge that the principle of state sovereignty poses for a normative account of extraterritorial

[80] Jones, 'Group Rights and Group Oppression', 377.

[81] Raz and Margalit, 'National Self-Determination', 139.

[82] Admittedly, it may be objected that there might be some communities within a state who have fewer qualms than most about foreign powers interfering. Welsh nationalists, for instance, might resent English rule so much that they would prefer to have a foreign power dealing with criminal wrongs. As will be argued in Chapter 3 below, it does not follow from this proposition that Welsh nationalists have a sufficiently important interest in German or French criminal law being in force in Wales to confer upon these extraterritorial authorities the power to punish offences perpetrated in Wales. In any event, this book does not assume the moral legitimacy of existing territorial boundaries, only the fact that they exist.

punishment. It identifies a particular interest that explains holding extraterritorial bodies under a prima facie immunity against dictating criminal rules on its territory. It is against this immunity that any extraterritorial body (be that a state or an international court) will have to justify holding the power to punish an offender to individuals in the state in which the offence was committed. But it also accounts for this immunity being held *pro tanto*, that is, insofar as this extraterritorial body cannot claim a collective interest sufficiently important to override that immunity.

2

An Interest-Based Justification for the Right to Punish

1. The Right to Punish

To explain the extraterritorial scope of the right to punish it may be argued that we need to look at the reasons that justify a particular state or some other authority holding the power to punish a particular individual. I will argue for this proposition in the next four chapters. For present purposes it may suffice to note that this position is fairly common in discussions regarding other aspects of the scope of a state's right to punish, such as sentencing severity, or the kinds of penalties that might be morally warranted.[1] Deterrence, retribution, and moral reform standardly lead to different normative implications in particular situations. They deal differently, for instance, with an otherwise peaceful offender who has murdered an unfaithful partner or with a recidivist shoplifter. Accordingly, our enquiry must begin by the normative justification of the right to punish.

This chapter will provide an explanation for the proposition 'state S has a moral right to punish offender O'. But to do this, it is necessary first to present a more detailed analysis of the structure of this particular right. This will have significant implications for the account of extraterritorial punishment put forward in this book. Following Wesley Hohfeld, the proposition 'X has a right to φ' may take the form of a claim, a liberty, a power, or an immunity. Within this framework, the right to punish involves first and foremost a normative power. When an individual is convicted in a criminal trial, she enters the courtroom holding certain rights and leaves it with some of her rights altered.[2] Usually she would be imprisoned, some of her property would be taken away, or some other burden will be imposed upon her.[3] However, when we say that a state has the

[1] Michael Moore goes as far as arguing that retributivism determines, in fact, also *what* we should punish (Michael S Moore, *Placing Blame: A Theory of Criminal Law* (Oxford: Clarendon Press, 1997), 169–70). For critical remarks, see Leo Zaibert, *Punishment and Retribution* (Aldershot: Ashgate, 2006), ch 6.

[2] This normative change (criminal sanction) must not be conflated with the force exercised to enforce it. I assume, throughout, that officials of the legal system concerned are authorized (ie, morally justified) to use force to enforce this decision within the territorial boundaries of the political organization to which they belong.

[3] As a matter of fact, many more rights are altered depending on the jurisdiction and the legal order such as eg a person's rights regarding the education of her children, some of her political rights,

right to punish an offender, we not only mean that it holds the normative power to alter her rights in this harmful way, but also that it is permissible for the state to do so. As argued in Chapter 1, however, the fact that someone holds such a power to modify these rights does not per se entail a liberty to do so. These notions are of a different order. Thus, a justification for this moral right would characteristically also require an account of state S being at liberty to punish a particular individual.[4]

Finally, it would hardly make sense to say that a state has a right to punish an offender if the exercise of this normative power and its liberty were not protected by certain claim-rights. First, it usually requires a claim against the offender and other parties interfering or resisting its exercise by, for instance, threatening the jury. Secondly, in contemporary societies individuals are also under a duty to contribute financially and in some other ways to the exercise of this right. People are usually under a duty, inter alia, to attend court as witnesses, to hand in any evidence that a tribunal requests, to act as members of the jury, and so on. To sum up, the right to punish is a complex molecular right. Yet we need not address each one of its incidents here.[5] We need only concentrate, for the purposes of this book, on a state's power and its liberty to punish an offender. Moreover, the power involved in this molecular right is of particular importance for us here as all the normative work needed to examine the issue of extraterritoriality is connected with this particular incident.

According to the theory of rights endorsed here, each of these two incidents will have to be explained by reference to the interests of certain individuals. Thus, this chapter examines some of the leading justifications for legal punishment under this interest-based framework and finds them wanting. The reason for this is that they either fail to identify a particular interest which would be sufficiently important to warrant the protection of a right, or the interest on which they are based would lead to harsher and morally unacceptable practices. This chapter will argue, by contrast, that a state's prima facie power to punish an offender is based on the collective interest of individuals in that state in its criminal laws being in force. This is because having a system of criminal rules in force constitutes a public good that contributes to the well-being of individuals who live under it in a certain way. Furthermore, legal punishment of the guilty is also morally permissible because criminal wrongdoers forfeit their claim-right against the state punishing them.

her right to privacy, etc. The power to alter these rights is different to the power considered here but a full account of this issue is beyond the scope of this book.

[4] This is the core incident of the right to punish in Alan John Simmons, *The Lockean Theory of Rights* (Princeton: Princeton University Press, 1992), 162. For a criticism of this view, see Daniel McDermott, 'The Duty to Punish and Legitimate Government', *J of Political Philosophy* 7/2 (1999). However, unlike mine, McDermott's point is not that as a matter of analytical jurisprudence the right to punish is a power-right. Rather, he argues that 'punishment requires the existence of some sort of authoritative hierarchical relationship in order to qualify as punishment' (ibid). This insight is captured in Chapter 6 and stands, I shall argue there, on different considerations.

[5] A complete justification for the institution of legal punishment would also need to examine, inter alia, whether a state is under a duty to exercise this particular power. In other words, whether punishment is also morally required. That issue is beyond the scope of this enquiry.

Accordingly, a state not only holds a prima facie power to punish an offender, it is also prima facie at liberty to do so.[6]

Two points of clarification are in order. First, we must distinguish between contingent and non-contingent justifications for legal punishment and stress the importance of providing a unitary, non-contingent explanation for this moral right. The notion of contingency is used here in the restricted sense of arguments that apply in some circumstances in which punishment seems warranted, but are unable to accommodate other standard cases. A contingent explanation is unsatisfactory even if, when it works, it would be more appealing than an alternative non-contingent one. Preferring a non-contingent argument is not just a matter of personal taste. A unitary justification contributes significantly to the clarity and workability of the argument.

Secondly, a convincing normative justification for legal punishment needs to rely on a clear and descriptively appealing conceptual analysis of what legal punishment is. This conceptual rigour is particularly important in the area of legal punishment, since a common problem has been the strong tendency to conflate conceptual elements with normative ones.[7] Punishment constitutes the distinguishing feature of any system of criminal law.[8] As such, it entails some sort of external behaviour. In the traditional Flew-Benn-Hart definition, legal punishment constitutes an evil or a deprivation of a good (1), visited intentionally *qua* evil by human beings other than the offender (2), on someone 'considered' an offender (3), for his offence (4), by a human agency which is authorized by the legal order (5).[9] But also, punishment is standardly said to involve also an expressive or communicative element.[10] Legal punishment is not only a deprivation of a good, inflicted by an authority for a violation of a rule, but also, and crucially, a kind of language. It is an act of moral communication and, more precisely, of moral criticism. It expresses condemnation of the crime and communicates to individuals that the rule that

[6] In this chapter powers and liberties should be understood as prima facie powers and liberties. The fact that they are prima facie rights means that they are assigned in the abstract, without consideration of the particularities of the context.

[7] H L A Hart, *Punishment and Responsibility: Essays in the Philosophy of Law* (Oxford: Clarendon Press, 1978), 5. A further problem is that the concept of punishment is also used in many and diverse contexts in our social life. It belongs, comfortably enough, in educational and religious contexts, but also in relations between friends, couples, and even strangers. Some of the conceptual obscurities and problematic intuitions affecting the justification for legal punishment, I suspect, stem from the fact that it is difficult to isolate this practice from the moral intuitions or principles that work or shape punishment in other social contexts. Admittedly, it is not always clear one should do this, but at least it seems plausible that many of these practices are sufficiently dissimilar to merit their own set of rules governing them (on this, see Peter F Strawson, *Freedom and Resentment, and Other Essays* (London: Methuen, 1974), 19–20 and, strongly against the position advocated here, Zaibert, *Punishment and Retribution*).

[8] The US Supreme Court, eg, invokes the notion of punishment as the relevant criterion to decide whether a given sanction is criminal in nature. See *Kennedy v Mendoza-Martinez* 372 US 144 (1963).

[9] Hart, *Punishment and Responsibility*, 4–5.

[10] See, famously, 'The Expressive Function of Punishment' in Joel Feinberg, *Doing & Deserving: Essays in the Theory of Responsibility* (Princeton: Princeton University Press, 1974); and Antony Duff, *Punishment, Communication, and Community* (Oxford: Oxford University Press, 2001). I do not rely here on Duff's distinction between expression and communication.

the offender violated is in force. How deeply entrenched this communicative or expressive element is in the standard practice of legal punishment is insightfully shown by Nozick's observation that punishment is visited 'with the desire that the person know why this is occurring and know that she was intended to know'.[11] But also, legal punishment is visited with the desire that society at large know that punishment is taking place and why.

The coexistence of these two elements (a certain external behaviour and a symbolic or communicative element) is crucial to understanding what legal punishment is. Yet one must not understand legal punishment as constituted by an element of hard treatment and another element expressing censure. Rather, it is the hard treatment itself or the external behaviour in general that usually expresses this condemnation or censure. In Feinberg's eloquent words, 'the very walls of his cell condemn him'.[12]

2. A Normative Justification for the Right to Punish

Our point of departure is, then, that the right to punish an offender is a complex molecular right. Analytically, it comprises first a normative power to change her moral boundaries in a way that entails visiting hard treatment or some other burden upon her.[13] The fact that someone holds this power means that someone else is under a liability to have punishment inflicted upon her. Furthermore, this right usually involves also being at liberty to change the offender's moral boundaries in this harmful way. Being at liberty to mete out punishment means that the offender lacks a claim-right against suffering the harm involved in legal punishment. I take it that a state has a power to punish a particular offender if and only if an aspect of someone's well-being (an interest of hers) is a sufficient reason for holding her under a liability for undergoing this kind of treatment. I also take it that a state is at liberty to exercise that power if no aspect of the offender's well-being is a sufficient reason for holding it under a duty not to do so.

2.1 The justification for the state's power to punish

The purpose of this section is, thus, to identify a particular interest in certain offenders being punished that is sufficiently important to be protected by a right. Let us begin with a simple case. In Dostoyevsky's *Crime and Punishment*, Raskolnikov famously killed a pawnbroker and her sister, who had no other family or descendants. Good or evil, these two women had a right to their lives, that is, they had an interest in remaining alive that was sufficiently important to put Raskolnikov,

[11] Robert Nozick, *Philosophical Explanations* (Oxford: Clarendon Press, 1981), 368.

[12] Feinberg, *Doing & Deserving*, 98.

[13] Conceptualizing this power as a right is not to say its exercise is discretionary. Powers can also be single rights in the sense that they can confer non-discretionary authority. Thus, under mandatory sentencing laws Judge A would have to exercise this power to sentence offender O whether he likes it or not.

inter alia, under a duty not to kill them. Moreover, their right standardly entailed also a right to self-defence. While Raskolnikov was threatening them with his axe, this fundamental interest arguably granted them a liberty to repel his attack even at the cost of his life. On similar grounds, it would have been permissible for Ivan and Olga, who were just passing by, to use force against Raskolnikov to rescue the two sisters.[14] However, the problem begins once these two women are dead, for it cannot possibly follow that their interest in being alive can entail conferring a normative power upon third parties to inflict harm on Dostoyevsky's unusual hero. Eloquently, both the 'self-defence' and the 'defence of others' justifications in criminal law make it clear that this harm is permissible if and only if, inter alia, there is an imminent attack on someone's rights and the act of defence is a necessary means of rescue from that attack.[15] The sisters' right to life only allows this much.[16] Their interest in staying alive cannot ground a right to inflict suffering upon Raskolnikov. In this type of situation punishment simply arrives too late. Moreover, how inadequate this argument is as an explanation for the right to punish is further illustrated by the fact that this interest can only explain a first order incident, that is, a liberty to use force against the attacker. It remains unclear how the victim's interest in remaining alive can result in the offender being under a liability to have some of her fundamental rights altered in the way punishment requires.

My point, then, is quite simple. The difficulty in explaining the power to punish an offender from an interest-based perspective not only arises from the fact that it implies inflicting harm upon a human being but, more crucially, it concerns the fact that this suffering does not seem to be entailed by anyone's concrete interest. At least it is not entailed by the interest of the person whose rights the offender herself has violated, or has attempted to violate. Admittedly, this particular claim holds only insofar as the victim dies. Yet an argument for punishment that is unable to accommodate precisely the case of accomplished murder is not only contingent, but utterly unpromising. It would lead, for instance, to the absurd conclusion that if an individual were to commit a robbery, she could escape punishment simply by killing her victim.[17]

[14] This position assumes that most people would accept the claim that individuals have a moral right to resist, repel, ward off, or prevent otherwise irreparable unjust harm. On this see Suzanne Uniacke, *Permissible Killing: The Self-Defence Justification of Homicide* (Cambridge: Cambridge University Press, 1994), 227.

[15] For a succinct account, see Andrew Ashworth, *Principles of Criminal Law* (Oxford: Oxford University Press, 2006), 139–41.

[16] I assume for present purposes that the dead cannot have rights. Admittedly, this is a controversial stance to take (supporting this view see, Fabre, *Whose Body Is It Anyway?*, 22–3; against it, see Feinberg, *Harm to Others*). To challenge the view hereby advocated, however, it would not suffice to show that the dead can have rights; it would have to be argued that they have an interest in the offender being punished that is sufficiently important to confer upon the state, eg, the power to punish her. Insofar as the rescuer's liberty is grounded on the victim's interest *in being alive*, this seems unlikely.

[17] Extending the definition of a victim, eg, to her family (as in *Kurt, Re* (24276/94) [1998] ECHR 44 (25 May 1998), and *Barrios Altos* (*Chumbipuma Aguirre and others v Peru*) Inter-American Court of Human Rights (14/03/2001), Series C No 75 [2001] IACHR 5, among others) would not solve this difficulty because this rationale could eventually be extended to the killing of her family.

These considerations lead to three basic, albeit important, implications. First, a state's power to punish an offender cannot be straightforwardly based on the interest of actual victims. This is reflected in the fact that in most legal systems victims do not have the normative power to waive or promote the exercise of the state's right to punish, at least with regard to the vast majority of offences. If we are to identify the interest that can consistently ground this particular right, we need to look elsewhere.[18] Secondly, the justification for first order incidents, such as the liberty to protect an individual victim, should not be conflated with the justification for the normative power to punish the offender.[19] The liberty to intervene in state S for humanitarian reasons is independent from, and in fact belongs on a different level to, the extraterritorial *power* to punish offences committed in that state. Finally, the points made in the preceding paragraph highlight a significant advantage of the rights-based framework hereby advocated. Namely, that it requires not simply an argument that punishment is generally advantageous, but rather that it forces us to identify whose interest it serves and what interest this is. In Jeffrie Murphy's words, even if punishment of a person would have good consequences, the question is still what gives a particular state S the moral right to inflict it upon a particular individual.[20]

Furthermore, this interest-based framework also makes it implausible to argue that this normative power is justified exclusively by reference to the interests of the offender. Unless one subscribes to a platonic conception of the human being, in which some sort of equilibrium between her different 'parts' is intrinsically valuable, and assumes punishment would help to bring about this equilibrium, it would be too cynical to argue that the suffering involved in legal punishment would be justified by its contribution to the offender's well-being. In addition, if the power to punish her has to be explained by taking into consideration the interests of third parties, surely there must be some sort of forward-looking component to its justification.

2.1.1 The interest in retribution

Even those who deny any rational justification for criminal sanctions rely in one way or another on an argument of the kind identified above. For instance, Mackie argues that retributive punishment is not based on moral reasons, but on feeling or sentiment. The justification for legal punishment is based, fundamentally, on what he calls retributive emotion. Mackie offers a biological explanation in terms of standard

[18] This argument does not entail taking any stance *vis-à-vis* the rights of victims during a criminal trial. In fact, an interest-based theory of rights would at least be compatible with granting them several procedural rights, such as the right to attend the trial, introduce evidence, be legally represented, etc.

[19] This is a quite common conflation in the literature on International Criminal Law. See eg Robert D Sloane, 'The Expressive Capacity of International Punishment: The Limits of the National Law Analogy and the Potential of International Criminal Law', *Stanford J of International L* 43 (2007), 45–6.

[20] Jeffrie Murphy, 'Marxism and Retribution' in *Retribution, Justice and Therapy* (Dordrecht: Reidel, 1979).

evolutionary theory. He begins with the advantage to species and individuals of retaliatory behaviour and feelings, and proceeds on the basis of natural selection. This process ends with the socialization and moralizing of retributive emotion.[21] It might well be that his explanation is descriptively correct. However, it begs the fundamental normative question. What his explanation tacitly implies, and does not argue for, is that this emotion has arisen because retaliatory behaviour and feelings are advantageous. How are these advantageous, for whom, and how much, are precisely the questions any convincing account of criminal sanctions would need to address.

There are many different retributive arguments in the literature which provide an account of this forward-looking element.[22] Antony Duff, for instance, has argued that the central point of punishment is to persuade the offender to accept the condemnation for her crime and, in accepting it, to repent that crime and reform her future conduct.[23] Leaving aside both the kind of state this view presupposes or what to do with offenders who will not possibly reform (or even listen), it is hard to see whose interest would ground this necessity of a secular penance, and why this interest would be important enough to justify an offender's liability to suffering the harmful consequences that legal punishment involves.

Ted Honderich, for his part, suggests that the truth in retributivism may be that punishment is justified partly or wholly by grievance-satisfaction.[24] This seems more plausible. However, in a case such as Raskolnikov's it is unclear whose grievance this would be. The reader feels more grief for his fate, or for Sonia's, than for the two women. More importantly, perhaps, an argument needs to be made as to why we should protect this interest in the first place. The fact that we have this feeling does not entail that it merits the protection given by a right. Punishment cannot be valuable just because it is wanted.[25] Indeed, not many people would argue for a right to exercise vengeance upon an offender even if this were also deeply desired. Those who desire it must also believe it is valuable, and do so only on the condition that it is valuable. This is precisely what Honderich's argument needs, but fails to show.

2.1.2 The interest in having a system of criminal rules in force

The justification for the normative power advocated here is based, by contrast, on the claim that having a system of criminal law in force constitutes a public good that benefits the individuals who live under it in a certain way. This proposition

[21] John Mackie, 'Morality and the Retributive Emotions', *Criminal Justice Ethics* 1/1 (1982).

[22] I take retributivism in a broad sense here. There is a certain amount of controversy as to precisely which doctrines are strictly retributivist. For conflicting views see eg John Cottingham, 'Varieties of Retribution', *Philosophical Quarterly* 29/116 (1979); David Dolinko, 'Some Thoughts About Retributivism', *Ethics* 101/3 (1991); and Zaibert, *Punishment and Retribution*, ch 6.

[23] See Duff, *Punishment, Communication, and Community*. See also Uma Narayan, 'Appropriate Responses and Preventive Benefits: Justifying Censure and Hard Treatment in Legal Punishment', OJLS 13/2 (1993), 174. For criticism of this view, see Andrew von Hirsch, 'Punishment, Penance and the State' in Matt Matravers, *Punishment and Political Theory* (Oxford: Hart, 1999).

[24] Ted Honderich, *Punishment: The Supposed Justifications* (Harmondsworth: Pelican Books, 1984), 233–4.

[25] See on this my discussion of what kind of interest merit the protection of a right in Chapter 1.

rests on an analytical and a normative claim. Analytically, it implies that there is a necessary link between a legal system being in force and the state holding the power to punish those who violate those rules. It has been plausibly argued that a system of criminal law is in force if and only if both those subject to it and external observers have reasons to believe so.[26] For this to obtain, three conditions must be met: (a) those who violate these criminal rules should be punished; (b) they should be punished for having committed the offence; and (c) this punishment ought to be meted out by a body expressly authorized by *that* legal system. From a normative point of view, having in force a set of legal rules prohibiting murder, rape, and so on, contributes to the well-being of individuals by giving them a sense of dignity and security. The collective interest of individuals in a given society having in force a criminal law system is arguably sufficiently important to put others under a liability to be punished for violating any of those rules.

Let us concentrate, first, on the analytical limb of the argument. Legal systems are commonly regarded as social institutions meant to regulate behaviour and settle disputes within a society. However, unlike other public goods, such as bridges or a water-supply system, their existence is not easy to establish. They do not allow people to cross over a river or get drinking water out of a tap. Laws exist in an altogether different way. Usually, we say that they exist when they are in force.[27] The meaning of this proposition, however, needs elaboration. Most people will agree that for a legal system to be in force it needs to enjoy some level of compliance. Albeit necessary, this is hardly a sufficient condition. British citizens may conform to a significant extent to German criminal laws, but this hardly entails that those laws are in force in the UK. Moreover, the significance of conformity to the law should not be overstated. Raz has plausibly argued that for a legal system to be in force it is not necessary that the population at large follows the law, nor that the laws constitute valid reasons for action for the people subject to them.[28] Law-violations are quite common in every law-regulated society, and people usually act on extra-legal reasons (moral convictions, social condemnation, etc). Rather, for a legal system to be in force it is necessary that people believe that laws are valid reasons for action, that is, that they believe they are bound by them.[29] When we say that Italian laws are in force in Italy, it is because both individuals in Italy and external observers generally believe that these laws are binding there. In this particular sense we may claim, for example, that laws regulating the slave trade were in force in the Roman Empire.

The existence of a legal system, however, cannot depend merely on a psychological fact. Not any kind of belief will suffice. For instance, the fact that many American 'born again' Christians believe that the Laws of God are in force in the US does

[26] Raz, *Practical Reason and Norms*, 171. On this, see also, H L A Hart, *The Concept of Law* (Oxford: Clarendon Press, 1997). For standard criticisms, see J M Finnis, *Natural Law and Natural Rights* (2nd edn, Oxford: Clarendon Press, 2011); and Neil MacCormick, *Legal Reasoning and Legal Theory* (Oxford: Oxford University Press, 1978). For a good analysis of this issue, see Nicola Lacey, *State Punishment: Political Principles and Community Values* (London: Routledge, 1988), ch 4.

[27] See, eg, Joseph Raz, *The Authority of Law* (Oxford: Oxford University Press, 1979), 104.

[28] Raz, *Practical Reason and Norms*, 171.

[29] Ibid.

not entail that, as a matter of fact, this is the case. Therefore, we must provide an account of the kinds of reasons this belief must be grounded on for the legal system to be in force. To do this, Raz points to the role that courts—that is, law-applying institutions—play in a legal system.[30] Legal systems standardly contain not only norms guiding individuals' behaviour, but also an institutionalized way of creating laws and evaluating the conformity of that behaviour to the law. The existence of courts indicates that the legal system provides for an institutionalized way of determining legal situations. Their role is mainly to determine normative situations authoritatively, and to do so in accordance with pre-existing norms which they are bound to apply.[31] Moreover, courts apply legal rules to the exclusion of other conflicting considerations (unless the laws themselves allow them to do otherwise). Following Raz, we may argue that these exclusionary authoritative judgments constitute the basis on which officials, subjects, and external observers must ground their belief for the relevant legal system to be in force. Furthermore, these considerations account for the fact that the right to punish takes the form of a Hohfeldian power, and not merely a liberty.

Admittedly, criminal sanctions are but one type of these norm-applying decisions. They are, however, necessary for any criminal law system to be in force.[32] This proposition seems commonplace, but let me elaborate on the reasons why this is so. Possibly, some would think that this is mainly because punishment deters potential offenders and a system can be said to be in force only if it achieves a certain level of compliance. The argument would run along the following lines: even if moral inhibitions are sufficiently strong to keep most people from committing serious crimes, whether this would hold true in a society without a machinery of criminal punishment seems dubious.[33] That individuals would not be deterred in such a society, however, need not be so. Arguably, it is unclear whether this minimum level of compliance with basic moral norms would not also be achieved if, for example, there was an effective police force authorized to prevent crimes and to use a 'shoot to kill' policy against offenders caught red-handed. This, in fact, may be more effective than the existence of courts and prisons in ensuring general compliance with the law. The situation of violent struggle in Iraq in the aftermath of the 2003 Gulf War, where courts were somewhat functioning but police prevention was not, illustrates this point.[34]

By contrast, the exercise of the power to punish offenders is necessary for a system of criminal law to be in force essentially because it grounds the belief that

30 Ibid, 137. 31 Ibid, 134.

32 Raz argues that although sanctions are as a matter of fact necessary for a legal system to be in force, this is not logically so. Provided human nature were different, he claims, it would be possible to have a sanction-less legal system (ibid). This claim is beyond the scope of our enquiry. In fact, it would not really undermine the argument hereby advocated. One could simply stipulate that this argument holds provided that human nature is not radically different. This would make the argument advocated here liable to the charge of contingency, but this contingency would be of a kind that no moral argument can really escape.

33 Johannes Andenaes, *Punishment and Deterrence* (Ann Arbor: University of Michigan Press, 1974), 51, 124, and 128. Andenaes refers to cases in which due to police strikes or breakdown of the state there was a very significant increase in the number of offences.

34 It is also instructive to note what happened in East Timor after the Indonesian retreat.

the rules of the system are binding. It is usually accepted that when an offender O murders her victim V she not only causally determines V's death; she also violates the legal rule prohibiting murder or prohibiting violations of the right to life. Similarly, punishment comprises both an element of hard treatment and an expressive or communicative element of censure which, though conceptually distinct, go together in practice. Both these elements are necessary to ground the belief in the bindingness (that is, the existence) of the criminal laws. Expressing censure in a purely symbolic way would be perceived as mocking such a rule rather than affirming its existence. Only by depriving the offender of some good of hers would both subjects and external observers take the existence of that legal rule seriously. Punishment is therefore needed

> as a means of making the standards of the criminal law *real*: as a way of stating that the meeting of those standards is a matter of duty or obligation ... rather than merely a matter of exhortation or aspiration.[35]

The hard treatment element per se (as purely external behaviour) will not suffice either. To use von Hirsch's metaphor, treating offenders 'like tigers in a circus' by incapacitating them is merely like 'neutralising a risk'.[36] Such treatment denies rather than communicates the fact that they are bound by legal rules. It would make little sense to impose legal rules on tigers (or hurricanes for that matter) prohibiting them to harm individuals. It is therefore the symbolic element contained in legal punishment that precisely expresses or communicates the existence of the rule that has been breached. A response to criminal behaviour that lacks this expressive or communicative element, and thereby treats the offender as a pure risk, would simply not be able to convey the right kind of message.

Furthermore, as the definition of legal punishment provided above stipulates, for the offender being punished to ground the belief in the criminal law being in force, it has to be the case that punishment is inflicted upon her for her offence. This does not mean that she has to be in fact guilty of the particular wrongdoing for which she was convicted. As it will become apparent below, it might be that she is in fact innocent. Yet the reason she is being punished must be that she allegedly has, to the relevant standard of proof, perpetrated the offence. As Hart rightly points out, this is a conceptual not a normative point.[37] Convicting an innocent individual *qua* innocent would analytically undermine belief in the legal system being in force. Even the general perception that an individual is being punished for some reason other than the fact that she committed a criminal wrong would arguably undermine the message legal punishment needs to convey to the relevant stakeholders.[38]

Finally, for a criminal sanction to restore the belief in the legal system being in force, it is necessary that this power is exercised by someone expressly authorized by that legal system. Indeed, in most legal systems only if a court of justice sentences an offender, would its subjects and external commentators agree

[35] Lacey, *State Punishment*, 182 (original emphasis).

[36] Andrew von Hirsch, *Censure and Sanctions* (Oxford: Oxford University Press, 1993), 11.

[37] Hart, *Punishment and Responsibility*, 4–5.

[38] On this issue, see Chapter 6.

that this system's legal rule has been enforced.[39] Private retaliation and harms imparted by natural forces may be expressions of natural or poetic justice, but they cannot ground the belief that the relevant *legal* rule is in force. Similarly, the fact that German courts claim the power to punish every act of arson perpetrated in Korea would hardly ground the belief in *Korea's* criminal laws against arson being in force.[40]

The overall analytical claim on which this account rests is not entirely new to the literature on legal punishment.[41] However, this literature has often neglected that any such account would also need to provide a normative justification in support of it. Namely, it is not enough to explain how legal punishment effectively expresses or communicates the existence of a norm prohibiting murder, rape, or other crimes; we must also explain why the existence of such a criminal rule is sufficiently important to place a number of individuals under a liability to suffer the kind of harm entailed by penal sanctions.

It is submitted here that a state's power to punish is normatively explained by the interest of individuals in having a legal system in force containing rules that prohibit murder, rape, torture, and other wrongs. This is because such a system contributes to their well-being in at least one important way. In Feinberg's words, the criminal law

> not only regulates my liberty by imposing duties and extending liberties to me, it also confers rights on me against my fellow citizens and thereby protects me from them in the exercise of my liberties.[42]

The fact that we believe that these rules are in force means that we consider not only ourselves, but also people around us to be bound by them. The criminal law, thus, contributes to our sense of being right-bearers, and that the legal system takes the protection of our rights seriously. This is all it is implied by the proposition that it contributes to our sense of dignity and security. Admittedly, this is an empirical claim which cannot be fully demonstrated here. However, its plausibility can be convincingly defended on the basis of a few standard observations.[43]

The benefit that a system of criminal laws being in force provides to individuals in a given state is hardly trivial. Consider the alternative. In a society which only allows for private self-defence and retaliation as responses to wrongdoing the situation would quickly deteriorate and individuals would end up living in constant fear,[44] as living conditions in failed states tend to illustrate. Furthermore, legal

[39] This is an empirical claim, not a conceptual or a normative one. For an argument that this should (normatively) be the case, see Chapter 6.

[40] On this, see Chapter 3.

[41] See, notably, David Luban, 'War Crimes: *The Law of Hell*' in Larry May (ed), *War: Essays in Political Philosophy* (Cambridge: Cambridge University Press, 2008), 287; Mark A Drumbl, *Atrocity, Punishment, and International Law* (Cambridge: Cambridge University Press, 2007), 176; and Sloane, 'The Expressive Capacity of International Punishment', 85.

[42] Feinberg, *Harm to Others*, 8.

[43] This is not such a great handicap in this area. In Tallgren's words: 'Any analysis [of this issue] operates ... in an area of more or less justified belief' (Immi Tallgren, 'The Sensibility and Sense of International Criminal Law', *EJIL* 13/3 (2002), 590).

[44] See, famously, Hobbes' *Leviathan*, ch 13.

punishment contributes to our well-being in a way that neither effective policing, nor a system of civil compensation can. Regardless of how many resources we allocate to policing or of whether an offender would be liable to pay compensation to her victim, if no punishment awaits those guilty of criminal wrongdoing, individuals will probably not consider people around them ultimately bound by such prohibitions. In a Raskolnikov-type of case, for instance, no compensation or any other legal consequence would follow. Moreover, criminal punishment conveys an altogether different message to individuals in terms of the protection that the legal system affords their rights. Punishment, in Feimberg's words, is not a price tag paid for some already consumed good.[45] It conveys the message that the protection of the law is real.

Furthermore, a system of criminal laws being in force is arguably a necessary condition, even if not a sufficient one, to achieve a particular kind of public order. Public order is generally considered, in itself, of enormous significance to individuals' well-being. Yet my argument does not rely on just any kind of public order. Public order could be maintained by means such as terror, as the USSR under Stalin and many other brutal dictatorships aptly illustrate.[46] By contrast, when the criminal law operates in the way advocated here, that is, by a centralized authority enforcing rules against wrongdoing, it contributes to bringing about a kind of order based on the moral significance of the rights of individuals. This particular kind of public order is quite plausibly of the utmost importance for the well-being of individuals. And the reason why this is so is precisely that, unlike public order in dictatorial regimes, it contributes significantly to their sense of being right-holders and that the legal system takes the protection of those rights seriously. In sum, this sense of dignity and security is arguably an essential component of our well-being, and possibly a precondition for leading a minimally decent life. Thus, their interest in these rules being in force is sufficiently important to confer upon the state the power to punish criminal offenders. Thus, individuals' collective interest in criminal rules being in force prohibiting murder, rape, and so on is arguably sufficiently important to confer upon the state the power to punish offenders.

Let me tie up a few loose ends. First, this justification does not rely on the claim that punishing offenders will ground a belief in not ourselves being victims of criminal wrongdoing. Neither the criminal law nor any other available social institution would be able to achieve this. Rather, this argument relies only on the weaker claim that in the society in which we live we benefit from the fact that there are laws in force prohibiting, for example, torture, murder, rape, and so on. The interest we may have in minimizing such risks should not be conflated with our interest in having a system of rules that is binding upon individuals.

Secondly, the interest in there being a system of criminal rules in force is both a necessary and a sufficient condition for the allocation of this normative

[45] Feinberg, *Doing & Deserving*.

[46] Admittedly, this is a matter of degree. For even the most horrendous regimes do, as a matter of fact, enforce certain actual violations of basic rights.

power. Admittedly, there are beneficial by-products of having these legal rules in force. It is often argued, for instance, that punishment of criminal behaviour would enhance social cooperation. Laws against counterfeiting, fraud, and other related offences arguably contribute to facilitating trade and commercial transactions between parties. Punishment is also said to discourage certain violent reactions towards wrongdoing, such as private vengeance or self-help, to provide a public record of the wrong that has been committed, to contribute to restoring social cohesion, to appease the grievance desires of victims, and to provide the opportunity to the offender to reflect and resolve to reform.[47] Most significantly perhaps, legal punishment would deter criminal wrongdoing. Yet under the argument provided here none of these beneficial aspects of the institution of legal punishment are necessary to justify the allocation of this power.

Finally, this argument is not based exclusively on my personal interest in the system of criminal rules being in force, but rather on individuals' collective interest in this kind of good. As we saw in Chapter 1, collective rights are based on a joint interest that justifies the imposition of duties, no-rights, liabilities, and disabilities on others. Thus, the claim on which this account relies is that individuals' joint interest in having this set of rules in force is prima facie sufficiently important (in terms of its bearing on their well-being) to hold offenders under a liability to have hard treatment meted out to them.

This consideration helps to clarify the role that victims' interests play in the argument here advocated. Above, it was argued that the interest in being protected against a particular wrongdoing can, at best, provide a contingent autonomous justification for the state's power to punish an offender. And even this was incompatible with some of our central intuitions regarding the practice of legal punishment. Here it may be suggested that victims share with other individuals the interest in a set of criminal rules being in force. For the purposes of the justification of the power to punish, the difference with the relevant interest held by other individuals within the state would be a matter of intensity, not of the subject matter of the interest itself.[48]

By contrast, it could be objected that an offender may legitimately complain that she does not belong to the collective whose interest warrants conferring this power upon the state. This is because, the argument goes, it is not in *her* interest to be punished. Admittedly, an offender has a clear interest in not having hard treatment or moral condemnation inflicted upon her. But this says nothing against her (also) having a general interest in wrongdoers being punished. The former interest is analytically independent from the latter. When she arrives in prison, she arguably has an interest in the criminal rule against murder being in force on the premises. And this is because this rule would contribute to her sense of dignity and security. In short, an offender would also herself benefit from this public good. As a result, she cannot claim that she is being alienated from the collective whose interests explain the state's power to punish.

[47] Lacey, *State Punishment*, 183–4. [48] See n 18 above.

To conclude, the criminal law shares the main features of what is usually conceptualized as a public good.[49] In Raz's explanation,

> a good is a public good in a certain society if and only if the distribution of its benefits in that society is not subject to voluntary control by anyone other than each potential beneficiary controlling his share of the benefits.[50]

Examples of public goods are public transport or a water-supply system. But public goods need not be of this sort. Other kinds are things such as living in a tolerant society, the flourishing of the arts, etc. Public goods, in short, are all sorts of goods that have the capacity to benefit individuals collectively. Admittedly, they allow that someone may not profit herself from this good and, also, that different people may benefit from this good to different degrees.[51] Nonetheless, what defines this kind of good is the non-exclusivity of its enjoyment.

2.1.3 The interest in reducing crime

One may wonder whether norm projection or convincing individuals of the binding nature of the system of criminal laws is the most important reason we have for punishing offenders. At face value, the answer seems to be a plain no. Take deterrence, for example.[52] This theory broadly argues that punishment is justified by its consequences as a means of protecting individual's rights and other valuable goods. This is achieved, standardly, by deterring potential offenders. There is a reasonable degree of consensus that, to some extent, legal punishment does deter criminal behaviour. More precisely, the claim is that 'ordinary people can sometimes be deterred by both formal and informal sanctions'.[53] Is not protecting people's rights more important than re-establishing their confidence in a set of criminal prohibitions being in force? And, if so, should not this interest warrant the protection of

[49] I share with Nicola Lacey the sense that it is crucial to conceptualize the criminal law as a public good (see Lacey, *State Punishment*, ch 8). However, the liberal framework advocated here seems to do better than her preferred communitarian one, at least with regard to the territorial and extraterritorial scope of the power to punish. On the relevance of *belonging* to a community for an account of extraterritoriality, see Chapters 3, 5, and 6.

[50] Raz, *The Morality of Freedom*, 198. [51] Ibid, 199.

[52] This chapter concentrates only on this type of consequentialist justification due to its persistent influence and popularity particularly in debates regarding extraterritorial prosecutions. See, eg, Security Council resolutions creating the ICTY and ICTR (SC Res 827 (1993) and 955 (1994), respectively) and the Preamble of the ICC Statute; see also *Prosecutor v Rutaganda*, Case No ICTR-96-3-7 (Trial Chamber, 6 December 1999), § 456; and *Prosecutor v Delalic*, Case No IT-96-21-T (ICTY, 16 Nov 1998), § 1234. For its theoretical pedigree see eg Sloane, 'The Expressive Capacity of International Punishment'; Mark J Osiel, 'Why Prosecute? Critics of Punishment for Mass Atrocity', *Human Rights Q* 22 (2000); Mark A Drumbl, *Atrocity, Punishment, and International Law*; Theodor Meron, *War Crimes Law Comes of Age: Essays* (Oxford: Oxford University Press, 1998), 196. There are other consequentialist arguments, most notably Braithwhite and Pettit's influential republican theory of punishment that are beyond my scope (see John Braithwaite and Philip Pettit, *Not Just Deserts: A Republican Theory of Criminal Justice* (Oxford: Clarendon Press, 1990)).

[53] Andrew von Hirsch et al, *Criminal Deterrence and Sentence Severity: An Analysis of Recent Research* (Oxford: Hart, 1999), 1 and 33–7. They emphasize, however, that twenty years before, the overview carried out in the US by the Panel on Research on Deterrent and Incapacitative Effects of the National Academy of Science still showed some significant doubts regarding this issue (at 12–13 and 47).

a right? In effect, the interest in protecting individuals' rights is arguably stronger than the interest in having a system of rules in force (even if they are not mutually exclusive). However, I suggest that the former interest cannot really explain the state's power to punish an offender.[54]

It does not follow from the interest that individuals have in deterring potential criminals that we should assign the state a Hohfeldian power to punish offenders. Rather, this interest seems to warrant conferring upon it a different type of right. If the 'more' punishment is exacted, the stronger the deterrent effect, we should have no trouble endorsing Feuerbach's classic formula according to which the risk for the law-breaker must be made so great, the punishment so severe, that he knows he has more to lose than he has to gain from his crime. In this light, it is somewhat dubious that our interest in preventing crimes explains offenders being under a liability to have legal punishment inflicted upon them. Rather, this interest is more clearly served by a liberty to stop and harm them, rather than by a power to punish them.

There are several examples in the international sphere that illustrate this point well. NATO's military intervention against Serbia, for one, had a much stronger impact on stopping the crimes being perpetrated in the former Yugoslavia against, say, the Albanian Kosovar population, than the establishment of the International Criminal Tribunal for the former Yugoslavia (ICTY) or any other threat of extra-territorial punishment. Indeed, the massacres in Srebrenica occurred two years after the creation of the ICTY, and the atrocities in Kosovo were perpetrated almost six years later. Similarly, President Reagan characterized the US air raid on Libya on 15 April 1986, as being a 'pre-emptive action' that would provide Colonel Kadhafi 'with incentives and reasons to change his criminal behaviour'.[55] To put it bluntly, then, deterrence would advocate summary executions or pre-emptive military strikes rather than costly criminal trials and long prison sentences.

Moreover, the connection between the power to punish an individual and deterrence must be critically examined in light of the admittedly limited empirical data available. Deterrence depends on two separate and accumulative causal links. First, the visitation of punishment needs to result in actual deterrence of potential offenders. Secondly, the deterrence of potential offenders should cause a reduction in the overall number of offences.

The first causal link is of particular relevance here.[56] The link between the visitation of legal punishment and the actual deterrence it achieves is significantly

[54] This chapter provides reasons against deterrence as an adequate justification for the power to punish an offender in its own terms. Chapter 3 will examine deterrence in the context of the extraterritorial application of domestic criminal laws.

[55] Cited in D J Harris, *Cases and Materials on International Law* (London: Sweet & Maxwell, 2004), 936.

[56] The second link is affected by phenomena such as 'destigmatization', 'deterrence decay', mass incarceration, etc. See eg von Hirsch et al, *Criminal Deterrence and Sentence Severity*, 8 and Daniel Nagin, 'Criminal Deterrence Research at the Outset of the Twenty-First Century' in Michael Tonry (ed), *Crime and Justice: A Review of Research* (Chicago: University of Chicago Press, 1998). On the detrimental effects of mass incarceration in the US see James P Lynch and William J Sabol, 'Assessing

conditioned by the fact that deterrence is a subjective phenomenon. Accordingly, what matters is not so much the actual infliction of punishment but, rather, what potential offenders believe the threatened consequences to be and how they evaluate them.[57] Available empirical studies suggest that the relationship between actual behaviour and future consequences (offences and punishment in particular) is far more complex than is intuitively thought, and that it sometimes conflicts with the principles that traditional deterrence has embraced.[58] Behavioural studies argue that it is not clear that potential offenders take into consideration future consequences often enough when deciding to commit an offence.[59] This is even more so in violent crimes, where an emotional component is usually involved.[60]

This criticism could be raised even more forcefully in the context of genocide, crimes against humanity, war crimes, or other crimes committed extraterritorially. As Roberts and Carver suggest,

> Rational calculation is especially liable to be displaced where perpetrators link criminality with personal survival or the defence of their national or ethnic identity, and where immediate group norms exert more direct influence over behaviour than phenomenologically distant international legal codes.[61]

Thus deterrence is weak in such contexts due, inter alia, to the limitation of resources and limited number of prosecutions, the lack of political legitimacy of most extraterritorial courts from the point of view of the targeted groups or individuals, but also to the collective nature of these crimes and the psychological pattern of the leaders.[62] Admittedly, we lack empirical studies that corroborate these hypotheses. Yet given the doubts that studies raise in purely domestic settings, we have good

the Effects of Mass Incarceration on Informal Social Control in Communities', *Criminology and Public Policy* 3/2 (2004).

[57] Von Hirsch et al, *Criminal Deterrence and Sentence Severity*, 6–7.

[58] Paul H Robinson and John M Darley, 'Does Criminal Law Deter? A Behavioural Science Investigation', *OJLS* 24/2 (2004), 182.

[59] On top of the standard characteristics that make potential offenders a group less inclined to think about future consequences of their conduct (risk seekers, impulsiveness, and alcohol and drug consumption), several studies include other temporary states of mind that are likely to drive out rational considerations of punishment. These include desires for revenge or retaliation, rage or anger, paranoia, manic depression, and other personality features that would not be considered illnesses, ie low ability to delay gratification or lack of self-control (ibid, 179–80). Von Hirsch and his co-authors refer in this sense to the strong presence of need or even 'desperation' and the conscious decision not to dwell on the possibility of getting caught leading to these same results (von Hirsch et al, *Criminal Deterrence and Sentence Severity*, 36).

[60] See Stephanie Carmichael and Alex R Piquero, 'Sanctions, Perceived Anger, and Criminal Offending', *J of Quantitative Criminology* 20/4 (2004) on the relevance of anger in particular. I do not know of other studies working on the basis of other emotional states.

[61] Lucy Carver and Paul Roberts, 'Penal Law and Global Justice' (2008), unpublished manuscript cited with permission from the authors, 30.

[62] See eg Sloane, 'The Expressive Capacity of International Punishment', 72–3; Tallgren, 'The Sensibility and Sense of International Criminal Law', 571–2. As Drumbl suggests, 'many perpetrators *want* to belong to violent groups', and they often believe 'they are acting for the benefit of the collective, not their own personal gain' (Drumbl, *Atrocity, Punishment, and International Law*, 171, with reference to Jaime Malamud-Goti, 'Transitional Governments in the Breach: Why Punish State Criminals', *Human Rights Q* 12/1 (1990)).

grounds to suggest that whether deterrence is achieved in this type of context is a far more tenuous and complicated process than initially assumed.[63]

Finally, if still committed to translate this interest into a normative power, the obvious problem that the deterrence theorist will face is its well-known inflationary character. Deterrence seems committed to the claim that the 'more' punishment is exacted, the stronger the deterrence effect of criminal law would be and, as a result, the fewer violations of these rights and goods would result. In particular, the deterrent effect has been said to depend on the certainty, severity, and celerity of the punishment.[64] The problem here is that such an argument would be committed to justifying and endorsing every bit of harm inflicted, as long as it does not outweigh the harm prevented. As suggested, this reasoning would be particularly problematic in the domain of international crimes such as genocide, war crimes, and crimes against humanity. Accordingly, deterrence may advocate a power to punish that is entirely incompatible with the way in which this power is currently construed. It would, for instance, offer no argument against altering an offender's moral boundaries in ways that allow for corporal punishment, including torture. Under certain circumstances, such as in the context of mass atrocities, it would probably warrant conferring a power to alter not only the offender's moral boundaries, but also those of her family and friends.

To clarify, all these implications should not be construed in deontic terms. The point here is that deterrence fails to account for certain key features of the normative power to punish offenders as it currently stands—that is, what states can validly do—not that it leads to morally impermissible outcomes.[65]

2.1.4 Three objections

Before closing this section three lines of criticism against the argument presented so far must be carefully considered. On the one hand, it may be argued that the explanation for the power to punish hereby advocated stands on instrumental grounds. This would make it liable to the charge of contingency raised above against victim-based arguments. In effect, this account entails that punishment is only of derivative value. Its value depends on it contributing to the well-being of individuals. Yet despite being instrumental, the connection between punishing offenders and reasserting our confidence in the bindingness of a legal rule is intrinsic and necessary. That is, there are neither epistemological difficulties nor standard cases for which this justification does not hold. Whenever offenders are punished for their offence and by a body expressly authorized by the relevant legal system, it is clear that the rule that was violated has been enforced. This necessarily conveys the message that the rules that were violated are in force. Moreover, these legal rules being in force prohibiting murder, rape, and so on necessarily contribute to individuals'

[63] In fact, studies do not talk about causality but rather about the weaker notion of correlation. On this and on the particular problem of simultaneity see von Hirsch et al, *Criminal Deterrence and Sentence Severity*, 17 and 20.

[64] Bentham, Jeremy, *The Rationale of Punishment* (London: 1830), ch VI.

[65] On the relevance of standard practices see Chapter 1.

sense of dignity and security. Thus, the instrumentality charge cannot ground its purported implication, namely, that an instrumental account of legal punishment will always be liable to the charge of contingency raised in this chapter—that is, not being able to explain all the standard cases.

On the other hand, it may be objected that the argument advocated here would collapse into a purely consequentialist account, therefore being liable to the criticisms raised above against deterrence. This perception, however, is based on a mistaken understanding of the role that consequences have in the argument presented. We may plausibly define a consequentialist doctrine as one in which 'the good is defined independently of the right' and which argues that 'the right is maximizing the good as already specified'.[66] Deontological theories, by contrast, should therefore be 'defined as non-teleological ones, not as views that characterize the rightness of institutions and acts independently from their consequences'.[67] In light of these rough definitions, the argument defended here does not define the good as individuals' well-being, and then try to maximize its overall level. Rather, the point is whether the interests of X, Y, and Z warrant conferring upon a particular state S the power to punish a specific offender O even if, overall, that would lead to a suboptimal level of well-being. In other words, although it takes consequences into consideration, this argument does not simply add them in a broad calculation of utility, crime-reduction, or overall well-being.

We must be careful not to misrepresent the specific interest on which the argument rests. The argument defended here does not explain state S's power to punish a particular offender O on the basis of an increase in the sense of dignity and security that individuals enjoy there. This would admittedly lead to trying to maximize this sense of dignity and security. Rather, the relationship of implication works in the opposite direction. It is because having certain criminal rules in force contributes to our sense of dignity and security that S holds the power to punish O. Thus, this argument relies on the interest individuals hold in these laws being in force rather than directly on the interest they have in their sense of dignity and security.

Accordingly, this justification is free from the harshness charge raised against deterrence. Individuals' belief in the existence of a rule need not entail a power to alter any right held by an offender, such as the right not to be tortured. A brutal penalty could express that a rule against, say, robbery is in force. And some people may even say that it would do so more forcefully than a prison sentence. However, this interest-based justification would not entail such power. For one, imprisonment and other more lenient penalties clearly suffice to communicate that a particular criminal rule is in force.[68] Moreover, when these more lenient means

[66] Rawls, *A Theory of Justice*, 22.

[67] Rawls adds: 'all ethical doctrines worth our attention take consequences into account in judging rightness. One which did not would simply be irrational, crazy' (ibid, 26).

[68] This point touches upon the question of cardinal levels of punishment: why imprisonment or fines instead of physical punishments or death? This is an extremely difficult question that is beyond the scope of this book. Indeed, the point here is not to defend imprisonment or any other specific penalty per se; rather, the point is only that although the argument here advocated requires some

work, one arguably lacks the power to use a harsher means. Most significantly perhaps, the power to inflict cruel or inhumane penalties or to punish individuals for acts committed by their relatives or friends would undermine, rather than support, the sense of dignity and security of individuals in any given state. Cruel penalties put into question our self-understanding as right-holders, and the role of legal rules as upholding and protecting those rights. That would be the case, for example, if the offender were tortured to death or the state were to sentence all her (innocent) family to forced labour.

There is one final objection to consider: that my argument commits me to the view that states hold the power to punish the innocent. As suggested above, the requirement that someone must be punished for her offence does not mean that she has, as a matter of fact, to have committed that offence. It means only that the fact that she is guilty is the reason for which she is being punished or, put differently, that a state can punish neither the innocent *qua* innocent, nor the guilty for the wrong reasons. Admittedly, this charge is accurate. Yet instead of considering it a fatal objection, I submit that with this feature lies a fundamental strength of the account of legal punishment advocated here.

Let me explain. By distinguishing between a state's Hohfeldian power to punish the innocent and it being at liberty to do so, this account can accommodate the fact that states hold the power to punish innocent people, while at the same time being able to claim, as I shall do in the next section, that punishing the innocent would be to act impermissibly. This means, in short, that the innocent's conviction and her sentence would be valid, that is, her moral and legal boundaries would be effectively modified by the relevant court.[69] However, it would be wrong for the state to punish her. There is simply no contradiction here. As stated in Chapter 1, sometimes it is possible to have a power which one is not at liberty to exercise or, in less technical language, a right to do wrong.

However, Chapter 1 also argued that there are certain situations in which the wrong involved in modifying certain rights is such that it precludes the modification itself.[70] This is not the case with punishing the innocent under the framework advocated here. But before arguing for this, it is worth situating this issue within the broader framework advanced in this book. My position is that for state S to have the power to punish a defendant O, not only someone's interest should be sufficiently important to confer upon S this power, but also S must have the authority to do so. As it will be argued at length in Chapter 6, S can claim the authority to punish O only when O receives a fair trial, she is convicted after a thorough investigation, and S is credibly punishing her because it is satisfied to the relevant standard of proof that O is guilty. Put differently, my account only commits me to the view that S has the power to punish the innocent when it makes

level of hard treatment (sufficient to convey the existence of a criminal rule), it does not lead to disproportionate or brutally harsh penalties.

[69] On why and under what conditions a state can claim the authority to punish the innocent, see Chapter 6.

[70] See section 2.1.

a reasonable and honest mistake.[71] This qualification removes much of the edge in this charge. Establishing a system of criminal laws ultimately entails accepting the possibility of punishing the innocent in some measure, at least with current levels of technology. Besides, as long as state S can justify to the innocent why she is being punished, and this justification is reasonable, her being punished would not undermine the sense of dignity and security that S's criminal laws being in force provide her, even if her conviction is mistaken.

Conversely, it may be the case that the interest that justifies conferring upon state S the power to punish O would simply override the interest on which O's claim-right against being punished rests. This would make it also permissible for S to punish the innocent. I will not rely on this type of overriding strategy to explain the permissibility of exercising the power to punish. But let me state here why this charge seems unwarranted. Even if we were to explain S's liberty to punish O by reference to the collective interest in having a system of criminal rules in force, this interest would hardly suffice to outweigh the interest of individuals in not suffering the type of censure and hard treatment that punishment involves. The consequences that legal punishment has for those who have it inflicted upon them are simply too severe, too profound to be outweighed by the interest of having a system of criminal laws in force. In particular, since the fulfilment of the later interest does not depend on it also being permissible for the state to punish O.

Accordingly, this separation between first and second order incidents—between powers and liberties—seems normatively sound. Furthermore, it helps us to explain at least two familiar features of criminal law systems. First, it follows that if the innocent can demonstrate that she was mistakenly convicted, she would be entitled to be compensated for the harm she suffered as a result of her incarceration. Moreover, if her innocence can be demonstrated she should be immediately released. Yet these new changes in her moral boundaries are not automatic. They would be the result of a further decision by a court of law, that is, an authority expressly authorized by the legal system, restoring her moral and legal boundaries.[72] Secondly, the legal power to release and compensate the innocent is required by the overall argument hereby advocated. It would no longer be the case that the innocent would be punished for her offence. Once her innocence has been demonstrated, her remaining in prison would undermine, rather than enhance, the sense of dignity and security of individuals living under that legal system. It is quite likely that a state that imprisons the innocent will be perceived as oppressive, and as a threat to individuals' fundamental rights.

2.2 The justification for the liberty to punish an offender

As suggested above, a complete justification for legal punishment does not merely need to argue that state S holds the power to punish offender O; it must also argue

[71] See Chapter 6, specially the discussion of the authoritativeness of mistaken decisions.

[72] Interestingly, states do not normally have the power to overturn convictions from other state's courts.

that it is permissible for S to do so. In Hohfeldian terms, the purpose of this section is to argue that state S is also at liberty to punish this offender. This argument can be made in two different ways. One way would be to argue that an interest of individuals in S is sufficiently important to put the offender under a no-right not to be punished. The other way would be to argue that this offender lacks herself a claim-right against having punishment inflicted upon her. In Razian terms, we can invoke an overriding consideration or a cancelling condition.[73]

Deterrence would provide an argument of the first kind. This book follows, by contrast, a cancellation strategy. This means arguing that an offender lacks a claim-right against being punished. There are at least two possible lines of argument one can use to make this case. One can either argue that the offender has forfeited her claim-right, or one can suggest that her general claim-right not to suffer this kind of treatment does not include protection against legal punishment. I shall defend a version of the forfeiture argument.[74]

Standardly, the forfeiture of a right makes reference to a right lost due to some crime or fault, breach or neglect of rules on the part of the person who is said to be responsible for it.[75] The concept of forfeiture is used in legal and moral discourse often enough not to warrant any kind of conceptual clarification here. The normative work forfeiture does, by contrast, needs to be carefully examined. Within the rights-based literature, Daniel McDermott provides an account of how this mechanism works in the context of legal punishment.[76] He argues that when Oscar wrongs Vanessa, say, by stealing £100 from her, she suffers two losses. First, she loses her money and, secondly, she does not receive the treatment due to her as a right-holder. As a result, Oscar incurred a debt for each of them. Just as he forfeited his right to £100, he forfeited his right to some moral good of his. However, unlike the £100, Oscar cannot restore to Vanessa the treatment he did not provide her. So in a moral community in which all members are entitled to certain benefits and burdens,

> By failing to provide their victims with the treatment they owe them as right holders, wrongdoers incur debts to their victims of the value of this moral good, and, as a result, they forfeit their rights to other, equally valuable, moral goods.[77]

Punishment is thus a means of denying these forfeited moral goods to the wrongdoers.[78]

Despite its strong intuitive plausibility, however, it seems that by using the notion of moral debt to justify Oscar's loss of his right, McDermott is unable to

[73] Raz, *Practical Reason and Norms*. See also Mitchell N Berman, 'Punishment and Justification', *Ethics* 118 (2008).

[74] For an example of the latter strategy, see Berman, 'Punishment and Justification'.

[75] Uniacke, *Permissible Killing*, 201.

[76] Daniel McDermott, 'The Permissibility of Punishment', *Law and Philosophy* 20 (2001), 424.

[77] Ibid.

[78] This argument should not be conflated with the unfair advantage theory defended at one point by Andrew von Hirsch and Herbert Morris, among others (see Andrew von Hirsch, *Doing Justice: The Choice of Punishments* (New York: Hill and Wang, 1976), and H Morris, 'Persons and Punishment', *The Monist* 52 (1968)). For criticisms, see Dolinko, 'Some Thoughts About Retributivism', and von Hirsch, *Censure and Sanctions*.

explain to whom that debt would be owed if Vanessa dies. Admittedly, if Oscar shoots her and she goes to hospital, he would incur a debt for hospital charges as well as other damages. *Pace* McDermott, he would also incur a moral debt for having violated Vanessa's rights. But in a Raskolnikov-type case, Oscar's material debt is extinguished with the sisters' death. Why would his moral debt not be extinguished precisely in the same way? McDermott's main strength, namely, the fact that 'there is nothing at all mysterious about the claim that committing a debt-generating act changes a person's moral status',[79] seems to condemn his explanation to contingency—particularly so as he explicitly rejects explaining this moral change by resorting to the idea that an offender incurs a debt towards the society in which she lives.[80]

Albeit ultimately unsuccessful, this approach shows precisely the kind of explanation one needs to provide. That is, what needs elucidation is the mechanism by which offender O committing a wrong results in a change in her moral boundaries that makes the state's punishment of her permissible. Two points need elaboration. First, it is often argued that an offender forfeits some of her rights. Yet it is very unclear what right an offender would allegedly forfeit, or better, what type of right this is. Most of the accounts in the literature fail to distinguish between first and second order Hohfeldian incidents. Accordingly, these accounts need the forfeiture argument to do all of the normative work, namely, to account for the offender's lack of an immunity *and* a claim-right against being punished. By contrast, in this account the forfeiture argument needs to explain only why the offender lacks a claim-right against the state exercising the power to punish her. By definition, to argue that an offender lacks the claim-right against being punished by state S, means only that S is at liberty to do so.

Secondly, state S holds the Hohfeldian power to punish an individual who is in fact innocent, namely, who by definition has not forfeited any claim-right of hers.[81] This is not just a normative claim but also, and crucially, a fairly accurate descriptive one. Accordingly, to argue that state S is under a duty not to punish an innocent defendant means that, whenever possible, S should restore her to the situation she was in before being punished, and when this is not possible it should compensate her for the wrong she suffered. Moreover, if state S's judge J knew that punishing her was wrong because she was innocent, judge J would be committing a wrongful act and could be criminally prosecuted. By contrast, to say that S is at liberty to punish a guilty defendant, or similarly that she lacks the claim-right against S doing so, is to say that she is owed nothing. So if she is convicted and afterwards pardoned she is not compensated for the time she spent in prison.

The lack of such a claim-right against being punished is all the forfeiture argument must account for. Let me now provide an account of how the forfeiture mechanism may work. This is a difficult and longstanding philosophical question.

[79] Daniel McDermott, 'Debts to Society', *J of Political Philosophy* 10/4 (2002), 441.
[80] Ibid.
[81] Subject to the state meeting the requirements for claiming authority to punish that innocent individual. On this, see Chapter 6.

It is behind, for instance, most attempts at capturing what it means for an offender to deserve being punished, or to claim that punishing her is intrinsically good. The doctrine of forfeiture of rights simply accounts for the fact that the protection that rights provide is not unconditional. Rather, it is usually conditional upon conduct. To give a quick example, if Amanda arrives late at the opera, she would probably be denied access to her seat. Her claim-right against being stopped at the door is not absolute; it is conditional upon arriving on time. The penalty for being late is, in the language of rights, that Amanda has forfeited the claim-right she had against the theatre management letting her in. This means that she is not being wronged by the doorman who refuses her entry; he is at liberty (and probably under a duty) to stop her. Accordingly, Amanda cannot claim compensation for having missed the show, nor is she entitled to receive seats for the next performance. The only remaining question is, then, whether such particular limitation to her right (being refused access) is a legitimate one to impose.

Analogously, we may say that individuals have generally a claim-right against being punished by the state. The state is under a duty not to punish them, and if it violates this duty, it should prosecute those who do so and (at the very least) it should compensate those who suffered this violation. But this claim-right is neither absolute nor unconditional. Individuals are entitled to its protection provided they do not perpetrate a criminal wrong. Furthermore, this limitation upon this claim-right seems, normatively, a legitimate one to impose. The reason for this may be disappointingly simple. It was argued here that legal punishment is a form of moral language that allows the state to censure an individual, and to convey to individuals generally the message that a set of legal prohibitions of murder, rape and so on are in force. With her act, the offender put into question the existence of the relevant prohibition; as a result, she cannot legitimately complain if she is strongly censured for her conduct, and reminded that this prohibition is also binding upon her. This simple point is what seems to account for the different entitlements between offenders and non-offenders from the point of view of their holding or not holding a claim-right against legal punishment being meted out by the state.

Before concluding, there are two important implications worth noting. First, to claim that O forfeited her claim-right against being punished does not necessarily entail that anyone is at liberty to do so. An offender O can be said to have forfeited her claim-right *in rem*, that is, against the world at large, or *in personam*, namely, against certain individuals or bodies.[82] Forfeiture arguments are normally construed in the former sense. Yet, as Fabre has suggested, it does not follow from the fact that an offender has forfeited her claim-right that no one punishes her, that anyone can do so. A more plausible version of the forfeiture argument would suggest that 'it is no longer the case that everyone is under a duty not to' punish her.[83] In other words, the forfeiture argument would explain why offender O has lost her

[82] On this distinction, see Chapter 1.

[83] Cécile Fabre, 'Permissible Rescue Killings', *Proceedings of the Aristotelian Society* 109 (2009), 153.

claim-right against a particular state (eg, Italy) punishing her, and not the world at large. The reason why a liberty is conferred upon Italy (and not, eg, Colombia) may be explained by other considerations. In this account, it would be explained by the interest that justifies Italy in particular holding the power to punish her.

And finally, this explanation does not lead to the implausible position that denying that an offender holds a claim-right against being punished amounts to denying her having an interest in not being punished. The fact that an interest warrants the protection of a right should clearly not lead us to conflate the two. Most probably the offender would still have an interest in not being punished, just as the latecomer to the opera would maintain her interest in seeing *Carmen*. The only thing they have lost, according to the view hereby defended, is the moral shield that protected those interests.

3. Conclusion

This chapter argues that in order to provide an explanation for the proposition 'state S has the moral right to punish individual O' we need to distinguish between the different incidents that form this molecular right. Yet it only puts forward an argument for S's power and its liberty to punish O. I argued that S's power to punish O should be explained by reference to the collective interest of individuals in S in its criminal laws being in force. This is because a system of rules being in force prohibiting murder, rape, and so on constitutes a public good that contributes to their well-being. By contrast, S's liberty to exercise this normative power against a particular offender has been explained by her having forfeited her claim-right against being punished.

Let me close this chapter by further elaborating how this general argument is situated *vis-à-vis* other accounts in the literature. The argument advocated here is a version of a hybrid, or dualist, justification of which the most famous and influential examples are those of Herbert Hart and John Rawls.[84] However, it is unique in its use of the Hohfeldian analysis of rights. The main defence of this argument will be made throughout the book, when it is put to use to explain the extraterritorial scope of this particular power. For present purposes, however, its reliance on Hohfeld provides it with a crucial advantage over standard dualist accounts. On the one hand, Hohfeld's analysis accounts for the precise normative implication of each of the arguments presented in this chapter. While the initial argument explains why offender O is under a liability to be punished, the argument developed in section 2.2 explains her lack of a claim-right against having her moral boundaries redefined in the way punishment requires. This cannot really be said of Hart's famous distinction between the general justifying aim of the institution of punishment and the right principles of its distribution. On the other hand, the

[84] Hart, *Punishment and Responsibility*; and John Rawls, 'Two Concepts of Rules' in Robert M Baird and Stuart E Rosenbaum (eds), *Philosophy of Punishment* (New York: Prometheus Books, 1988). For a more recent version see von Hirsch, *Censure and Sanctions*.

analysis favoured here provides a clear criterion of how the different arguments relate to each other. The fact that liberties and powers are of a different order is an important feature of Hohfeld's analysis of rights. This means for our purposes that in some cases state S would have the power to do something which it is not at liberty to do. Put briefly, this argument is able to explain why states are commonly seen as holding the right to punish innocent individuals, while at the same time being able to maintain that it would be wrong for them to do so.

3

Extraterritorial Jurisdiction over Municipal Crimes

> The Spaniards violated all rules when they set themselves up as judges of the Inca Atahualpa. If that prince had violated the law of nations with respect to them, they would have had a right to punish him. But they accused him of having put some of his subjects to death, of having had several wives, &c—things, for which he was not at all accountable to them; and, to fill up the measure of their extravagant injustice, they condemned him by the laws of Spain.[1]

1. The Existing Legal Framework

As a matter of law, states characteristically claim the power to punish certain municipal offences committed extraterritorially. Under the Sexual Offences Act 2003, for example, English and Welsh courts have the power to punish nationals or residents of these countries who commit certain types of sexual crimes, for instance, on a holiday trip to South-East Asia. Similarly, under article 113–7 of its Penal Code, France claims jurisdiction over any felony committed anywhere in the world when the victim was a French national at the time the offence took place. Most states criminalize conduct such as the counterfeiting of their currency, espionage, or treason regardless of where they are performed. In short, although the criminal law is usually regarded as primarily territorial in its application, these types of provisions are relatively standard in the vast majority of states.

The extraterritorial scope of states' power to punish is ultimately governed by international law. States are free to decide whether and when they will exercise this right, but they can do so only within the constraints imposed by the international

[1] Emmerich de Vattel, *Law of Nations; or, Principles of the Law of Nature, Applied to the Conduct and Affairs of Nations and Sovereigns* (New York: AMS Press, 1773), 110. Although this quote shows precisely what is at stake in this chapter, a point of clarification is in order. Vattel got the facts wrong, possibly following the, at his time, well-known account of Garcilazo. The Inca Atahualpa was not tried through a fair procedure as sometimes suggested but rather executed, in haste, on expediency reasons. Francisco Pizarro and some of his men feared an attempt to rescue him while waiting for reinforcements. Moreover, he was allegedly executed for offences against Pizarro and the Spaniards, not for offences against his own people. Incidentally, Pizarro's decision was heavily criticized in Spain on the ground that he lacked the right to try a king. For a good account of this story see J Hemming, *The Conquest of the Incas* (London: Papermac, 1993).

legal system.[2] By and large, there are currently three different grounds or principles on which a state can base its power to punish an offender extraterritorially for a domestic offence. These are commonly known as the principles of nationality, passive personality, and protection, and they rely, respectively, on whether the offence was committed by one of its nationals, as under the Sexual Offences Act cited above, against one of its nationals, as in the French provision, or against the sovereignty or national security of that state, as with the counterfeiting of national currency.[3]

This chapter examines the moral foundations of this well-established legal framework and finds them lacking. By contrast, it advocates a more restricted scope for states' power to punish municipal offences extraterritorially. Section 2 argues that the territorial scope of a state's power to punish is determined by the reasons that justify that particular state holding the power to punish wrongdoers generally.[4] It provides an explanation for the primarily territorial character of domestic criminal law based on the normative justification for the power to punish advocated in Chapter 2. The remainder of the chapter will contend that although states have the power to punish certain offenders extraterritorially on grounds of protection, that is, for crimes which affect their sovereignty or security (section 5), doing so on the basis of the nationality of the offender or that of the victim would be *ultra vires* (sections 3 and 4, respectively). It will be argued that the arguments on which the nationality and passive personality principles are standardly defended either beg the fundamental question which they are meant to answer or collapse into much broader claims of extraterritorial jurisdiction that few of their supporters would be prepared to endorse. Section 6 examines two possible lines of criticism to the framework put forward. It rejects the claim that the theory advocated here is too restrictive and, as a result, unconvincing in a world in which crime is increasingly becoming globalized. Finally, it argues that other justifications for the right to punish available in the literature, on the whole, do not fare as well as the argument defended here in explaining the way in which international law regulates states' extraterritorial criminal jurisdiction for municipal crimes.

2. The Territorial Scope of the Power to Punish

The territorial scope of a state's criminal law is commonly regarded as a manifestation of its sovereignty. This entails that a state has the normative power to prescribe criminal rules which are binding on every person who is, for whatever reason, on its territory. Crucially for our purposes, it also entails the normative power to punish

[2] Joseph H Beale, 'The Jurisdiction of a Sovereign State', *Harvard L Rev* 36/3 (1923), 243.

[3] Sometimes other bases of jurisdiction are articulated, such as the floating territorial principle, jurisdiction on embassies abroad, in aircrafts, and so on (B J George Jr, 'Extraterritorial Application of Penal Legislation', *Michigan L Rev* 64/4 (1966), 609; and Michael Hirst, *Jurisdiction and the Ambit of the Criminal Law* (Oxford: Oxford University Press, 2003), esp ch 6). These 'quasi-territorial' bases of jurisdiction are not covered in this book.

[4] This chapter examines the grounds on which the courts of a state S can claim jurisdiction to punish a given offender. The question of a state's authority to punish will be examined in Chapter 6.

anyone who violates its criminal rules within its territorial borders. In Locke's words, the issue at stake here is

> by what Right any Prince or State can put to death, or punish an Alien, for any Crime he commits in their country. 'Tis certain their Laws by virtue of any sanction they receive from the promulgated Will of the Legislative, reach not a Stranger.[5]

I shall not address the issue of when a particular offence can be said to be committed on the territory of a particular state. That is a complicated enough question the consideration of which merits treatment beyond the object of this enquiry.[6] We will examine the standard cases in which, for example, both the conduct of the offender and its result (eg, the victim's death) occurred on the territory of a given state. As a legal basis for criminal jurisdiction, territoriality raises little controversy.[7] However—or perhaps precisely for this reason—any justification for the power to punish concerned with evaluating its extraterritorial application needs, first, to be able to account convincingly for this basic principle.

It is submitted here that in order to account for the territorial scope of a state's right to punish, we need to look at the reasons that justify that particular state initially holding the power to punish wrongdoers. In Chapter 2 I argued that the power to punish offenders is based on the claim that having a system of criminal law in force constitutes a public good that benefits the individuals who live under it in a certain way. This proposition involves a jurisprudential and a normative claim. From the point of view of analytical jurisprudence, it implies that there is a necessary link between a system of criminal laws being in force and the state holding the power to punish offenders. From a normative point of view, I argued that having a set of legal rules in force prohibiting murder, rape, and so on contributes to the sense of dignity and security of individuals in any particular society. Ultimately I suggested that the collective interest individuals have in this system being in force, that is, binding on them, is sufficiently important to warrant conferring upon the state the power to punish offenders. As it stands, this argument clearly accounts for the territorial scope of this power. A state's normative power to punish a given offender is justified by the collective interest of individuals in that state in having a system of laws in force prohibiting, murder, rape, etc. It is the people in France who have an interest in the French criminal law system being in force.

This readily explains, for instance, why France holds the power to punish offences committed by or against foreigners on its territory.[8] Offences against foreigners committed in France do, as a matter of fact, undermine France's criminal laws

[5] John Locke, *Two Treatises of Government* (Cambridge: Cambridge University Press, 1988), §9, 273.

[6] The standard doctrine distinguishes between subjective and objective territoriality, and the more controversial effects doctrine. On this, see the classical piece by Michael Akehurst, 'Jurisdiction in International Law', *BYIL* 46 (1972–1973), 145 and, more recently, the monograph by Hirst, *Jurisdiction and the Ambit of the Criminal Law*, chs 3 and 4 (from a UK perspective).

[7] See eg 'Draft Convention on Jurisdiction with Respect to Crime', *AJIL* 29 (Supp 1935), 480; and Brownlie, *Principles of Public International Law* (Oxford: Oxford University Press, 2003), 299.

[8] This is an important aspect of this argument because, as I shall argue in section 6 below, it creates a significant difficulty for one of the most influential arguments for legal punishment available in the literature.

being in force, thus affecting this public good. When A murders B in France, she puts into question the existence of France's legal rule prohibiting murder. This reasoning holds even if both of them are foreigners who happened to be on French territory (eg, on holiday). Moreover, it would hold even if the victim is targeted because he is not a member of the territorial state. If an English football fan is killed after a match in Germany by German fans, this would certainly undermine the confidence of the people in the rule against murder being in force in Germany. This explains why states, which are often portrayed as self-interested machines, characteristically prohibit the murder of any person on their territory, and not only the murder of their nationals or residents.[9]

Ultimately, it is submitted that the collective interest that explains conferring upon the territorial state the power to punish anyone who commits a crime on its territory is also shared by individuals who happen to be there accidentally, or for a very short period of time. It is the interest of every individual in a given state that collectively grounds that state's power to punish, not merely the interests of its nationals or permanent residents. To illustrate: Manuel is a Colombian national. When he travels to Italy on holiday, he has an interest in people there abiding by most of the Italian criminal laws. While walking down an alley in Rome or dining in a jovial *trattoria* in Naples, Manuel has an interest in Italy's criminal laws prohibiting murder, theft, etc being in force. Although temporally limited—after all, he will probably be out of the country in a matter of days—this interest is arguably as strong as the interest of any other Italian national or permanent resident sitting next to him. During his stay, his interest is therefore part of the collective interest that justifies Italian courts holding a power to punish those who violate Italy's criminal rules.[10]

These considerations, then, fully explain the territorial scope of the criminal law system to the extent that it involves a state holding a normative power to punish anyone who violates its criminal law within its borders. Let us now examine whether this state can claim an exclusive right to do so, or whether other states could claim the power to exercise their criminal jurisdictions concurrently. I suggest here that extraterritorial states are under a prima facie disability to punish offences perpetrated abroad. This claim needs to take into consideration two concurrent arguments.

First, one may argue that the population in a given state lacks an interest in enforcing its domestic criminal laws on the territory of a foreign state. That would be true in most cases, but not in all. People living in Uruguay do not usually have an interest in the Uruguayan criminal laws being in force in Sweden that is sufficiently important to warrant conferring upon Uruguay a power to punish offences committed on Swedish territory. To that extent, this argument entails

[9] As argued in Chapter 2, we must not conflate the belief that a rule is in force with the somewhat different one that one, *in particular*, is less vulnerable to being a victim of a criminal offence. Criminal laws can ground the former belief, but not the latter.

[10] Although perhaps not central to my argument, this position allows for the claim that the interests of temporary visitors also matter. This position is not only compatible but arguably required by the moderate cosmopolitan position endorsed in Chapter 1.

that Uruguay itself lacks the prima facie power to do so. But this explanation only provides for a conditional conclusion. Under certain circumstances (some of which will be explored below) individuals living in Uruguay may have an interest in their criminal laws also being in force in Sweden. A standard case could be the counterfeiting of Uruguayan currency. Hence this argument explains only why states may lack extraterritorial criminal jurisdiction in those cases in which individuals in their territory lack a collective interest in their criminal laws being in force abroad.

Secondly, we also need to consider the interests of individuals in the state in which the offence was perpetrated (the territorial state). In Chapter 1 I argued that states hold a right to self-government. This right does not merely include the power to criminalize certain behaviours; it also entails a prima facie immunity against other states dictating and enforcing their criminal rules on the territory of a foreign state. This entails, for instance, that the UK has a prima facie immunity against Sri Lanka dictating criminal rules that apply on UK territory (and vice versa). However, it was also argued that this prima facie immunity is neither absolute nor unconditional. It is limited, inter alia, by the interests of individuals outside the territorial state. Accordingly, the interest that explains this immunity does not necessarily preclude an extraterritorial state holding a power to punish a particular offender for crimes committed on the territory of another state in every possible case. It only creates a further argumentative threshold that the justification for extraterritorial punishment must meet.[11]

3. The Nationality Principle

Let us now examine the moral credentials of the 'nationality principle'. The issue at stake here is whether states have the normative power to punish an offender for a crime she committed on the territory of another state, on the ground that the offender is a national of the extraterritorial state. This basis of criminal jurisdiction often comes accompanied by other considerations. Most commonly, it is provided for offences that affect the security of the state,[12] or that are committed against a national of the extraterritorial state. For the sake of clarity, we may consider cases in which the nationality of the offender constitutes the sole basis of criminal jurisdiction. Other grounds of extraterritorial criminal jurisdiction will be examined below, under the passive personality and the protective principles.

Akin to the principle of territoriality, the nationality principle is also relatively uncontroversial under existing international law.[13] In fact, it has been generally

[11] A note of caution is in order here. Just as I have argued that only a certain specific interest can explain a state's power to punish a particular offender, it is not the case that any interest that individuals in other states may have would suffice to override the prima facie immunity of the territorial state. See sections 4, 5, and 6 below.

[12] See *United States v Bowman* 260 US 94 (1922).

[13] See Sir Arthur Watts and Sir Robert Jennings, *Oppenheim's International Law*, vol 1, *Peace* (Harlow: Longman, 1992); and Akehurst, 'Jurisdiction in International Law'. For more cautious positions, albeit considering it uncontroversial, see Brownlie, *Principles of Public International*

recognized that the original conception of law was personal, and that only the appearance of the territorial state gave rise to the right to subject aliens to the *lex loci*.[14] Recently, this basis of jurisdiction has been growing significantly in some states, and some lawyers even advocate making it a general basis for criminal jurisdiction in the UK.[15] Although many countries have self-imposed restrictions on the application of this basis of jurisdiction it is generally argued that, as a matter of law, there is no rule against extending it as far as those countries see fit.[16]

A first conceptual difficulty with this principle is that the word 'nationals' has different meanings when used in public international law and international political theory.[17] Lawyers mean membership of a state, whereas political theorists often concentrate on the moral relevance of nations. We need not enter that debate here. The nationality principle only makes reference to membership of a state, not of a nation. By way of stipulation I will use the term 'nationals' here to refer only to the citizens of a state. A further point of clarification concerns the extension of this principle to residents. In an early work in this area, Donnedieu de Vabres pointed out that, historically, it was the domicile of the accused rather than her nationality which provided the basis of this type of jurisdiction.[18] Although nowadays this principle is taken to mean that states have the right mainly to prosecute their nationals,[19] the generally accepted position is that residence may suffice for jurisdiction, and that on occasion, states do adopt such an approach.[20]

It is submitted here that a state's normative power to punish is explained by the collective interest of individuals in that state in having a system of criminal laws in force. This argument is incompatible with the nationality principle. To put it simply, there seems to be no way in which Spain's criminal rules being in force require punishing an offender for a robbery she committed in Paraguay, simply on the ground that she happens to be a national of Spain. For one thing, it seems odd

Law, 301–2; and Antonio Cassese, *International Criminal Law* (Oxford: Oxford University Press, 2003), 281.

14 James Leslie Brierley, 'The Lotus Case', *LQR* 44 (1928), 155–6.

15 See the Sexual Offences Act 2003, the Landmines Act 1998, and the Nuclear Explosions (Prohibition and Inspections) Act 1998. Also, P Arnell, 'The Case for Nationality Based Jurisdiction', *ICLQ* 50 (2001), 961.

16 Regarding self-imposed restrictions, in some countries the law requires that the offence be a crime under the law of the state in whose territory it was committed (eg, Egypt; see Cassese, *International Criminal Law*, 281). In others, it is only provided for serious offences.

17 Agruably, nationality has no uniform definition even in international law (Harvard Research in International Law, 'The Law of Nationality', 23 *AJIL* (Supp 1929) 21).

18 Henri Donnedieu de Vabres, *Les Principes Modernes Du Droit Pénal International* (Paris: 1928), 66–8.

19 'Draft Convention on Jurisdiction with Respect to Crime', 533. The only exception to this being, plausibly, stateless persons. In the Draft Convention on Jurisdiction with Respect to Crime the only persons assimilated to nationals are those aliens who 'discharge ... a public function which [they were] engage[d] to perform for that State' or who are personnel of a ship or aircraft of that state's flag (see Art 6).

20 See Ian Brownlie, *Principles of Public International Law* (7th edn, 2008), 303; Michael Akehurst, 'Jurisdiction in International Law', 156–7; and Watts and Jennings, *Oppenheim's International Law*, 469.

to say that the offender has violated the criminal laws of Spain. But even granting this proposition for the sake of argument, the collective interest of individuals in Spain in the sense of security and dignity that criminal laws being in force provide them does not seem to be affected by a robbery in Paraguay. Inhabitants of Spain may feel horrified by a particular crime committed outside its territory by a co-national, but their belief in the system of criminal rules under which they live being in force is not undermined by these offences. This conclusion is at odds with current international law as well as, to some extent, with commonsense morality. The remainder of this section critically examines the arguments put forward to justify this basis for extraterritorial criminal jurisdiction.

Nationality-based criminal jurisdiction has been defended, for instance, on the basis of the proposition that the right of an extraterritorial state to punish, for example, certain sexual offences committed by its members abroad is justified by the possibility of recidivism within that state.[21] A first remark is that, if anything, this argument provides a justification for punishing *only* that state's residents and *not* its nationals. It cannot explain, for example, why the UK would hold a power to punish a British national residing in Spain for an offence she committed in Spain (or France for that matter). This argument would therefore change the scope of this basis of jurisdiction in a way that, to some extent, would be controversial. That is, if applied consistently, nationality would cease to have *any* relevance for exercising the power to punish on the basis of this principle.

But even leaving this issue aside, the problem with it is that it seems to justify the power to punish on the basis of incapacitation or, to a lesser extent, the moral reform of the offender. At the level of philosophical argument this is problematic. Most legal and political philosophers reject these normative arguments as a plausible justification for legal punishment *simpliciter*. There is nothing in the extraterritorial application of criminal laws that would override these well-established moral considerations.

In a different vein, it has been claimed that nationality constitutes an 'evolution' from the 'narrow', 'self-interested' territorial purposes of the state.[22] The criminal law of England and Wales would now 'protect' children extraterritorially against, say, certain sexual offences committed by nationals or residents of those countries. However, if the exercise of criminal jurisdiction by an extraterritorial state is justified by the extra protection awarded to these children, it is open to question on what possible grounds this right could be limited to a state's own nationals or residents. A strict application of this argument would lead to the principle of passive personality, that is, jurisdiction based on the nationality of the victim (if victims in the territorial state are in a particularly vulnerable position), or eventually to universal jurisdiction if potential victims are scattered around the globe, but not to the nationality principle. To that extent, this argument can be readily rejected as a basis for jurisdiction based solely on nationality.

[21] Arnell, 'The Case for Nationality Based Jurisdiction', 961; and V Lowe 'Jurisdiction' in Malcolm D Evans (ed), *International Law* (Oxford: Oxford University Press, 2006), 347.

[22] Arnell, 'The Case for Nationality Based Jurisdiction', 960.

Some further arguments that try to ground this jurisdictional principle on an interest other than the interests of the members of the extraterritorial state reason on the basis of a *non sequitur*. For example, it has been based on the interest of the offender in having a fair trial, or not facing capital punishment.[23] This argument might show that certain states, namely those which cannot guarantee a fair trial or which provide for capital punishment, would lack the power to punish the offender.[24] But it simply does not follow from the fact that the territorial state is disabled from exercising the power to punish an offender, that the state of which she is a national itself holds that power.

Somewhat differently, the power of the extraterritorial state has been based on an interest of the members of the state in which the offence was perpetrated. The argument goes: the territorial state might have an interest in not being forced to face the option of either punishing the offender (and face diplomatic pressure and adverse international publicity) or simply releasing her.[25] This realpolitik argument is again based on a *non sequitur*. The territorial state may have an interest in avoiding such a nasty scenario, although this would probably depend on the identity of both states, as well as plausibly of the offender and the victim. But even if we accept that this is necessarily the case for the sake of argument, this claim does not warrant the stated conclusion. Rather, the interests of individuals in the territorial state seem to warrant conferring upon that state a power to decide whether to: (a) exercise its power to punish the offender itself (despite diplomatic pressure); (b) simply release her; or (c) authorize the extraterritorial state to punish her. This interest entails that it is up to the territorial state, and only up to this state, to decide. Thus, the interest of members of the territorial state cannot straightforwardly justify an extraterritorial state having an autonomous (unilateral) power to punish the offender in such circumstances. All it can show is that the territorial state should hold a normative power to authorize other states, such as that of which the offender is a national, to punish her.[26]

Other scholars are concerned with jurisdictional gaps and the need to fight 'impunity' or, as Cockburn LJ famously put it, some 'blot upon the law'.[27] Two different scenarios are often mentioned. First, we may face a situation in which the offence is committed on a territory on which no state has jurisdiction (*terra nullius*). For instance, the nationality principle was invoked as a basis for criminal jurisdiction when the offender, a US national, killed someone on a Guano Island.[28]

[23] Ibid, 959.

[24] In Chapter 6 I shall argue that states which cannot guarantee a fair trial would lack the power (authority) to punish offenders regardless of the basis of their jurisdiction. The question of capital punishment is, unfortunately, beyond the scope of this enquiry.

[25] Arnell, 'The Case for Nationality Based Jurisdiction', 960. *A contrario*, suggesting that an extraterritorial state may have an interest in punishing an offender to preserve its good relations with the state on whose territory the offence was committed, see Geoffrey R Watson, 'Offenders Abroad: The Case for Nationality-Based Criminal Jurisdiction', *Yale J of International Law* 14 (1992), 68–9. My rebuttal to both arguments is the same.

[26] This issue will be examined in more detail in section 6 below.

[27] *R v Wilson* (1887) 3 QBD 42 at 44.

[28] *Jones v United States* 137 US 202L (1890).

Yet even if we recognize the US has the power to punish her in this case on the ground that we have an interest in avoiding impunity, it does not seem to follow that only the state of which the offender is a national has a power to punish her. Rather, the logical implication of this argument is that any state would have the right to exercise criminal jurisdiction over that offender for her crime, that is, to universal jurisdiction.

A second, more difficult, scenario would obtain when the offender returns to her 'home' country after committing an offence abroad. Extradition laws in many states prohibit the extradition of nationals,[29] and this type of regulation is arguably consistent with international law.[30] This type of provision has been normatively defended on a number of different grounds. The most popular one is arguably the ultimate lack of confidence in foreign legal systems, but arguments also include the disadvantage of being 'tried in a foreign language, separated from friends, resources and character witnesses', or the likelihood of prejudice against foreigners.[31] Somewhat more recently, non-extradition of nationals has been defended by reference to the perspectives for moral reform of the offender. Namely, it has been suggested that it would be better that an offender is convicted by the courts of her community, and that she serves the sentence in facilities located within the state to which she belongs and would have to be reintegrated to afterwards.[32] More importantly for our purposes, the rule on non-extradition of nationals has traditionally been closely connected to the principle of nationality. In French law, Plachta suggests, there was historically a 'causal' connection between the prohibition of extradition of nationals and the law giving France the power to punish them for offences perpetrated extraterritorially.[33] Analytically, he suggests, these two principles or rules should be regarded as correlative.[34]

The rule of non-extradition of nationals, however, does not provide us with a consistent explanation of the nationality principle. First, the moral basis of this rule is doubtful. A careful consideration of the relevant arguments is beyond the scope of this enquiry. Yet it seems to be a widely held view among scholars that the legal prohibition of the extradition of nationals is unjustified at the bar of justice; it is,

[29] Many of them have constitutional rules stating such prohibition while others do so by statute. See, eg, Harvard Research, 'Draft Convention on Extradition', *AJIL* 29 (Supp 1935), 123–5; and Christopher L Blakesley, 'A Conceptual Framework for Extradition and Jurisdiction over Extraterritorial Crimes', *Utah L Rev* (1984), 709.

[30] See, eg, Michael Plachta, '(Non-)extradition of Nationals: A Neverending Story?', *Emory International L Rev* 13 (1999), 78.

[31] Royal Commission on Extradition, Report of the Commissioners (1878), cited in the 'Draft Convention on Extradition', 127. See also, Martin T Manton, 'Extradition of Nationals', *Temple LQ* 19 (1935), 24; and Sharon A Williams, 'Nationality, Double Jeopardy, Prescription and the Death Sentence as Basis for Refusing Extradition', *International Rev of Penal Law* 62 (1991), 260–1.

[32] See Zsuzsanna Deen-Racsmány, 'Modernizing the Nationality Exception: Is the Non-extradition of Residents a Better Rule?', *Nordic J of International Law* 75 (2006), 30 and references in n 3 therein.

[33] Plachta, '(Non-)extradition of Nationals', 118–19.

[34] Ibid, 119. Against this view, see C Shachor-Landau, 'Extra-Territorial Penal Jurisdiction and Extradition', *ICLQ* 29 (1980), 275.

in the words of some, 'an illegitimate relic of nationalist sentiments'.[35] Moreover, the power to refuse extradition and the power to punish an individual are logically independent from each other. The fact that individuals in state S may have an interest in not extraditing an offender that is sufficiently important to grant that state a right (or even put it under a duty) not to do so, is unrelated to the question of whether they have an interest that is sufficiently important in that state punishing her. Some states systematically refuse to extradite individuals in the absence of a self-assumed conventional obligation[36] and this does not provide them with the power to punish offences perpetrated (both by nationals and non-nationals) in countries with which they do not have an extradition agreement. Contrariwise, states that *do* allow for the extradition of nationals also often claim (justifiably from a legal point of view) the power to punish their nationals for offences they may have committed extraterritorially.[37]

But even if we grant for the sake of argument both the moral basis and the correlativity points, the rule of non-extradition of nationals by itself would not lead us to grant a state the power to punish an offender extraterritorially on the basis of her nationality. Admittedly, the Harvard Research Code suggests that 'if a requested State fails to surrender its national, it shall try him itself'.[38] Now, states are arguably under a legal duty not to extradite individuals for reasons other than their nationality, several of which are indeed morally appealing, such as the risk of being tortured or suffering cruel or inhuman treatment (this may include being sentenced to death), or of being unfairly tried in the requesting state.[39] If having a moral duty not to extradite offender O sufficed to confer upon the requested state the power to punish her itself, the nationality of the offender plays no significant part in the argument in support of conferring on that state a power to punish O. A more plausible rationalization of this situation would be to suggest that the power of the extraterritorial state to punish O is normatively explained by reference to the power held by the territorial state requesting her extradition. But this would be an instance of what has been called 'vicarious' or 'representational' jurisdiction rather than jurisdiction based on the nationality principle.[40] Nationality, or even

[35] Cited in Ethan A Nadelmann, 'The Evolution of United States Involvement in the International Rendition of Fugitive Criminals', *NYU J of International Law & Politics* 25 (1993), 847. The Harvard Research in International Law has argued that 'the exception of nationals from those whom it is the duty of a State to extradite is so inadequately supported by the reasons given for it, and is so generally condemned by thoughtful students' that should be entirely abandoned by states (in 'Draft Convention on Extradition', 123, and at 128–9 for detailed criticism of the rationales cited above). For more contemporary views see Plachta, '(Non-) extradition of Nationals', 113–14 (at fn 137); and Shachor-Landau, 'Extra-Territorial Penal Jurisdiction and Extradition', 286–7.

[36] Deen-Racsmány, 'Modernizing the Nationality Exception', 33.

[37] England is but one example (see, eg, Ryngaert, 'Jurisdiction in International Law', 90).

[38] 'Draft Convention on Extradition', 126.

[39] On this see *Soering v United Kingdom*, 161 ECtHR Series A, reprinted in 28 *ILM* 1063 (1989). See also John Dugard and Christine Van den Wyngaert, 'Reconciling Extradition with Human Rights' *AJIL* 92 (1998), 187–212 and Garreth Peirce, 'America's Non-Compliance', *London Review of Books* 32/9 (2010), 18–22.

[40] Christopher L Blakesley and Otto Lagodny, 'Finding Harmony Amidst Disagreement Over Extradition, Jurisdiction, The Role of Human Rights, and Issues of Extraterritoriality Under International Criminal Law', *Vanderbilt J of Transnational Law* 24/1 (1991), 38 and Jürgen Meyer,

residence, has no bearing on the conferral of the power to punish O to the state which apprehended her on this alternative basis.[41]

Finally, it has often been argued that the nationality principle is based on the special relationship that links individuals to the state of which they are members. This relationship is usually referred to as allegiance.[42] This argument depends on what exactly this relationship amounts to. A first consideration that needs to be made is that none of the well-known arguments defending the intrinsic 'ethical significance' of nationality seem to entail the application of a state's criminal laws to its nationals abroad.[43] These arguments are meant to explain why states have the duty to give priority to their own nationals in matters such as the protection of their interests or, at least, the right to do so.[44] Therefore, they do not directly support the principle of nationality.[45]

Alternatively, we may build this allegiance relationship under the terms of a 'mutual exchange of benefits' scheme.[46] Defenders of this argument would suggest that because the offender receives protection and other benefits from the state of which she is a national, she also has to bear the burdens of her membership to that state.[47] A first objection against this argument is that it does not seem to apply to every state. Indeed, not every state seems to confer enough benefits upon its members to claim from them a duty to bear their burdens while abroad. Members of a state who had to flee on humanitarian or economic grounds, for example, would seem to be excluded from this argument. Crucially, however, even if an individual is under certain obligations towards her state of nationality, this approach still begs the crucial question. Namely, it does not explain what the interest of the people in that state is that justifies

'The Vicarious Administration of Justice: An Overlooked Basis of Jurisdiction', *Harvard International LJ* 31 (1990), 110.

[41] On the principle of vicarious jurisdiction, see section 6 below.

[42] See, eg, *Blackmer v United States* 284 US 421, 427 (1932) and *United States v King* 552 F2d 833, 851 (9th Cir 1976), quoted in Watson, 'Offenders Abroad', 68. If this were the only justification for the right to punish in these cases, it seems that this would exclude the practice of some states that claim jurisdiction over an offender even when she acquired their nationality after she committed the crime (see art 5 of the French *Code d'Instruction Criminelle,* quoted in 'Draft Convention on Jurisdiction with Respect to Crime', 522).

[43] I borrow the expression from David Miller, 'The Ethical Significance of Nationality', *Ethics* 98/4 (1988).

[44] On this, see standardly David Miller, *On Nationality* (Oxford: Oxford University Press, 1995); Samuel Scheffler, *Boundaries and Allegiances: Problems of Justice and Responsibility in Liberal Thought* (Oxford: Oxford University Press, 2001); and Yael Tamir, *Liberal Nationalism* (Princeton: Princeton University Press, 1993).

[45] If anything, they may provide an argument for the principle of passive personality, ie, the right of the extraterritorial state to protect the victim (wherever she is) by punishing those who violate her rights. Claims of that kind will be examined below.

[46] Miller, *On Nationality*, 61. This is, roughly, how fair play theories of punishment justify this power. See, eg, Richard Dagger, 'Punishment as Fair Play', *Res Publica* 14 (2008). They too are liable to this line of criticism.

[47] Interestingly, until well into the 20th century many European powers had 'national courts' in the territories of other states (eg, Persia, China, the Ottoman Empire, etc) to try their citizens for crimes committed there. This jurisdiction, however, was based on capitulation treaties and not on a right held by the European powers themselves. See W E Grisby, 'Mixed Courts of Egypt', *LQR* 12/3 (1896), 252 and A M Latter, 'The Government of the Foreigners in China', *LQR* 19/3 (1903), 316.

someone being under the specific duty to comply with its criminal rules while being abroad. Consider the following case: a French national travels to Mumbai and robs a bank. When he is back in Paris, he is prosecuted under the French criminal law and punished. It is unclear here what is France's interest in this individual respecting its criminal laws abroad. Certainly, the power to punish this offender cannot be based on individuals in France enjoying the sense of dignity and security that their system of criminal laws being in force provides them. This robbery has not undermined the bindingness of France's criminal rules, or affected the sense of dignity and security they provide to people in France in any meaningful way. Furthermore, other interests that France may put forward would collapse into unappealing justifications for the power to punish (incapacitation or moral reform), or into some form of universal jurisdiction (deterrence or retribution).[48] In other words, unless there is a specific element in the offence itself (say, its effects or purpose) that affects the public good that individuals in the extraterritorial state themselves enjoy, that state would lack the power to enforce its criminal rules against a national of that state who acted abroad.

A defender of the allegiance argument may reply that individuals in a given state would at least have an interest in the offender not being able to make *fraude à la loi* of such state, namely, go abroad to do something criminalized at home. This argument, again, does not seem to stand on the ground of the nationality of the offender but on the ground of her residence. But leaving this issue aside, it seems persuasive. However, it appears to get its intuitive plausibility from something other than the nationality of the perpetrator or, for that matter, her permanent residence. Suppose an offender goes with her victim to the border of state S, tricks her into stepping across into state T, beats her up, and then both return to S. Would not individuals in S have an interest in seeing the offender punished in order to be reassured that the laws are effectively in force? Arguably they would. But this again responds to territorial considerations. Individuals in S have an interest in not being tricked or forced into a position in which S lacks the power to punish the offender. Their sense of dignity and security *while in S* requires this. However, this has nothing to do with the nationality of the offender or her permanent residence. The rationale for conferring upon S the power to punish an offender in such circumstances would also hold if both the offender and the victim happened to be tourists on holiday.

It may be concluded, after much argument, that as a basis for criminal jurisdiction the nationality principle is altogether unjustified at the bar of justice. Moreover, most of the arguments that are usually put forward to defend this widely accepted legal right either beg the relevant question, or ultimately justify conferring upon an extraterritorial state the power to punish domestic offences on other more controversial grounds, such as universality or passive personality.

[48] See section 6 below on deterrence and retribution.

4. The Passive Personality Principle

We turn now to examine whether a state should have the power to punish an offender extraterritorially on the ground that the victim is a member of that state. This basis of criminal jurisdiction is among the most contested in contemporary International Law.[49] It is the only regular basis of extraterritorial criminal jurisdiction not included in the 1935 Harvard Draft Convention on Jurisdiction with Respect to Crime. However, it has been increasingly adopted by states.[50] Ultimately, it may be argued that there currently seems to be no rule under international law prohibiting this basis for criminal jurisdiction over domestic offences.[51]

To examine whether the justification for punishment outlined in this book endorses the passive personality principle the question is, once again, whether the members of a state have a collective interest in that state's criminal laws being in force abroad *vis-à-vis* offences committed against a co-national. In the previous section, I argued that individuals in any given state lack an interest in having that state's criminal laws enforced against them or their co-nationals (or co-residents) abroad. The opposite proposition, however, might seem promising. It is submitted that this is not the case. Advocates of the passive personality principle would need to show that, in fact, an offence committed abroad affects the sense of dignity and security of individuals in the state claiming such extraterritorial power by putting into question the bindingness of its criminal rules. Yet if a German citizen is assaulted by a group of infuriated monks while visiting a Tibetan monastery in the Himalayas, this would hardly affect the confidence of individuals in the German criminal laws being in force.

More generally, it is not even true that German citizens abroad have an interest in the German criminal law being in force extraterritorially sufficiently important

[49] The authors in Oppenheim say it is inconsistent (Watts and Jennings, *Oppenheim's International Law*, 468), and F A Mann suggests it 'should be treated as an excess of jurisdiction' (Mann, 'The Doctrine of Jurisdiction in International Law' in *Further Studies in International Law* (Oxford: Clarendon Press, 1990), 92). It was heavily criticized by Judge Moore in the *Lotus* case, and even there the majority, which accepted that Turkey had the right to punish Mr Demons, did not fully endorse the principle of passive personality (*SS Lotus* (*France v Turkey*), *PCIJ Reports*, Series A no 10, 19 (1927)).

[50] The Harvard Research project (1935) contains a list of 28 states that have adopted this principle; many of them still endorse it (see Watts and Jennings, *Oppenheim's International Law*, 472). France, eg, objected to the application of this principle by Turkey in the *Lotus* case. Before 1975, it recognized jurisdiction on this basis but it was rarely applied. To do so it required a decision of the *Ministère Public* that it was in the public interest to do so. This occurred when the offence had some territorial effects or endangered the security of the state. To that extent, it is hard to say that jurisdiction was based on passive personality alone. France's Criminal Procedure Law provides for its criminal jurisdiction over crimes (as opposed to *délits*) committed extraterritorially against its nationals (art 689 of *Code the Procedure Pénal* referring to art 113–7 of *Code Pénal*). On the conflicting views exposed by relevant state officials upon adoption of art 113–7, see Eric Cafritz and Omer Tene, 'Article 113–7 of the French Penal Code: The Passive Personality Principle', *Columbia J of Transnational Law* 41 (2002–3), 587–8.

[51] For a list of countries that have adopted this basis for jurisdiction see, Geoffrey R Watson, 'The Passive Personality Principle', *Texas International LJ* 28 (1993), 13 (fn 76).

to confer upon Germany the power to punish offenders in this type of case. The German criminal law cannot provide abroad the benefits that justify Germany's criminal jurisdiction at home. While walking through an alley in Buenos Aires it would be awkward for a German citizen to feel that his rights are granted or protected by the German criminal law. This would hold even if the German criminal law system did provide, as a matter of law, for extraterritorial criminal jurisdiction on the grounds of passive personality.[52] While an individual is abroad, the only system of criminal law that can meaningfully contribute to her (relative) sense of dignity and security is the criminal law of the territorial state. Put differently, the power to punish is explained here by reference to a public good, and this public good benefits the individuals that happen to be within a particular territory. Because of the features of this public good, it cannot be enjoyed extraterritorially. In fact, this is the case with most public goods offered by the state, such as public health or transport. It therefore must follow that under the argument advanced in this book states lack the power to punish offenders extraterritorially on the ground that the victim is their national.

But what if there is no territorial state that provides this public good? There are several places in which no territorial system of criminal law is in force. Cases that come to mind immediately are Antarctica or some small island in international waters.[53] Would states have a power to punish violations to their own criminal rules extraterritorially on *terra nullius* on the ground that the victim of the offence is their national? To answer this question we have to examine, once again, whether individuals in state S have a collective interest in S's criminal law system being in force in those areas where no territorial system is in force. Arguably people in, say, Japan would lack an interest in Japan's criminal law system being in force in Antarctica sufficiently important to ground someone's liability to be punished for a murder of a Japanese national committed in Antarctica. This is because the fact that a Japanese national is killed there does not seem to affect the sense of dignity and security that the Japanese enjoy in Japan. Ultimately, Japanese criminal laws cannot really be in force in Antarctica as such, at least while it maintain its current legal and demographic situation. This does not mean that, absent a territorial authority, no authority should have the power to punish a given individual for an offence perpetrated in Antarctica. Japan could claim criminal jurisdiction, for example, over a military expedition or base in Antarctica. It only entails that the fact that victim is a national of a given state S does not seem to do any justificatory work in terms of providing S, in particular, with the power to exercise its criminal jurisdiction on *terra nullius*.

The line of argument followed in this section is connected to one of the standard objections against the passive personality principle, namely, that perpetrators would normally not be able to anticipate that they will be subjected to a foreign criminal law.[54] Although not incompatible with that view, the argument advocated here does not rely on the proposition that these prosecutions would necessarily be

[52] See, eg, *United States v Columba-Colella* 604 F2d 356 (5th Cir 1979), at 360.
[53] See *Jones v United States*.
[54] Watson, 'The Passive Personality Principle', 22–5.

unfair to wrongdoers, but rather suggests that nationals of state S while abroad would not have a valid and convincing reason to consider people around them bound by the criminal rules of their home country. Someone may still object that neither of these two objections would obtain if an individual is targeted precisely because of her nationality. In effect, the principle of passive personality has been notoriously popular in cases involving terrorist acts, which are sometimes characterized by this feature.[55]

However, this defence of passive personality seems to stand on a conflation. Geoffrey Watson suggests that '[i]n terrorism cases, the exercise of passive personality jurisdiction flows naturally from the foreign affairs power [of the US],' only to add that '[a] terrorist crime against an American abroad affects United States security interests in a way that a common crime does not'.[56] This latter qualification seems to imply a crucial distinction. It indicates that the reason why the state of nationality of the victims of, say, hostage taking may be ultimately justified in prosecuting this type of act, is that the state itself is being coerced into doing or refraining from doing something that it would not otherwise do. The terrorist attack against members of the Israeli team while attending the Munich Olympic Games, and the hijacking of the *Achille Lauro* by members of the Palestine Liberation Front illustrate this well. As Watson seems to admit, the extension of the scope of the power to punish in these situations would not be based merely on the nationality of the victim, but rather on the protection of the sovereignty and security of the state.[57] As such, these cases provide no support for the principle of passive personality; they should rather be examined under the protective principle, discussed in the next section.[58]

There are, of course, situations in which a victim of a terrorist act just happens to be a national of S, but has not been targeted as such. The attack would not even have to have been directed against her state. This would be the case, for instance, of a non-US national who happened to be working in the World Trade Center on 9 September 2001. If her country of nationality were to claim the power to punish the perpetrators of that act, it would then be relying strictly on the principle of passive personality.[59] Unlike the cases of terrorist acts discussed so far, in this

[55] The US relied (partially) upon this principle in *United States v Yunis* 681 F Supp 896 (1988), to try a Lebanese national for hijacking a Jordanian airliner in which three US citizens were travelling, even if it had objected to Mexico exercising extraterritorial criminal jurisdiction on this basis in the *Cutting* incident of 1887 (US Department of State, *Report on Extraterritorial Crime and the Cutting Case, in Foreign Relations of the United States*, 751–867). See, also, §402 of Restatement (Third) of The Foreign Relations Law of the United States (1987) and *United States v Vasquez-Velasco* 15 F3d 833 (9th Cir 1994), at 839–42.

[56] Watson, 'The Passive Personality Principle', 33.

[57] This is a somewhat common conflation. See, eg, the claim that passive personality is triggered when state officials are assaulted and murdered abroad (John G McCarthy, 'The Passive Personality Principle and its Use in Combating International Terrorism', *Fordham International LJ* 13 (1989–90), 300).

[58] See, eg, Watson, 'The Passive Personality Principle', 10 and Gerald P McGinley, 'The Achille Lauro Affair—Implications for International Law', *Tennessee L Rev* 52 (1984–5), 712.

[59] There is admittedly a third possibility. Some scholars may argue that terrorist acts should, in fact, warrant conferring universal jurisdiction over their perpetrators. This line of argument is unfortunately beyond the scope of the present work.

instance the state's power would have to be based on the special relationship that states have with their citizens. This leads us to the arguments proposed by those who defend the ethical significance of nationality.

Advocates of this position generally endorse the proposition that individuals have certain special obligations towards their co-nationals.[60] Although the obligations vary with regard to the duties each gives rise to, it seems safe to assume that all of them entail that states have a special obligation to protect the interests of their nationals. This special obligation implies that they also have a right to do so.[61] If the nationality bond intrinsically requires a state to fulfil these special duties, it seems that the proponents of special obligations to co-nationals are committed to extending this protection abroad.[62] So far, so good. However, to assert a power to punish on the basis of this proposition is a *non sequitur*. The liberty to protect their nationals does not per se entail a second order power to punish those who violated their rights. As argued in the previous chapter, we are usually ready to recognize that a state has the power to punish someone for a homicide even if the victim's rights can no longer be protected. To go from protection to punishment a further argument is needed. The only way in which we could meaningfully bridge this gap is to say that legal punishment is justified by its deterrent effects or eventually by incapacitation.

I shall address deterrence as an argument for the allocation and scope of the power to punish in the last section of this chapter.[63] As for incapacitation, it may be doubted that it is considered a serious explanation for the moral power to punish at all. As is commonly suggested, it violates the offender's status as a person by treating her merely as a tiger in a circus.[64] Yet the problem for our purposes is that it also leads to problematic jurisdictional implications. After all, what difference does it make in which country an offender is kept as long as she is incapacitated? If anything, then, incapacitation as a general justification for the power to punish would collapse into a rule favouring universal jurisdiction over domestic offences.

5. The Protective Principle

The protective principle is invoked when a state claims extraterritorial criminal jurisdiction to punish someone for an offence against its security, integrity, sovereignty, or important governmental functions.[65] It is beyond the scope of this

[60] The standard arguments are made by Miller, *On Nationality*; Scheffler, *Boundaries and Allegiances*, 60, 79; Tamir, *Liberal Nationalism*, 137.

[61] This argument is used in Cassese, *International Criminal Law*, 282.

[62] Watson, 'The Passive Personality Principle', 18.

[63] On my critique of deterrence as a general justification for the power to punish, see Chapter 2.

[64] Andrew von Hirsch, *Censure and Sanctions* (Oxford: Clarendon Press, 1993), 11.

[65] See Christopher L Blakesley, 'Extraterritorial Jurisdiction' in M Cherif Bassiouni (ed), *International Criminal Law* (Ardsley: Transnational Publishers, 1998), 54; and Jackson Nyamuya Maogoto, 'Countering Terrorism: From Wigged Judges to Helmeted Soldiers—Legal Perspectives on America's Counter-Terrorism Responses', *San Diego International LJ* 6 (2004–2005), 258. This

enquiry to clarify which offences do in fact meet the test of affecting these goods, or which goods in particular warrant states having jurisdiction on these grounds. It may suffice for present purposes to concentrate on certain offences for which the principle is standardly invoked, such as those committed against a state's governmental authorities, its military forces, and the counterfeiting of currency or public documents issued by the state.[66] It seems safe to argue that currently this basis for criminal jurisdiction is reasonably well established under international law.[67] It should be noted, however, that states have had diverging attitudes towards this principle. While continental Europe and Latin America have often advocated this basis of jurisdiction, the Anglo-American world has traditionally been reluctant to accept it. Yet more and more often the US and the UK have tended to come to terms with it and use it for their own purposes.[68] There are several arguments that purportedly justify states having extraterritorial criminal jurisdiction on grounds of 'protection'. Among the most popular ones are self-defence, deterrence, and protection *stricto sensu*. I shall not deal with them here in any detail. Rather, I will present my own argument for that conclusion. The reason for this is that although the present account differs from them in terms of the specific consideration on which they rest, it coincides with the conclusion they all reach.[69]

The justification for a state's power to punish advocated in this book is based on the collective interest of individuals in that state in there being a system of criminal laws in force on its territory. This system is a public good that provides them with a relative sense of dignity and security thereby contributing to their well-being. The relevant question is thus whether individuals in state S have a collective interest in

principle has also been extended to the 'protection' of the interests of members of military allies; France and the Communist countries constitute regular examples of this (see Akehurst, 'Jurisdiction in International Law', 159).

[66] The first 'modern' version of the principle of protection was reputedly the French Procedural Code of 1808, which authorized the extraterritorial prosecution of aliens for crimes 'against the security of the State, of counterfeiting the seal of the State, the national currency, national documents, or banknotes authorized by law' (cited in Monika B Krizek, 'The Protective Principle of Extraterritorial Jurisdiction: A Brief History and an Application of the Principle to Espionage as an Illustration of Current United States Practice', *Boston U International LJ* 6 (1988), 339).

[67] See the 'Draft Convention on Jurisdiction with Respect to Crime', 543 and 551, for a list of 43 states that provided for it either in their current legislation or in their pending criminal codes. More recently, see art 694 of the French *Code de procedure penal*. The US Omnibus Diplomatic Security Act of 1985 is broadly based on the protective principle, although it also relies on the principle of passive personality. For an dissonant voice, see Manuel R García-Mora, 'Criminal Jurisdiction over Foreigners for Treason and Offences against the Safety of the State Committed Upon Foreign Territory', *U of Pittsburgh L Rev* 19/3 (1957–1958), 567.

[68] At least until the late 1950s, the UK and the US both seemed to have rejected this basis of jurisdiction unless a bond of allegiance between the offender and the sovereign was found. Treason seemed to have been the overarching concern. I believe that *Joyce v DPP* [1946] AC 347 should be understood as an example of this principle being relied on by a British court. Hirst, however, rejects this understanding of Joyce (see his, *Jurisdiction and the Ambit of the Criminal Law*, 49).

[69] On deterrence as a justification for the protective principle see Recent Developments, 'Protective Principle of Jurisdiction Applied to Uphold Statute Intended to Have Extra-Territorial Effect', *Columbia L Rev* 62/2 (1962), 375. Self-defence, eg, was articulated in the *Bayot* case (Ann Dig 109 (No 54) *Cour de Cassation*, France, 22 February 1923) and the *Fornage* case (*Cour de Cassation*, 84 *J du Palais* 229, 1873). For a careful, though not necessarily critical, treatment of the other arguments see García-Mora, 'Criminal Jurisdiction over Foreigners'.

S's criminal laws being in force extraterritorially *vis-à-vis* certain offences against, for example, the security and political independence of the state. I contend they do. Let me illustrate this point:

The scene was Washington, November and December 1921. The world's naval powers had come to negotiate limits to shipbuilding to prevent a runaway naval race and save money. The point in contention was the ratio of tonnage afloat between the three largest navies, those of Britain, the United States, and Japan. The US proposed a ratio of 10:10:6.... But the Japanese were unhappy and would not budge from their insistence on a 10:10:7 ratio.... Calculations difficult to summarize here meant that Western navies would be at a disadvantage in Japanese waters with a 10:10:7 ratio, but would have ships enough to dominate even far from home ports if they could insist successfully on 10:10:6.... Two years earlier after months of work [Herbert O] Yardley had solved an important Japanese diplomatic code; ... on December 2, as the naval conference struggled over its impasse on the ratio, a copy of a cable from Tokyo was delivered to Yardley's team and deciphered almost as quickly as a clerk could type. The drift of the message ... was an instruction to Japan's negotiators to defend the ratio tenaciously, falling back one by one through the four positions only as required to prevent the negotiations from breaking down entirely. As Yardley later described ..., position number four was agreement to the 10:10:6 ratio. 'Stud poker,' Yardley wrote, 'is not a very difficult game after you see your opponent's hole card.' So it proved. On December 12 the Japanese caved.[70]

Arguably, this act of espionage is as harmful to Japan's interests (and those of the Japanese) as acts of espionage against Japan committed on its own territory.[71] In other words, it makes little difference where the secret message was intercepted. But then, if Japan should arguably have the power to punish those who carry out acts of espionage against Japan on its territory, it must follow that it would also have to hold this power extraterritorially. Unlike cases of theft or murder against an individual victim, espionage against state S, even if carried out extraterritorially, will affect the interests of individuals in S. For them to be able to enjoy the sense of dignity and security that that criminal rule being in force provides, the rule has to be binding on offenders irrespective of where the act of espionage is committed. Furthermore, this argument does not collapse into a wider basis of extraterritorial jurisdiction. Individuals in S have an interest in S prosecuting and punishing espionage against state S, but not against state T. In our example above, China would lack the power to prosecute any American official. Finally, S would hold this extraterritorial power regardless of whether or not the state on whose territory the act of espionage was committed itself decides to prosecute the perpetrator.[72]

[70] Taken from T Powers, 'Black Arts', *New York Review of Books* 52/8 (2005).

[71] I deal here only with espionage in times of peace. Espionage in the context of armed conflict has its own specific rules.

[72] Interestingly, the US prosecuted and convicted Alfred Zehe, an East German national, for espionage related to documents concerning US anti-submarine warfare perpetrated in Mexico and East Germany (*United States v Zehe* 601 F Supp 196 (D Mass 1985)). Zehe was ultimately returned to East Germany in exchange for Americans being held there. For an analysis of the case, and of the evolution and application of the principle of protection in US law, see Krizek, 'The Protective Principle of Extraterritorial Jurisdiction'.

It should be noted, however, that this basis of criminal jurisdiction has not been free from criticism. The underlying preoccupation focuses on the rights of those individuals subjected to this type of prosecution. On the one hand, it has been argued that these trials will be necessarily biased or politically conditioned.[73] This objection, however, affects only some of the offences that usually give rise to the protective principle, but not necessarily many others, such as counterfeiting currency or public documents, or even perjury to the detriment of national authorities abroad. More importantly, perhaps, even with regard to those offences for which this objection may have some bite, such as treason, espionage, or crimes with a political element in general, the difficulty it creates has nothing to do with the *extraterritorial* character of the prosecution. Rather, it affects this kind of trial, period. The Dreyfus affair in late nineteenth-century France and, more recently, the trials against Mossaui in the US, and members of the Basque separatist movement ETA in Spain illustrate this neatly.[74] Ultimately, this consideration does not undermine the collective interest that justifies a particular state holding the power to punish individuals for this type of crime, nor does it present a countervailing interest of sufficient entity to provide the offender with an immunity against that power. Rather, it seems to affect the conditions that any given body (be it territorial or extraterritorial) must fulfil in order to claim, itself, the normative power to punish this type of offence. Lack of impartiality may affect the moral credentials of a state's authority to punish an offender, not the fact that it has a sufficiently weighty reason to do so. Accordingly, this issue belongs with the examination of that authority in Chapter 6.

On the other hand, it has been argued that this type of jurisdiction lends itself to inadmissible extensions.[75] This is historically true. Jessup cites a case in which, during the Nazi period, a German court approved the prosecution in Germany of a Jewish alien who had extramarital intercourse with a young German woman in Czechoslovakia on the ground that it affected the 'purity of the German blood'.[76] Salman Rushdie's death fatwah constitutes another powerful illustration of this danger. Without going that far, many provisions which invoke the protective principle are unacceptably vague. For example, the Hungarian Penal Code at some point provided for extraterritorial jurisdiction over any act against 'a fundamental interest relating to the democratic, political and economic order of the Hungarian People's Republic'.[77] As it is often said, however, the fact that a given state can abuse a right it has is hardly a conclusive argument against it initially holding that right. These examples show cases of blatant abuse of this doctrine, but they say very little about its application to offences that do in fact affect the security or political independence of the state. In other words, these considerations may have some bite

[73] García-Mora, 'Criminal Jurisdiction over Foreigners'.

[74] On the ETA trials and its complaints see eg *Adolfo Araiz Flamariqe et al* in the Spanish Constitutional Court (STC 136/1999 in BOE no 197, 18 August 1999, 26–96).

[75] García-Mora, 'Criminal Jurisdiction over Foreigners', 583.

[76] Philip C Jessup, *Transnational Law* (New Haven: Yale University Press, 1956), 50.

[77] In Akehurst, 'Jurisdiction in International Law', 58.

at the level of institutionalization of the principle of protection, but they have very little to say on its credentials as a matter of normative principle.

Finally, we may consider whether a state's laws prohibiting criminal acts which affect its sovereignty, security, or important governmental functions being in force extraterritorially can provide individuals in that state with any sense of dignity and security. Above I argued that the public good that punishment provides, benefits the individuals on the territory of the state where they happen to be. For instance, it was claimed that a German citizen, while abroad, cannot enjoy the sense of dignity and security provided by the German criminal laws in Germany, but rather, it is the criminal laws of the country where she is (the territorial state) being in force that would contribute to her sense of dignity and security.[78] This may seem to undermine the argument advocated in this section.

Yet in this particular type of case we are not considering the sense of dignity and security that the German criminal laws provide to, for example, Germany's Chancellor abroad. Angela Merkel herself, on a visit to Patagonia, would have an interest in Argentina's criminal laws being in force. These rules would contribute to her sense of dignity and security. Rather, the protective principle is explained by the sense of dignity and security that a criminal prohibition provides to the German people *in Germany* regarding their Chancellor, while she is abroad. The Germans have, themselves, an interest in making it their business to punish anyone who commits such an act, irrespectively of where this act takes place and of the concurrent power held by the territorial state. It is submitted here that German criminal law is perfectly able to contribute to the sense of dignity and security of its nationals with regard to their Chancellor. Finally, the reason why the Germans might have an interest in Germany punishing such an act concerns Merckel's political status, not her nationality. They would have the same interest if their Chancellor happened to be Austrian or Peruvian. It is the position the victim holds in state S's government that explains S's power to punish the offender extraterritorially.

Accordingly, it is the case that individuals would have a collective interest in an extraterritorial state punishing an offender on the ground of protection sufficiently important to confer upon that state the prima facie power to do so. Yet as it was argued in Chapter 1, the territorial state would have a prima facie immunity against extraterritorial states exercising their criminal jurisdiction over offences committed in their territory. This means that there would be a conflict of rights. It seems plausible to suggest that the interest that explains, say, France's prima facie power to punish an offender for the counterfeiting of French passports in Paraguay is sufficiently weighty to override Paraguay's prima facie immunity. As explained in Chapter 1, Paraguay's immunity is not absolute; it is limited both by the interests of individuals abroad, and by the fundamental interests of Paraguayans. The French have an interest in there being a criminal rule in force against the counterfeiting of French passports that is sufficiently important to confer upon France the power to punish the perpetrator even when the offence is committed abroad. Individuals in Paraguay, moreover, would not have their right to self-government unduly

[78] See section 4 above on passive personality.

curtailed by France's strict application of the principle of protection to this type of case. Whether or not Paraguay itself decides to criminalize the counterfeiting of French passports, the interest of individuals in Paraguay in it being a self-governed entity does not seem to include the right to shield individuals committing crimes against vital interests of foreign states from extraterritorial prosecution. The general acceptance of this basis of extraterritorial jurisdiction under international law seems to confirm this rather uncontroversial point.

6. Two Possible Objections

Before concluding this chapter, we need to examine two possible objections to the account of extraterritorial punishment for domestic offences advocated here. On the one hand, many people would find it simply too restrictive. They will protest, for instance, that by preventing states from exercising their criminal jurisdiction extraterritorially on grounds other than protection, this approach would preclude joint efforts by states to fight certain forms of criminality. This is particularly sensitive in a world in which the forces of globalization seem to have bolstered transnational crime.[79] This, however, is not what my argument entails. True, it warrants putting states under a prima facie disability to punish offenders for an offence committed outside their territory unless the offence threatens their security, sovereignty, or political independence. However, I have also suggested that under certain circumstances individuals in state S would have an interest in an extraterritorial state being able to enforce S's criminal laws.[80] This interest, moreover, could well be sufficiently important to warrant conferring upon S the normative power to authorize an extraterritorial state to do so, and thereby waive its immunity against having foreign criminal rules enforced on its territory.[81] But this is simply not the same as arguing that the extraterritorial state, itself, has the unilateral power to punish an individual for such offences. My argument entails only the former proposition.

Let me put this in more concrete terms. Under the argument advocated here, states hold a normative power to grant each other extraterritorial criminal jurisdiction for acts committed on their respective territories. The Conventions of the Council of Europe on Cybercrime (2001) and on Action against Trafficking in Human Beings (2005), and the 2003 UN Convention against Corruption are but a few examples of this. States can also consent to (authorize), as they sometimes do, a particular state or states exercising jurisdiction on their territory in the context of an extradition treaty, and even on an ad hoc basis. They can either provide a foreign state with full power to exercise extraterritorial criminal jurisdiction, or subject it to certain limitations.[82]

[79] See, eg, Misha Glenny, *Mcmafia: A Journey through the Global Criminal Underworld* (New York: Knopf Books, 2008).

[80] See section 3 above on the nationality principle.

[81] On the general compatibility of this claim with International Law, see Cryer et al, *International Criminal Law and Procedure*, 39–40.

[82] For instance, they may limit this authorization to certain crimes, or certain offenders, etc.

In some cases, to use Chief Justice Taft's words, some offences 'are such that to limit their [prosecution] to the strictly territorial jurisdiction would be greatly to curtail the scope and usefulness of the statute'.[83] In other cases, there will be great incentives for states to make treaties authorizing as many states as possible to exercise this type of extraterritorial jurisdiction. Take the regulation of corruption. If developing country S only confers the power to punish upon developed country T, companies in countries U, V, and so on would most likely be able to secure valuable contracts at the expense, exclusively, of the companies in T (and individuals in S). Neither the interests of individuals in S nor those of individuals abroad would be best served by a narrower (bilateral) conferral of extraterritorial jurisdiction.[84] These considerations, however, do not per se warrant extraterritorial states having criminal jurisdiction over this type of crimes. They provide only prudential reasons. It would be up to the state where the offence was perpetrated, and only up to that state alone, to decide whether an extraterritorial state will hold a (concurrent) power to punish an offender for an offence she committed in its territory. This explanation thereby accommodates what we may call internationalized or transnational criminal law, that is, domestic criminal laws that are enforceable extraterritorially by domestic courts on the basis of an agreement between states.[85]

The objector may still suggest that this framework would not be able to accommodate the principle of 'vicarious' or 'representational' jurisdiction, a somewhat neglected basis of criminal jurisdiction in common law countries.[86] This principle provides an extraterritorial state with the power to punish an offender in its custody, when her extradition has not been requested by the state with traditional jurisdiction over the case, or when there are legal obstacles to agreeing to such a request.[87] As such, it has often been considered subsidiary to non-extradition, and not directly dependent on the authorization of the territorial state.

We need not, however, take this analysis of the principle of vicarious jurisdiction at face value. As argued in section 3 above, the power to punish an offender and the power to refuse extraditing her are logically and normatively independent. It follows then that such an extraterritorial power simply cannot be normatively justified on the basis of non-extradition.[88] It must be explained by reference to someone's concrete interests. Moreover, if refusing to extradite an offender sufficed to confer upon an extraterritorial state the power to punish an offender, any state would be able to claim universal jurisdiction over domestic offences by simply

[83] *United States v Bowman*, 98. Although in this case the court left open the question of whether this basis of jurisdiction applied also to aliens, the reasoning seems to lead inevitably to that conclusion.

[84] On this, see, eg, Ilias Bantekas, 'Corruption as an International Crime and Crime against Humanity', *J of International Crim Justice* 4/3 (2006), 467.

[85] This proposition, however, does not cover 'purely' international crimes such as aggression, genocide, war crimes, and crimes against humanity. On this, see Chapters 4 and 5.

[86] For the connection between 'vicarious' jurisdiction and transnational criminal law, see Blakesley and Lagodny, 'Finding Harmony Amidst Disagreement', 36.

[87] Ibid, 38.

[88] For a similar point see, Albin Eser, 'Common Goals and Different Ways in International Criminal Law: Reflections From a European Perspective', *Harvard International LJ* 31 (1990), 119.

apprehending the suspect and refusing to extradite her. This claim is not only incompatible with international law, but also unconvincing at the bar of justice.

By contrast, authorization accounts for a large number of cases in which this basis of jurisdiction is claimed. Often enough, vicarious jurisdiction is agreed upon by states, either in an extradition treaty or through the rule of *aut dedere aut judicare* in a multilateral convention.[89] It may also be provided for under reciprocal legislation,[90] or implicitly when refusing to request the extradition. In any event, authorization by the state which has jurisdiction over the offence is perhaps the sole consistent normative explanation of the power to punish offences extraterritorially in cases other than protection. The arguments often used in defence of this principle simply point at the practical convenience of this type of arrangement to minimize the tension resulting from a refusal to extradite an alleged offender, or as a simple institutional arrangement to punish a fugitive who managed to cross an international border into a state with no extradition treaty with the territorial state.[91] They are therefore concerned only with issues of institutionalization, and largely beg the underlying question of principle. In sum, then, the framework hereby advocated can account for certain instances of the principle of 'vicarious' jurisdiction; when this principle is claimed unilaterally by the extraterritorial state, that is without any form of authorization, it would have to conclude that it is *ultra vires*.

A second possible line of criticism to the framework advocated in this chapter concerns whether other justifications for legal punishment are, overall, better suited to explain the way in which extraterritorial punishment is currently regulated as a matter of both domestic and international law. If this were the case, these alternative arguments would probably have to be preferred over the one advocated here for their explanatory power. There are, however, two common problems with most arguments available in the literature. First, the consideration(s) on which they rely lack any clear connection to the territorial scope of the power to punish. And, secondly, they are usually unable to account for the specific considerations (nationality or protection) on which extraterritorial jurisdictional bases are grounded. This is true of most consequentialist and deontological considerations such as deterrence, incapacitation, moral reform, retribution, and so on. Regardless of their interplay within each theory, it is simply not true that they are more

[89] This principle should not be conflated with the principle of universal jurisdiction, which will be examined in Chapter 5. Universal jurisdiction is not based on the representation of the territorial state, but rather claimed as an autonomous power to punish the offender by an extraterritorial body. It therefore does not require, eg, that the principle of double criminality is satisfied. On this distinction see Christoph Safferling, 'International Decisions: Public Prosecutor v. Djajic' *AJIL* 92 (1998), 529–30; Rüdiger Wolfrum, 'The Decentralized Prosecution of International Offences through National Courts' in Yoram Dinsten and Mala Tabory (eds), *War Crimes in International Law* (Boston: Martinus Nijhoff, 1996), 235; and Jain Cameron 'Jurisdiction and Admissibility Issues under the ICC Statute' in Dominic McGoldrick, Peter Rowe, and Eric Donnelly (eds), *The Permanent International Criminal Court: Legal and Policy Issues* (Oxford: Hart, 2004), 79. For a portrayal of 'vicarious jurisdiction' as a form of universality see 'Draft Convention on Jurisdiction with Respect to Crime', 573.

[90] Geoff Gilbert, *Responding to International Crime* (2nd edn, Leiden: Martinus Nihoff, 2006), 91.

[91] Ibid; and Blakesley and Lagodny, 'Finding Harmony Amidst Disagreement', 39.

attuned with our current practices. As will be argued below, most justifications for legal punishment tend to advocate broader jurisdictional rules than those provided under international law today: they risk collapsing into universal jurisdiction.[92] Moreover, when certain considerations are introduced to limit the extraterritorial scope of a state's power to punish, these theories end up being too restrictive or in any event less attuned with some of the core features of the distribution and scope of states' power to punish as currently regulated.

But first I must show that the argument advocated in this chapter does not lead to any of these unfortunate implications. It has been argued that Finland's power to punish is justified by the collective interest of individuals in Finland in having in force a system of laws prohibiting murder, rape, and so on. The question is thus, once again, whether individuals in Finland have a collective interest in Finland's domestic criminal laws being binding universally. From the arguments stated so far it should be clear that this is not the case. When discussing the nationality and passive personality principles I claimed that there seems to be no way in which Finland's criminal rules being in force requires punishing an offender for a robbery she committed in Nepal. For one, it seems odd to say that she has violated the laws of Finland. But more importantly, the sense of dignity and security that the Finnish criminal laws being in force provides individuals in Finland is not affected by a robbery in Nepal. Individuals in Finland may feel sympathetic to the victims of a crime committed elsewhere or even horrified by it, but the system of criminal rules under which they live is not put into question by that offence. Therefore, Finland would simply lack the power to punish offenders for domestic offences universally.

How would a deterrence-based theory analyse this situation? As argued in Chapter 2, the central claim on which deterrence is grounded is that punishment is justified as a means of protecting individual's rights and other valuable public goods by deterring potential offenders. It is the protection provided that justifies the suffering inflicted upon an offender. Regardless of whether we can limit some of its unappealing implications by introducing deontological considerations, deterrence seems inevitably attached to the following reasoning: the 'more' punishment is exacted, the stronger the deterrent effect of criminal law would be and, as a result, the fewer violations of these rights and goods would obtain. In particular, the deterrent effect has been said to depend on the certainty, severity, and celerity of the punishment.[93] It surely seems that allowing every state to exercise its criminal jurisdiction over any given offence will contribute to the certainty of the punishment. More importantly, perhaps, it would contribute to the *perceived* certainty. It is obviously beyond the scope of this enquiry to even begin to consider how strong this extra deterrent effect would be. That would probably depend on the type of crime and the type of offender; shoplifting and money-laundering may well be differently affected. In any event, if we accept that there will be some

[92] Justifications for punishment are notoriously complex and varied. I simplify here the literature in a way that takes into consideration at least some of the most relevant arguments on which contemporary justifications rely.

[93] Jeremy Bentham, *The Rationale of Punishment* (London: 1830), ch VI.

extra deterrence, any justification that relies on deterrence would be committed to granting every state the power to punish any particular offender.[94] This surely would not prove it wrong but it is hardly an implication their advocates would be prepared to endorse.

Of course, the consequentialist theorist might respond that this would be too quick. Deterrence is only one consideration that must be included in a broader calculation of utility, namely, we need to balance it against other countervailing considerations, such as for instance the friction that the exercise of universal jurisdiction for domestic offences would create between states. With this further consideration in mind, we may admit that a consistent consequentialist would be able to deny that deterrence is committed to conferring upon states a power to punish that is universal in scope. This restatement is certainly more plausible, but it is ultimately unconvincing for two reasons. First, although successful in restricting the extraterritorial scope of the power to punish, this move may end up being too restrictive. For instance, if avoiding international friction overrides deterrence in the overall calculus of utility, it follows that the UK would be unjustified in punishing Russian agents for the alleged murder of Litvinenko, which was perpetrated in central London.[95] This by itself, casts some doubts on how successful this restatement ultimately is; the doubts grow when we take into consideration another important feature of the right to punish.

Indeed, my second point against this more elaborate version of deterrence concerns what may be considered to be, ultimately, an advantage of the language of rights over unfettered consequentialism. If the balance between conflict avoidance and deterrence is in favour of the former, the consequentialist would be committed to the view that an extraterritorial state S is unjustified in punishing an offender. By contrast, to say that S holds the power (the right) to punish such an offender means that it is up to S, and only up to S, to decide whether to exercise it, even at the expense of creating friction with some other state. Thus, the rights-based account endorsed in this book is able to explain an important feature of the current practice of legal punishment. Namely, that provided that individuals in state S hold a sufficiently weighty interest in S punishing a particular offender, this confers upon S the right to decide whether or not to punish such offender, even when this would lead to a suboptimal level of utility.

Interestingly, retributivist justifications for legal punishment seem to face a similar difficulty. A central tenet of retributive justifications for legal punishment is that 'the state is justified in punishing an offender because she deserves to be punished'. A distinction is warranted here: some retributivists argue that this proposition only explains why it is permissible to visit legal punishment upon offenders.[96] In the language of rights that we have been using so far, this argument explains why offenders lack a claim-right not to be punished. It does not explain

[94] See, similarly, Walter W Cook, 'The Application of the Criminal Law of a Country to Acts Committed by Foreigners Outside the Jurisdiction', *West Virginia LQ* XL/4 (1934), 328.

[95] For good coverage of this affair see, generally, <http://topics.nytimes.com/topics/reference/timestopics/people/l/alexander_v_litvinenko/index.html> (last accessed 19 August 2010).

[96] McDermott, 'The Permissibility of Punishment'.

why any given state has the normative power to do so. This version of retributivism is not committed to universal jurisdiction but it does not, either, provide a complete justification for the institution of legal punishment. In fact, it has little to say about the issue at hand.

A second type of retributivist suggests that desert is both a necessary and a sufficient condition for conferring upon state S the power to punish a given offender. The problem with this is that regardless of what is the precise explanation of the propositions 'the state has the power to punish an offender because she deserves to be punished' or 'inflicting punishment to the guilty is intrinsically good', they seem to warrant the conclusion that states should have the power to punish offenders irrespective of where the offence was committed. This follows, at least, as long as retributivism is not able to qualify that tenet by claiming that these offenders deserve to be punished *by state S*. But retributivists characteristically do not take that approach. Take for example Ted Honderich's claim that the truth in retributivism is that punishment is justified by grievance satisfaction.[97] Arguably, to the victim and all those who sympathize with him it would make little difference, in terms of grievance satisfaction, just which state does in fact punish the offender, as long as she is effectively punished. It seems, then, that most retributivists will also be committed to defending states holding criminal jurisdiction regardless of where the crime was committed.[98] Moreover, the nationality of both offender and victim seem entirely unrelated to the reason why any particular state holds the power to punish a particular offender.

The remainder of this section concentrates on two arguments that may provide a better answer to this problem: von Hirsch and Ashworth's liberal argument for legal punishment, and Antony Duff's influential more communitarian approach.[99] Von Hirsch and Ashworth see punishment as mainly explained in terms of censure, though their justification is supplemented by an element of deterrence. Deterrence, as we have seen, cannot help them to circumscribe the territorial or extraterritorial scope of states' power to punish. Accordingly, the censure-based element of their justification must do the explanatory work. On the particular issue at stake here their argument goes as follows: (a) offences are moral wrongs; (b) by censuring the offender, punishment provides recognition of the conduct's wrongfulness; (c) this recognition should be made by a public authority and *on behalf of the wider community*, because it relates to basic norms of decent interaction among individuals;[100] (d) the state is, so the argument goes, the only body capable

[97] Honderich, *Punishment: The Supposed Justifications*, 233–4.

[98] Nozick's argument that punishment connects the offender with 'correct values' will be liable to this charge (Robert Nozick, *Philosophical Explanations*). And so would be M Moore's claim that the criminal law is to 'attain retributive justice' by 'punish[ing] all and only those who are morally culpable in the doing of some morally wrongful act' (*Placing Blame: A Theory of Criminal Law*, 33–5). Moore is, however, one of the few theorists who would be comfortable with this implication.

[99] See, respectively, Andrew von Hirsch and Andrew Ashworth, *Proportionate Sentencing: Exploring the Principles* (Oxford: Oxford University Press, 2005) and Duff, *Punishment, Communication, and Community*.

[100] They refer here to citizens rather than individuals (von Hirsch and Ashworth, *Proportionate Sentencing*, 30). However, this cannot be meant in any meaningful way. Otherwise, one would have

of providing such public valuation of the offender's conduct.[101] The main difficulty their argument faces is that it does not identify the wider community on whose behalf censure should be conveyed. This may be because their main underlying concern is to establish that legal punishment is the business of the state rather than of private individuals. However, what it means for our purposes is that they fail to explain which state it is the business of.

Von Hirsch and Ashworth consider themselves conventional liberals. The community they seem to have in mind is that of a group of individuals who share some basic norms of decent interaction. But then this community would have to include every individual worldwide. After all, most moral wrongs do not depend upon territorial boundaries or political allegiances. On these grounds, it would be up to them to explain why an extraterritorial state would not be in a position to provide a public valuation of an offence perpetrated abroad. The decision of both the territorial state and that in which the offender happened to be arrested would arguably amount to a public recognition of the conduct's wrongfulness. If, as they say, the disapproving response to the conduct should not be left to victims and others immediately affected, they would need to provide an argument explaining why it should have to be left to the immediate state, that is, the one on whose territory the offence was perpetrated.

By contrast, Duff's Communitarian theory of punishment does not necessarily collapse into universal jurisdiction. Duff has influentially argued that the central point in punishing a wrongdoer is to persuade her to accept the condemnation for her crime and, in accepting it, to repent that crime and reform her future conduct.[102] I will not examine the soundness of that argument here; our main interest is in appraising Duff's position in light of extraterritoriality. Duff sees punishment as a secular penance the main purpose of which is to communicate censure to moral agents. He is therefore very much concerned with being able to reach the offender's moral conscience. For the punishment to reach the offender's moral conscience, the punishing agent needs to have the moral standing to censure her for her wrong. This moral standing depends on it fulfilling two conditions. First, it must have the appropriate relationship to the offender, or to her action in question. This implies the existence of a political community on behalf of which punishment is imposed, that is, a linguistic community that shares a normative language and a set of substantive values sufficient to render mutually intelligible the normative demands that the law makes on its citizens. Secondly, such state must not have lost that standing as a result of some (wrongful) previous dealing with the offender.

to infer from this argument that as long as the 'indecent' interaction is towards an alien, the criminal law would have nothing to say on this. Their own liberal stance would be inconsistent with that proposition.

101 Ibid, 29–31 (emphasis added).

102 See Antony Duff, *Punishment, Communication, and Community* (Oxford: Oxford University Press, 2001). See also Uma Narayan, 'Appropriate Responses and Preventive Benefits: Justifying Censure and Hard Treatment in Legal Punishment', OJLS 13/2 (1993), 174.

Duff's argument does better than most of its rivals in this context. This is arguably because he conceives the question about the justification for legal punishment as not only being about whether it is permissible to punish someone, but rather, and crucially, about whether some particular body has the right to do so. Again, the answer to this latter question depends crucially on what, on Duff's account, constitutes a political community. If he makes the requirements too thin (namely, mutual recognition and protection of basic human rights) then he would have to admit that almost any body would have the moral standing to censure offenders, and as a result he would end up advocating universal criminal jurisdiction for every wrong that ought to be criminalized. But this is arguably not what he has in mind. Duff seems to be talking of a thicker notion of political community. He explicitly advocates a conception of political community based on

> an idea of people living together (as distinct from merely beside each other) in a society defined by some set of shared values and understandings that might be implicit, inchoate or disputed, but without which society, politics and law would be impossible.[103]

Accordingly, his argument would be safe from advocating too broad a principle of distribution of criminal jurisdiction in the international society.

Duff has recently elaborated on his explanation of when a particular body has the appropriate moral standing to bring the offender to account for her offence.[104] He mainly relies on a theoretical point about the conception of responsibility which is consistent with, but does not necessarily depend on, his normative justification for legal punishment. This conceptual point is the crucial aspect of his account on which the notion of appropriate moral standing seems to rest. Duff argues that the concept of responsibility has a relational dimension. An offender is responsible for X *to Y*, or better, she is responsible *as W* for X *to Y*. To illustrate: as a university teacher, there are only certain bodies or individuals who can call Sam to account if, say, he delivers an ill-prepared lecture. He will not be accountable to 'a passing stranger, or to [her] aunt, ... or to the Pope'.[105] Duff uses this model to argue explicitly against a territorial conception of criminal jurisdiction. ' "[A]cting within a specified geographical area *X*" does not by itself have the normative significance that an answer to the "as what" question requires.'[106] Rather, individuals should respond 'as citizens' of a political community. It is the fact that they belong to the political community that makes them accountable to a particular state for a criminal offence. On this basis, Duff argues that '[t]he wrongs that properly concern a political community, as a political community, are those committed within it by its own members'.[107]

This conception, Duff admits, requires an obvious qualification: it needs to extend to visitors and temporary residents, as well as citizens.[108] But this causes

[103] Duff, *Answering for Crime: Responsibility and Liability in the Criminal Law* (Oxford: Hart, 2007), 44.

[104] Antony Duff, 'Criminal Responsibility, Municipal and International' (unpublished manuscript: 2006, cited with permission from the author). See also his *Answering for Crime*, chs 1 and 2.

[105] Duff, 'Criminal Responsibility', 5.

[106] Duff, *Answering for Crime*, 44.

[107] Duff, 'Criminal Responsibility', 13.

[108] Duff, *Answering for Crime*, 54–5.

problems. Duff's argument for a certain offender being accountable to a particular state is that she belongs to that political community, that she is a citizen of that state. But visitors and temporary residents are not citizens. With regard to them he claims that they should, as guests, 'be accorded many of the rights and protections of citizenship, as well as being expected to accept some of its responsibilities and duties'.[109] Duff does not elaborate on this. He only stipulates that

> This is not to revert to a geographical principle that grounds jurisdiction in the territorial location of crime: what makes normative sense of jurisdiction is still the law's identity as the law of a particular polity.[110]

But this is a crucial part of his argument. Being a guest is, both in terms of the application of the criminal law, and in everyday moral situations, a spatially determined notion. I am a guest at your house only when I am physically at your house. But Duff's whole point is to argue against this kind of criterion. Thus, if he wants this analogy to work he needs to explain why this is not simply falling back into a territorial conception of the criminal law.

One way to make sense of this extension is by recourse to consent. When O enters state S, he may argue, she consents to abide by its rules.[111] It is, however, questionable whether such a reliance on consent would not ultimately undermine the weight that belonging to a political community has in Duff's general argument. After all, being a citizen of S is hardly a matter of pure choice in the vast majority of countries. What is more, this claim would mean that individuals who have not validly consented to entering S would not be bound by S's criminal rules at all. Surely Duff would not want to argue that Adolph Eichmann or Mr Alvarez Machain were not bound by the Israeli or American prohibition of murder, rape, and so on while in Israel or the United States.[112]

A more promising argument for this extension, although one that Duff would probably himself reject, seems to rely on the benefits accorded to certain individuals in terms of rights and protections. Yet this reliance on the benefits that S provides to individuals seems ultimately to undermine Duff's overall explanation. If all we need for someone to be accountable to state S is that she receives certain rights and protection from S, the notion of citizenship, that is, that she belongs to that political community, ceases to do any justificatory work. Residents and even people on holiday receive important benefits from the state where they happen to be simply by being there. If, by contrast, Duff wants to maintain that criminal responsibility

[109] Ibid, 54. [110] Ibid, 55.

[111] This view has been defended, for instance, by Samuel Pufendorf. He wrote that

> A stranger who, in the guise of a friend, enters a state whose policy has been the friendly reception of foreigners, even without giving any expression of his fealty, is understood to have expressed tacitly, by his act of entering the country, his willingness to conduct himself by the laws of that state.

See his *De jure Naturae et gentium* in James Brown Scott (ed), *The Classics of International Law* (trans C H and W A Oldfather) (Oxford: Clarendon Press, 1934 [1688]), 403.

[112] Both were allegedly abducted and illegally transferred to the forum state. On this, see Chapter 6.

is a relational concept and it makes that offender responsible *to S* on the ground that she is a citizen of S, he seems committed to the claim that temporary residents and visitors are not accountable to S.

The best way of making sense of Duff's position is, arguably, to take his analytical point about the concept of responsibility together with his normative justification for inflicting legal punishment upon an offender. After all, an offender being responsible for a particular act to a particular person or community is not, or not yet, paramount to being liable to that person or community visiting legal punishment upon her. One might well be responsible for a criminal wrong without being liable to be punished. A standard example would be when an offender agrees to testify against a mafia organization and is granted immunity from prosecution. Duff suggests that a given state S having the moral standing to punish an offender is necessary for S to be able to reach her moral conscience. If being able to communicate moral censure to an offender is what justifies the state meting out legal punishment to her, then Duff would be committing himself to the implausible view that only if this offender is a citizen of S would S be justified in punishing her. But this explanation is unhelpful. It is not at all clear why the United Kingdom would not be able to reach the moral conscience of an Italian rapist just because he is Italian.

Finally, Duff's conception does not really provide a convincing explanation of some other standard instances of states' power to punish certain offenders. On the one hand, Duff is reluctant to endorse the principles of nationality and passive personality. He argues that

> one could ... plausibly hold that we are not answerable to our fellow citizens for wrongs that we commit abroad, and that while we may expect our fellow citizens to have some collective concern at least for serious wrongs that we suffer abroad, that concern should not extend to calling the wrongdoers to account.[113]

Duff might still want to claim an analytical advantage over the territorially based account advocated here:

> the point is that extra-territorial jurisdiction over crimes committed by or against the polity's members makes straightforward sense if we take citizenship to be the basis of criminal responsibility—whereas if we start with a territorial criterion of jurisdiction they will seem much more puzzling.[114]

But that does not seem true of the territorial conception advocated in this book. There is nothing analytically mysterious in examining whether individuals in France themselves have an interest in France's criminal rules being in force in Nepal important enough to confer upon France the power to punish an offence committed in Nepal by or against a French national. The claim here is that as a matter of fact they simply seem to lack such interest.

On the other hand, his position would fail to explain other aspects of the scope of the power to punish as currently regulated. For example, his account would

[113] Duff, *Answering for Crime*, 54. [114] Ibid.

have difficulties in explaining what under international law is called the principle of objective territoriality.[115] This jurisdictional basis entails that a state would have jurisdiction over an offender when the result of her conduct occurred on its territory despite the fact that her conduct was performed abroad. A standard example is when A shoots B across a national border, the state where B died claiming jurisdiction to prosecute A.[116] This principle can be applied to many other more pressing issues such as Internet fraud, money-laundering, and terrorism. Duff would thereby have difficulties in explaining why Scotland had the power to punish anyone (at least anyone who is not a Scottish national) for the Lockerbie incident. Also, Duff's model of civic criminal responsibility would face difficulties explaining the principle of protection.[117] Namely, it would have difficulties explaining why, for example, Uruguay has the power to punish an Italian national for counterfeiting Uruguayan currency in France. After all, the perpetrators of these offences lack the relevant relationship to Uruguay or Scotland, respectively, and it can hardly be argued that they have received any specific benefit or protection from these countries. It might even be the case that they have never been to Uruguay or Scotland at all. And yet, these jurisdictional bases are not only well established as a matter of law; they also seem based on widely held intuitions about the appropriate scope of states' power to punish.

7. Conclusion

The central findings in this chapter are relatively straightforward. I have argued that international law theory fails to provide a convincing explanation for some of the existing bases of extraterritorial jurisdiction over municipal crimes. In order to examine the extraterritorial scope of states' power to punish offenders we need to look at the reasons that justify them holding that power in the first place. The justification for the power to punish advocated in Chapter 2 fully accounts for states' power to punish offences committed on their territory or against their sovereignty, security, or important governmental functions (protective principle). However, it is incompatible with states holding an extraterritorial power to punish an offender on grounds of her nationality or that of the victim (nationality and passive personality principles). The last section of this chapter examined two possible lines of criticism to the account of extraterritorial criminal jurisdiction over domestic offences developed here. It first rejected the claim that the framework put forward is too restrictive by explaining how the justification for legal punishment advocated here can accommodate collaborative efforts to tackle transnational crime through international agreements. Finally, it

[115] See, eg, Brownlie, *Principles of Public International Law* (Oxford: Oxford University Press, 2003), 301ff.

[116] See, eg, *State v Hall* 114 NC 909, 19 SE 602 (1804) for exactly this situation, albeit between the US states of North Carolina and Tennessee.

[117] See section 5 above.

examined whether competing justifications for legal punishment available in the literature have more promise in terms of being able better to explain how international law regulates extraterritorial punishment. Ultimately, I have argued that even refined consequentialist and deontological theories ultimately do not fare as well as the argument advocated here in accounting both for the existing legal framework regulating this area, and for our core intuitions regarding the appropriate scope of states' power to punish.

4
A Jurisdictional Theory of International Crimes

> Nothing is more pernicious to an understanding of [international crimes such as genocide] ... than the common illusion that the crime of murder and the crime of genocide are essentially the same. The point of the latter is that an altogether different order is broken and an altogether different community is violated.[1]

1. Stating the Problem

In the previous chapter I argued that as a matter of normative argument state's power to punish an offender for crimes such as robbery, assault, fraud, and so on, is primarily territorial. That is, an extraterritorial state would lack this normative power, unless the offence threatens its sovereignty, security, or important governmental functions (the 'principle of protection'). I also argued that neither the nationality of the offender nor that of her victim would suffice to explain why a given state ought to have the power to punish that particular offender extraterritorially. Nonetheless, this general position needs to be qualified. These jurisdictional rules apply only to municipal offences. They do not purport to apply to offences such as genocide, war crimes, or crimes against humanity, which we may call, for present purposes, 'international crimes'. That there is currently such a thing as an international crime as a matter of international law is hardly controversial. Paradigmatic examples of prosecutions for this type of crime are the trial of Milosevic in The Hague, the extradition proceedings against former Chilean dictator Pinochet in the UK, and the indictment of the current President of Sudan before the International Criminal Court (ICC). The issue at stake in this chapter is, generally, what makes a particular offence an international crime. That is, what distinguishes international offences from domestic ones. A more specific question then arises: is it possible to provide a cogent theory of international crimes able to accommodate, for example, genocide, war crimes, and crimes against humanity?

This chapter, then, is concerned with identifying the specific features of international offences that explain why the state on whose territory the crime was

[1] Hannah Arendt, *Eichmann in Jerusalem: A Report on the Banality of Evil* (New York: Penguin Books, 1994).

committed lacks the exclusive power to punish those responsible for it. This is not yet an endorsement of the thesis that international crimes warrant giving states universal criminal jurisdiction. That position will be advocated in the following chapter. It is worth clarifying further the distinction between the different arguments. This chapter will only argue that individuals in the territorial state lack an interest in *that* state holding a prima facie immunity against extraterritorial authorities punishing an offender for an international crime committed there. This means that at least some extraterritorial authority holds the power to punish her. Chapter 5 will provide an account of the jurisdictional rules applicable to this type of offence. It will be argued that the ICC as well as every state should hold at the bar of justice the power to punish an offender for an international crime regardless of where it was committed. These distinct issues are often conflated. As a matter of philosophical argument it pays to examine them separately.

Before going any further two points of clarification are in order. First, the aim here is not to elucidate the main features of existing offences under international law or to provide justification for the criminalization of specific acts. Rather, the issue at stake concerns identifying a specific feature or set of features that would explain why jurisdiction for these offences should be broader than the territoriality and protective principles advocated in the previous chapter for municipal crimes. Put differently, the main task in this chapter is to provide an intelligible rationale for the settled instances of international offences, rather than to provide a test that will solve hard cases.

Secondly, it is important to specify further what is in need of normative elucidation. After all, both domestic and international offences can be characterized as behaviours that warrant meting out legal punishment to their perpetrators. There are, however, a number of normative implications specifically attached to the notion of 'international crimes'. Crucially, tribunals can hold individuals accountable even in the absence of any traditional link or *nexus* with the perpetrator, the victim, or the offence. This means that a given state can punish an individual for an international crime even if the offence was not committed on its territory, against its sovereignty, or by or against one of its nationals. Accordingly, I shall use here the concept of an international offence in a narrow, jurisdictional sense, as crimes that warrant conferring upon some authority extraterritorial criminal jurisdiction. My aim is to isolate this issue from other significant normative and legal features commonly associated with this type of crime, such as the possibility of granting amnesties or pardons by the territorial state, the inapplicability of statutes of limitation, or the law on state or diplomatic immunity.[2] Put simply, this chapter is about explaining why Belgium can legitimately claim the power to prosecute and

[2] See the 1968 Convention on the Non-Applicability of the Statutory Limitations to War Crimes and Crimes against Humanity (adopted by GA Res 2391) and the parallel European Convention of 1974. See also, ICC Statute, Arts 29 and 27(2) and, eg, the Argentine Supreme Court decision in *Arancibia Clavel*, Argentine CSJN, Decision no 259, 24 August 2004, and the French Court of Cassation in *Barbie*, 78 ILR 125. More recently, the Audiencia Nacional of Spain refused to extradite former Argentine President Maria Estela de Perón, precisely on the grounds that because the offences she was requested for were not crimes against humanity (and therefore international offences) the statutes of limitation applied and Argentina lacked jurisdiction to try her. See (in Spanish) <http://

punish two Rwandan nuns for participating in a genocide in Rwanda, but cannot prosecute and punish a single case of rape or murder perpetrated in El Salvador.

This way of framing the question might be controversial. It may be objected, for instance, that by focusing exclusively on this jurisdictional aspect I am using a single normative implication to conceptualize international crimes instead of providing a sound analysis of the concept itself. In other words, this way of proceeding could be said to put the cart before the horse. Admittedly, my approach implies a criticism of part of the existing literature,[3] because it suggests that it is ultimately unhelpful to try to determine what humanity stands for in the notion of crimes against humanity, and then to explain all their normative implications on the basis of this connection. Instead, I seek to isolate a specific implication often associated with this type of offence—extraterritorial prosecution—and provide a normative argument to account for it.[4] This is not such a controversial stance to take. As argued by Abi-Saab,

> The concept of war crimes was ... initially related, in international law, to the delimitation of the penal jurisdiction of States to prosecute and punish, rather than to the definition of the incriminated acts and the attendant penalties.[5]

Moreover, my approach gains some support from the fact that these offences are referred to as international crimes, and that prosecutions for them are often resisted and criticized precisely because of their extraterritorial character.

The quest for a unified explanation of international crimes is an important one. Highlighting this normative issue contributes to answering the question whether there should be a system of international criminal law at all. And arguably, it has become more pressing as a result of states increasingly claiming an extraterritorial power to punish offenders for crimes other than piracy under international law. Among the arguments commonly articulated as an explanation for the particular jurisdictional regime attached to international offences are: that they are analogous to piracy in some specific respect; that they are perpetrated in places where law enforcement is simply too weak; that they harm or violate humanity itself; and that they shock the conscience of humankind. For clarity of exposition, I shall divide these arguments into two main groups. Section 2 examines arguments claiming that international offences are analogous to piracy in some relevant sense and, as a result, subject to the same jurisdictional rules. Section 3 addresses the arguments purporting to explain them in terms of harm to humanity. Ultimately, these two

www.elpais.com/articulo/internacional/Audiencia/Nacional/rechaza/extraditar/Isabelita/Peron/elpepuint/20080428elpepuint_15/Tes> (last accessed 1 August 2010).

[3] Two exceptions are May, *Crimes Against Humanity* and Cryer, *Prosecuting International Crimes*, 75.

[4] For examples of this approach see David Luban, 'A Theory of Crimes against Humanity', *Yale J of International Law* 29 (2004) and Richard Vernon, 'What Is Crime against Humanity?' *J of Political Philosophy* 10/3 (2002).

[5] Georges Abi-Saab, 'The Concept of "War Crimes"' in Sienho Yee and Wang Tieya (eds), *International Law in the Post-Cold War World: Essays in Memory of Li Heopei* (London: Routledge, 2001), 100. Admittedly, this notion originally extended the states' criminal jurisdiction to try only enemy combatants or civilians.

families of arguments will be found wanting. Section 4 presents a jurisdictional theory of international crimes. It argues that what justifies making a criminal rule into an *international* criminal rule is the fact that it cannot really be in force on the territory of a given state if it has to rely exclusively on being enforced by that state. Section 5 examines whether we can apply this normative and conceptual framework to war crimes. Finally, section 6 deals with the objection that international criminal law does not really need a theory of international crimes.

2. Piracy-Based Explanations and the History of International Crimes

Piracy was undisputedly the first international offence in the specific sense used here. Pirates have traditionally been referred to as *hostis humani generis* and their actions considered cognizable by any state which holds them.[6] Although scholars point to the slave trade as another classic example of an international offence, piracy has proved extremely enduring and influential both in theory and practice. Scholars, theorists, and courts have therefore often tried to explain the main features of international offences, and in particular their distinct jurisdictional regime, by reference to one or more of piracy's specific features.[7] Characteristically the arguments take the form: piracy is and ought to be an international offence; war crimes, genocide, crimes against humanity, and the like share feature 'x' with piracy; thus, they should also be international offences. There are two different kinds of problems with these arguments. Some misguidedly link universal jurisdiction to a particular feature 'x' that piracy arguably shares with other international crimes but which does not really explain its jurisdictional regime; others, by contrast, fail to make that link altogether and argue on the basis of a *non sequitur*.

Willard Cowles has provided one of the few explanations of why war crimes must be considered international offences.[8] His argument is not purely normative; rather he also seems to rely on historical and legal considerations. However, it is a good example of the kind of argument with which this section is concerned. Cowles represents what we may call for present purposes the 'scene of the crime' theory. He argues that the 'origin of the jurisdiction over the war criminal must

[6] This position on piracy as a matter of what we currently call Public International Law goes back at least as far as Grotius. But it has been suggested that this view essentially goes back to the period before Alexander (Max Radin, 'International Crimes', *Iowa L Rev* 32 (1946–1947), 41). On piracy, see generally Alfred P Rubin, *The Law of Piracy* (Irvington-on-Hudson: Transnational, 1998).

[7] See, eg, *Israel v Eichmann*, 36 ILR 277 (Supreme Court of Israel, 1962); and Judge Moore's dissenting opinion in the *Lotus* case (*France v Turkey*), PCIJ, Series A no 10 (1927), 70. See also Luc Reydams, *Universal Jurisdiction: International and Municipal Legal Perspectives* (Oxford: Oxford University Press, 2003), 58.

[8] In effect, as I argue in section 3 below, most of them were tailored specifically to tackle crimes against humanity. For another argument on war crimes, though less appealing, see Thomas H Sponsler, 'The Universality Principle of Jurisdiction and the Threatened Trials of American Airmen', *Loyola L Rev* XI (1968–1969).

be sought in the ancient practice of brigandage'.[9] He suggests that the concept of the war criminal is a legal construction of the twentieth century. Previously, war criminals acting both in a public and a private capacity were considered brigands. And brigandism, like piracy, 'stem[s] from the fundamental fact of the lack of governmental control in the areas of [its] operations'; brigands flourish where political order and law enforcement are lacking, typically in times of war.[10] It is in this sense that war crimes are very similar to piratical acts: in both situations there is 'a lack of any adequate judicial system operating on the spot where the crime takes place' and 'both the pirate and the war criminal take advantage of this fact, hoping thereby to commit their crimes with impunity'.[11] Thus, Cowles concludes,

> The jurisdiction, exercised over war crimes, has been of the same nature as that exercised in the case of the pirate, and this broad jurisdiction has been assumed for the same fundamental reason.[12]

Cowles's argument is historically informed, and certainly appealing. However, I suggest it is ultimately unsuccessful. The reason for this is that it relies too heavily on the pedigree of piracy as an international offence: Cowles is so concerned with showing that war crimes can be assimilated to piracy, that he overlooks the justification for initially considering piracy an international offence. On his view, international offences are those which are perpetrated in places where governmental control is lacking, and where offenders can expect to act with impunity. Whether this argument suffices as a historical reason for making piracy an international offence is questionable. Many other offences were often perpetrated on the high seas, such as assault or murder unaccompanied by robbery, and these were not subjected to extraterritorial jurisdiction. Neither the fact that piracy or war crimes are difficult to prevent and punish, nor the fact that they are committed in areas where there is little state authority seems to suffice as an explanation of why they were in fact made into international offences. In fact, war criminals can also operate within a very rigid legal and organizational structure—Nazi troops being only one example of this.

Whether Cowles's argument succeeds as a normative explanation of the jurisdictional regime of international offences is even more dubious. Although he does not say so explicitly, his argument seems to be that where law enforcement is very weak or lacking, such as on the high seas or in times of war, the standard bases of jurisdiction for domestic offences would fail to deter potential offenders. This is implied by the assertion that in such contexts brigands and war criminals

[9] Willard B Cowles, 'Universality of Jurisdiction over War Crimes', *California L Rev* XXXIII/2 (1945), 181.

[10] Ibid, 193.

[11] Ibid, 194, 217. Cowles points to other features of brigandism which, to some extent, might explain the expansive jurisdictional rules on it: 'it is motivated by no public cause and ... authorized by no state', or it 'has been to a large extent international in character', ie, international borders are ideal for the brigand, and 'bands of brigands are often made up of members of more than one nationality' (at 184, 185, and 186 respectively). But ultimately he relies on the 'scene of the crime' consideration to justify its particular jurisdictional regime.

[12] Ibid, 217.

expect to commit their crimes with impunity. Admittedly, allowing extraterritorial states to punish a war criminal would normally increase deterrence. However, as argued in Chapter 3, deterrence as a general justification for the power to punish would collapse the distinction between municipal and international offences by providing extraterritorial states with criminal jurisdiction over both of them. As a result, Cowles's argument is not really an explanation of what makes war crimes and piracy international offences.

The second, and perhaps more influential, version of these piracy-based explanations is the 'nature of the crime' theory.[13] It is often argued that the 'heinousness' of an offence is what justifies a state with 'no connection' to it holding the power to punish the offender. This proposition has a number of different formulations. The Preamble of the ICC Statute, for instance, talks about 'unimaginable' atrocities. Similarly, it has been argued that international offences are characterized by 'a level of callousness that embodies the very essence of evil itself',[14] or that they 'shock the conscience of mankind',[15] that they have an 'added dimension of cruelty and barbarism'[16] capable of 'tear[ing] the roots of civilized society',[17] and so on.

The heinousness argument, however, is not used by itself to justify the particular jurisdictional rules often associated with international offences but rather connected to the piracy analogy. Under this argument, it is the nature of piratical acts, in particular, their heinousness—rather than the location of the crime—that makes them cognizable by an extraterritorial authority.[18] An attraction of this approach, Eugene Kontorovich suggests, is that by arguing that the heinousness of the crime explains the power to punish international offences extraterritorially, advocates of the piracy analogy put their opponents in the uncomfortable position of having to either question the heinousness of, for example, systematic torture, or concede that it should be treated like piracy.[19]

Kontorovich himself argues against this use of the piracy analogy. He correctly suggests that heinousness could not have been the actual reason why piracy was

[13] Stephen Macedo, *Universal Jurisdiction: National Courts and the Prosecution of Serious Crimes under International Law* (Philadelphia: University of Pennsylvania Press, 2004).

[14] Laurence Thomas, 'Forgiving the Unforgivable' in Eve Garrard and Geoffrey Scarre, *Moral Philosophy and the Holocaust* (Aldershot: Ashgate, 2003).

[15] *Prosecutor v Tadic*, Case No IT-94-1-AR72 (1995) at §57. See also, Michael Walzer, *Just and Unjust Wars: A Moral Argument with Historical Illustrations* (New York: Basic Books, 2000), 107.

[16] *Regina v Finta* [1994] 1 RCS at 818.

[17] Christopher C Joyner, 'Arresting Impunity: The Case for Universal Jurisdiction in Bringing War Criminals to Accountability', *Law and Contemporary Problems* 59/4 (1996), 171.

[18] Eugene Kontorovich, 'The Piracy Analogy: Modern Universal Jurisdiction's Hollow Foundation', *Harvard International LJ* 45/1 (2004), 205. For examples of explicit endorsements of this analogy, see Diane F Orentlicher, 'Settling Accounts: The Duty to Prosecute Human Rights Violations of a Prior Regime', *Yale LJ* 100 (1991), 2557. See also, 1 *Law Reports of Trials of War Criminals* 35, 42 (1947) (Brit Mil Ct Almelo), cited in Kontorovich, 'The Piracy Analogy', 195. This reasoning has been followed, for instance, by US courts in *Extradition of Demjanjuk, Re* 612 F Supp 544 (ND Ohio 1985). The most famous case in which the US claimed extraterritorial jurisdiction over acts of torture, namely *Filártiga v Peña-Irala* 630 F2d 876 (2d Cir 1980), is not directly relevant for our purposes here, as it deals with civil jurisdiction, and therefore not with the scope of the US power to punish.

[19] Kontorovich, 'The Piracy Analogy', 208.

initially considered an international offence. When similar acts were perpetrated by privateers, that is, state-licensed pirates, they were repatriated rather than subjected to universal criminal jurisdiction.[20] Moreover, acts of piracy were never really considered particularly heinous. Piracy ultimately amounted to a particularly troublesome variety of robbery.[21] And although the *locus* where it was committed made it hard to prosecute, this was certainly not enough to put its heinousness on a par with offences such as state-sponsored rape or the poisoning of water supplies.[22]

Thus, once the problems of the piracy analogy are understood, the argument from heinousness seems to lose whatever it was that explained precisely why *extraterritorial* bodies would have the power to punish those responsible for international crimes. There is no evident connection between the heinousness of a particular crime and the scope of a state's power to punish a particular offender. And yet, it is precisely this connection that a theory of international crimes needs to explain.

3. International Offences as 'Crimes against Humanity'

Arguably, the most elaborate arguments for international offences have been developed within what we might call the paradigm of 'crimes against humanity'.[23] This paradigm is not necessarily focused on the legal category of crimes against humanity, as distinct from war crimes, genocide, or crimes against peace (aggression). Rather, it often implies the particular view, traceable perhaps to The Hague Convention's Martens Clause, that international crimes harm or violate humanity itself.[24] This harm to humanity purportedly explains why an extraterritorial state or an international tribunal would be entitled to punish their perpetrators. Interestingly, it is in the context of crimes against humanity as a legal category (namely, distinct from war crimes, genocide, or crimes against peace) that scholars

[20] Ibid, 210ff.

[21] See *United States v Palmer* 16 US (3 Wheat) 610 (1818), cited in ibid, 225.

[22] Both already mentioned by Vattel in *Law of Nations*, book III, §§ 145, 157. Conversely, it might have been precisely because piracy was not as heinous as murder or rape that states were willing to accept extraterritorial jurisdiction over it: '[u]niversal jurisdiction over murder would usurp this deeply felt responsibility and thus antagonize the nation with traditional jurisdiction.' See Kontorovich, 'The Piracy Analogy', 229 citing *United States v Furlong* 18 US (5 Wheat) 184 (1820). In this case, the court argued:

> Robbery on the seas is considered an offence within the criminal jurisdiction of all nations .... Not so with the crime of murder. It is an offence too abhorrent to the feelings of man, to have made it necessary that it also should have been brought within this universal jurisdiction (id).

[23] Cf the writings of Anupam Chander, 'Globalization and Distrust', *Yale LJ* 114 (2005); Adil Ahmed Haque, 'Group Violence and Group Vengeance: Toward a Retributivist Theory of International Criminal Law', *Buffalo Crim L Rev* 9 (2005); Vernon, 'What Is Crime against Humanity?' 283; Luban, 'A Theory of Crimes against Humanity'; May, *Crimes Against Humanity*. I shall concentrate mainly on the last two.

[24] Preamble to the 1899 Hague Convention (II). See also *Prosecutor v Erdemovic*, Case No IT-96-22 (Trial Chamber, Sentencing Judgment (29 November 1996)), §28.

and tribunals have been pressed to distinguish municipal from international offences.[25] War crimes and crimes against peace, by contrast, entered the constellation of international offences largely uncontested. Many argue that the first criterion used to internationalize crimes against humanity was precisely the 'war nexus'.[26] In any event, crimes against humanity have now established themselves as a category of international offences in their own right and, some would argue, they could eventually become synonymous with them.[27]

Crimes against humanity can be quite schematically defined as the commission of certain inhumane acts (such as murder, torture, rape, and so on) as part of a widespread or systematic attack directed against a civilian population.[28] Accordingly, the crimes against humanity paradigm revolves around the notion that crimes against humanity are group crimes in the sense that they are either committed by certain groups or against them. Its advocates usually also rely on the fact that they entail some egregious form of wrongfulness. I will argue that the different arguments under this account fail on two grounds. First, they are ultimately unable to identify a convincing rationale for making crimes against humanity cognizable by some *extraterritorial* authority. Secondly, when they do provide an explanation of this feature, the explanation collapses the distinction between domestic and international offences by advocating extraterritorial prosecutions for both.

A first general line of argument relies on the proposition that crimes against humanity are international offences because they are perpetrated by states or state-like organizations against groups under their control. That is, the consideration that turns them into international crimes is the group-character of the perpetrators. There are several versions of this argument. For the sake of clarity of exposition, we may divide them into three: (a) the analytical claim that an extraterritorial authority would have the power to punish an offender for an international crime on the ground that the territorial state has forfeited its immunity against it doing so; (b) the normative argument that the extraterritorial state's power to punish is based on the interests of potential victims in the territorial state and in other states affected; and (c) the argument that this power must be explained by reference to the individual interest of every single person on earth (ie, member of humankind).

Let us first examine the claim that when security forces or state officials in state S perpetrate crimes against humanity against part of S's own population, S lacks the right against other parties interfering in its internal affairs by, in particular,

[25] Phillis Hwang, 'Defining Crimes against Humanity in the Rome Statute of the International Criminal Court', *Fordham International LJ* 22 (1999); Beth Van Schaack, 'The Definition of Crimes against Humanity: Resolving the Incoherence', *Columbia J of Transnational Law* 37 (1999).

[26] See, eg, M. Cherif Bassiouni, *Crimes Against Humanity in International Criminal Law* (2nd edn, The Hague: Kluwer, 1999), 70–7 and Roger Clark, 'Crimes Against Humanity' in George Ginsburgs and V N Kudriavtsev (eds), *The Nuremberg Trials and International Law* (London: Martinus Nijhoff, 1990), 190–2.

[27] William J Fenrick, 'Should Crimes against Humanity Replace War Crimes?', *Columbia J of Transnational Law* 37 (1998–1999). For the view that war crimes are more appropriate as synonyms of international offences see Gerry Simpson, *Law, War and Crime* (London: Polity Press, 2007).

[28] See Art 8 of the Rome Statute of the ICC.

punishing the perpetrators.[29] This claim is intuitively plausible. Why should such a state retain a right against this type of interference? The problem, though, is that there is no explicit explanation why the territorial state has forfeited its prima facie right against a certain extraterritorial body, in particular, punishing the perpetrators. Accounting for this implication is harder than it might initially appear. Let me illustrate this by reference to an interpersonal example. If A attempts to kill B by shooting at her, A would arguably lack a right against third parties intervening to save B's life (by killing A if necessary). This is often explained by arguing that A forfeited her right against being attacked.[30] However, once the threat is over, a third party would need a different kind of justification to use force against A (for our purposes, by punishing her).[31] This is precisely the kind of argument that justifications for legal punishment provide and the question this argument begs. The argument being considered can only explain why the territorial state may have forfeited its first order Hohfeldian claim-right against a third party intervening on humanitarian grounds to stop the perpetration of crimes against humanity on its territory. But this proposition cannot account for the territorial state's loss of its second order immunity against foreign bodies punishing the offender.[32] So we are left exactly where we started, namely, with the need to provide a normative justification for conferring upon an extraterritorial state or international tribunal the power to punish offenders for crimes against humanity.

A second version of the argument based on the group-character of the perpetrators purports to explain a state's extraterritorial power to punish crimes against humanity by reference to the interests of potential victims. The claim is that when such crimes are perpetrated by a state or state-like entity, this is likely to affect people besides the actual victims. Accordingly, the international community 'would have a legitimate basis for intervention so as to protect the larger community also likely to be harmed by the plan'.[33] This argument is open to the criticism sketched in the previous paragraphs that the actual physical protection afforded to potential victims, either by way of deterring or incapacitating offenders, cannot withstand scrutiny as a justification for a state's extraterritorial power to punish the perpetrators. Larry May, who is one of the main advocates of the position under discussion, might retort that these sorts of '[g]roup-based harms are of interest to the international community because they are more likely to ... risk crossing borders and damaging the broader international community.'[34] A problem

[29] Luban, 'A Theory of Crimes against Humanity', 109. This is also what Larry May calls the 'security principle' (see his *Crimes Against Humanity*, 63–9).

[30] See Judith Jarvis Thomson, 'Self-Defense', *Philosophy & Public Affairs* 20 (1991), 283–310 and Suzanne Uniacke, *Permissible Killing: The Self-Defence Justification of Homicide* (Cambridge: Cambridge University Press, 1994).

[31] On this, see Chapter 1.

[32] May is consistent here. As explained in Chapter 1, he conceives of a state's sovereign right to non-interference in terms of first order Hohfeldian incidents. However, I have argued throughout this book that failure to distinguish first and second order incidents obscures significant features of the right to punish (and of the right to self-government). On this see Chapters 2 and 1, respectively.

[33] May, *Crimes Against Humanity*, 88.

[34] Ibid, 83. See also his 'Humanity, International Crime, and the Rights of Defendants', *Ethics and International Affairs* 20/3 (2006), 374.

with this further claim, however, is that even if this is the case, it does not yet explain conferring the power to punish the perpetrators upon an *extraterritorial* state. Let me explain. If crimes against humanity committed in Argentina risk affecting potential victims in Chile, Uruguay, or other Latin-American countries, as the Plan Condor did,[35] this may well explain Chile and Uruguay's power to punish individuals responsible for such crimes. But it does not, or not yet, explain conferring upon, say, Australia the power to do so. This argument seems to get its intuitive pull, again, from *territorial* considerations thereby failing to address the precise issue at stake, namely, extraterritoriality.[36]

The third argument based on the group character of the perpetrators may help to account for this issue. International crimes have also been explained by recourse to the interests of every individual on earth: it is argued that crimes against humanity harm humanity in the sense that they are both crimes against our shared humanness and against humanity understood as humankind. The aspect of our humanness that is affected by crimes against humanity is our character as political animals.[37] Human beings, the argument goes, are political rather than social animals (eg, ants) in the sense that we need some form of artificial coercive organization. But politics can go horribly wrong and end up in the most atrocious crimes. Accordingly, 'because we cannot live without politics, we exist under the permanent threat that ... the indispensable institutions of organized political life will destroy us.'[38] Crimes against humanity so defined pose a 'universal' threat that every individual human being (humankind) has an interest in repressing. Thus, the interest that justifies making them into international offences is the 'interest in expunging [them] from the repertoire of politics' because 'in a world where crimes against humanity proceed unchecked, each of us could become the object of murder or [persecution]'.[39]

It may well be that individuals both within the territorial state and outside it have an interest in those responsible for international crimes being punished. We need to take a closer look, however, at the particular interest on which this account rests. Luban's claim seems to rely on the proposition that every human being has an interest in crimes against humanity being punished irrespective of where they were perpetrated simply because anyone could be a victim of these offences. We are all hostages of some political organization, and politics can potentially always go horribly wrong. Thus, any state—not just the territorial state—should have the power to punish an offender for this type of offence. However, we also inevitably live next to each other, and every human being could also be a victim of murder, assault, theft, etc. Moreover, the chances of being a victim of any of these

[35] See, eg, Marcos Novaro and Vicente Palermo, *La Dictadura Militar 1976/1983: Del Golpe de Estado a la Restauración Democrática* (Buenos Aires: Paidós, 2003), 122–3.

[36] It may argued that crimes against humanity would also cross borders in the sense that they would very likely cause large numbers of refugees and asylum seekers to arrive in neighbour states. Given that May is hereby talking about the group-based character of the victim, this kind of consequence for individuals in neighbour states does not appear to be the kind consideration he has in mind.

[37] Luban, 'A Theory of Crimes against Humanity', 110.

[38] Ibid, 90–1. [39] Ibid, 138.

municipal offences are, in a significant majority of states, far greater than those of being a victim of crimes against humanity. Accordingly, insofar as this argument is grounded on the individual interest that each human being holds in not being the victim of a criminal offence, it collapses the distinction between international and municipal offences by advocating extraterritorial prosecutions for both.

The reader might find this response unfair. Clearly there is a significant disanalogy between offences committed by states or state-like organizations and those committed by individuals acting alone: while the territorial state can prevent/punish domestic offences, who would be able to stop/punish state officials from/for perpetrating crimes against humanity against its subjects? Though I readily admit that this disanalogy holds, I dispute that it undermines the previous objection. If the problem is that while some agent (the territorial state) can prevent a single murder, no one can prevent crimes against humanity, the solution seems to be to grant an extraterritorial body the right to do so. However, and as explained above, the right to stop atrocities occurring in a given state involves only a *liberty* (and at best a claim-right) to intervene on humanitarian grounds, that is, a first order Hohfeldian incident, not (or not yet) a *power* to punish those responsible for them. Ultimately, this power seems to rely on the claim that every human being has an interest in *deterring* potential perpetrators of crimes against humanity. This is the only way in which the criminal law may try to 'expunge these acts from the repertoire of politics'. Nevertheless, this shows precisely why the alleged implications of the disanalogy put forward disappear. To repeat, although deterrence can explain extraterritorial prosecutions in the case of crimes against humanity, it collapses the distinction between domestic and international offences by advocating extraterritorial prosecutions for both.

Crimes against humanity, however, have not been identified exclusively by the group-based character of their perpetrators. According to the second line of argument identified at the outset of this section, what also makes them international offences is that they are committed against individuals on the ground of their membership of a group or population. In Luban's words,

> in a world where crimes against humanity proceed unchecked, each of us could become the object of murder or [persecution] solely on the basis of group affiliation we are powerless to change.[40]

Similarly, Larry May argues that

> Humanity is implicated, and in a sense victimized, when the sufferer merely stands in for larger segments of the population who are not treated according to individual differences ..., but only according to group characteristics.'[41] This is because this type of offence is 'individuality-denying'.

Human beings have 'interests that people be treated primarily as fellow humans rather than according to their subgroup affiliations'.[42] And yet, these propositions

[40] Luban, 'A Theory of Crimes against Humanity', 138.
[41] May, *Crimes Against Humanity*, 85–6.
[42] May, 'Humanity, International Crime, and the Rights of Defendants', 374.

do not justify conferring upon an extraterritorial authority the power to punish perpetrators of this kind of crime. The crucial link is between the group-based character of the victims and the notion of harm to humanity. Ultimately, it is the claim that international crimes harm humanity that accounts for their specific jurisdictional regime.[43]

This link, however, is difficult to establish. The underlying rationale behind these claims would be that these crimes could happen to people for reasons that are beyond their control. In Frossard's words, the victim is killed 'under the pretext of having been born'.[44] But that someone is assaulted because she is tall, or short, or pretty does not seem to constitute a sufficient reason for triggering the extraterritorial prosecution of her attacker. Rather, it seems that what is doing the justificatory work here is the fact that the victim is a member of a vulnerable group or persecuted minority, rather than the fact that she is being targeted for reasons she cannot change. What matters is the fact that she is Jewish, or black, Muslim, or Albanian (in a world where these groups are persecuted) not the fact that she cannot change what she is.[45] Conversely, the argument seems unable to accommodate a situation in which the victim is attacked for belonging to a particular political party, or professing a certain religion (things she would eventually be able to change). Moreover, when victims are chosen because of their affiliation to a certain vulnerable group, it is that group that is harmed by the crimes, not humanity at large. As Andrew Altman has argued, when

> Jews or Muslims are being targeted ... it is not humanity that is thereby harmed but rather [Jews or Muslims].... Baptists in the United States, Confucians in China, and Hindus in India would not seem to be harmed. Indeed the form of religious hatred that would lead to anti-Semitic or anti-Islamic genocide hinges precisely on the notion that Jews or Muslims are different from the rest of humanity.[46]

Larry May provides a possible answer to this objection. He argues that just as we say that domestic crimes harm a particular national community, analogously crimes against humanity harm the world community (humanity as humankind).[47] This argument is based on the 'solidarity that we feel with fellow humans' on the basis of our 'common vulnerability to violence and harm'.[48] Humanity, then, is harmed when its members are harmed by not treating them as fellow humans but as merely members of other less inclusive communities, that is, when they are persecuted on the basis of group membership. But this further elaboration is unhelpful. First, there is no necessary link between victims belonging to a particular

[43] Ibid, 376.

[44] André Frossard, *Le crime contre l'humanité* (Paris: R Laffont, 1997), 70, cited in Martti Koskenniemi, 'Between Impunity and Show Trials', 6 *Max Planck UNYB* 6 (2002), 29.

[45] Interestingly, vulnerability is at the core of Larry May's conception of war crimes. See eg his *War Crimes and Just War* (Cambridge: Cambridge University Press, 2007), 20.

[46] Andrew Altman, 'The Persistent Fiction of Harm to Humanity', *Ethics and International Affairs* 20/3 (2006), 368–9. See also Luban, 'A Theory of Crimes against Humanity', 138.

[47] May, *Crimes Against Humanity*, 82.

[48] May, 'Humanity, International Crime, and the Rights of Defendants', 376.

sub-group and their humanity being violated.[49] Crimes which are not group-based may also harm our basic sense of solidarity towards human beings generally. They may also constitute 'violations of the human condition'. The case of Joseph Fritzl, who kidnapped and sexually abused his daughter for several years would be a clear example.[50] Conversely, few people would argue that every possible instance of 'hate crimes' or even gender-related crimes should be turned into international offences.[51] That a given individual is assaulted by a small racist gang because of being Jewish, or black, or Latino, in a quiet alley in Hamburg hardly entails, nor should it, that Germany lacks its prima facie immunity against an extraterritorial authority interfering in its domestic affairs.

Ultimately, as Massimo Renzo argues, the main shortcoming of this approach is not

> the answer it provides to the question of what kind of crimes can be said to harm humanity, but ... the very assumption that an adequate account of crimes against humanity will have to be given by answering this question.[52]

The harm principle has been plausibly described as a normative requirement that 'conduct should be criminalized only if it is harmful'.[53] Its function is therefore to set a limit to what conduct should be criminalized. Regardless of the intrinsic merits of such an approach, the issue at stake with international crimes does not seem to be whether crimes against humanity should be criminalized but, rather, who should have the power to do so. To that extent, its invocation in this context may be seen as misplaced.

May would probably argue, though, that the *international* harm principle is meant to do exactly that, namely, show that certain group-based crimes actually harm humanity, and that this justifies them being criminalized *by the international community*. But it is not entirely clear that this is what the international harm principle is supposed to do. The need for an international harm principle, May suggests, concerns the fact that

> international criminal prosecutions risk loss of liberty to the defendants, a loss that is of such potential importance that should not be risked unless there is also a harm to the international community.[54]

[49] The same can be argued against May's explanation of why war crimes harm humanity, ie, that they 'fail to treat humans with the mercy and compassion deserved by all humans' (ibid). He does suggest elsewhere, however, that most war crimes are international crimes in any event in virtue of their crossing of state borders (May, *War Crimes and Just War*, 40).

[50] On this case see <http://news.bbc.co.uk/2/hi/7371959.stm> (last accessed 1 August 2010).

[51] Furthermore, this argument implies that eg racially motivated crimes are more serious than crimes with other motivations, or even motiveless crimes, and this is not easy to argue.

[52] Massimo Renzo, 'A Criticism of the International Harm Principle', *Criminal Law and Philosophy* (forthcoming, 2011). See also, Antony Duff, 'Authority and Responsibility in International Criminal Law', section 3, in Samantha Besson and John Tasioulas (eds), *Philosophy of International Law* (Oxford: Oxford University Press, 2010).

[53] See Hamish Stewart, 'The Limits of the Harm Principle', *Criminal Law and Philosophy* 4/1 (2010), 17–35.

[54] May, *Crimes Against Humanity*, 70.

It is doubtful, however, that such a high threshold is necessary to justify before the offender the harm involved in punishment, particularly when May would usually accept that she should be liable to be punished for a domestic offence. And also, the harm principle seems to provide an answer to the question of why the offender would be liable to be punished *simpliciter*, not why she would be liable to be punished *by an extraterritorial authority*. It is difficult to go from the former conception to the latter on the basis of the idea of harm. As argued throughout this section, the notion that crimes against humanity harm the world community seems somewhat artificial.

More importantly, perhaps, the harm principle has traditionally been construed as requiring actual harm to individual persons, taken singly or collectively.[55] It is not easy to show that torture as part of a systematic attack against a population in South Africa actually harms individuals in Sweden or Japan. It is also unclear in what way the international community is harmed by a war crime perpetrated in an isolated conflict in Colombia. The only way of making sense of this claim seems to be by setting such a low threshold (ie, solidarity on the basis of our common vulnerability to violence or harm) that it would once again collapse the distinction we are trying to draw between crimes against humanity and many municipal ones. To that extent, this explanation is ultimately unhelpful as a criterion for making certain wrongs into international offences in the jurisdictional sense here advocated.

4. A 'Jurisdictional' Theory of International Crimes

Existing accounts of international offences, then, cannot really explain what distinguishes them from domestic crimes in terms of allowing for some form of extraterritorial jurisdiction. Admittedly, they provide certain important insights on which the argument provided here must draw, namely that international offences are committed by states or state-like entities, or perpetrated in places where law enforcement is particularly weak, or involve the most heinous acts committed against individuals who are in a position of vulnerability. However, they all fail in one central respect. They do not connect the fundamental considerations on which they rest with a plausible explanation of why some particular authority should hold the power to punish a particular offender.

In Chapter 2 I argued that a state's power to punish an offender is justified by the interest of individuals in that state in there being a system of criminal law in force. I now submit that there are certain criminal rules that cannot be in force in a given state unless at least some extraterritorial authority holds a concurrent power to punish those who violate them. These rules provide a foundation for international crimes. Let me illustrate this by reference to a particular crime against humanity: acts of torture perpetrated in S as part of a widespread or systematic

[55] See, Feinberg, *Harm to Others*, 26 and Raz, *The Morality of Freedom*, 414.

attack.[56] Plausibly, whenever acts of torture are perpetrated in S in the context of such an attack, it will necessarily be the case that S is either responsible for perpetrating, instigating, or allowing them, or is simply unable to do anything about them. As a result, the fact that S itself holds the power to punish this kind of act cannot really ground the belief of individuals in S in this criminal rule being in force. As Geras puts it,

> states and governments are themselves ... the very source of the calamities we are talking about ...; [thus, they] cannot be relied upon as the guarantors ... of last resort.[57]

Take for example the last Argentinean dictatorship (1976–83). As is well documented, the military had significant leeway to kidnap individuals, torture them, and in most cases make them disappear.[58] If a military squad knocked on someone's door or held someone captive in a clandestine detention unit, there was no recourse to the police, no hope of being rescued by the authorities, nothing except the sheer use of force in self-defence (and often not even this was a possibility). These squads were not, in any meaningful sense, *bound* by a criminal prohibition against doing what they were, in fact, ordered to do as a matter of policy. In this context, individuals in Argentina could not believe that the criminal rule against being kidnapped, tortured, and killed by these public officials was in force, even if such a rule was part of the substantive criminal code of the land.

However, this may seem too quick. Would not individuals in S have a conflicting interest against this kind of interference? In Chapter 1 I argued that individuals in S have an interest that is sufficiently important to confer upon S a prima facie immunity against extraterritorial authorities dictating or enforcing criminal laws on its territory. I now argue that in a situation such as the one described in the previous paragraph, Argentina would lack an immunity against an extraterritorial body punishing those responsible for these crimes against humanity perpetrated on its territory. In effect, S normally holds a prima facie immunity against an extraterritorial state punishing a given offender for a crime she committed on S's territory. This immunity is ultimately explained by the interest of individuals there in S being a self-governed entity. As argued in Chapter 1, however, this immunity is not absolute; it is limited both by the interests of non-members, and by the fundamental interests of the members of S. Arguably, individuals in S have a fundamental interest in there being a criminal rule in force in S against acts of torture, murder, and the like perpetrated as part of a widespread or systematic attack. Moreover, this interest is not only incompatible with S holding

[56] See Art 7.1 of the ICC Statute. I leave aside for present purposes the requirements of them being 'an attack directed against any civilian population' and the 'knowledge of the attack', as well as any further qualification stemming from Art 7.2.

[57] Norman Geras, *The Contract of Mutual Indifference: Political Philosophy after the Holocaust* (London: Verso, 1998), 4.

[58] See Jaime E Malamud-Goti, *Game without End: State Terror and the Politics of Justice* (Norman: University of Oklahoma Press, 1996) and Iain Guest, *Behind the Disappearances: Argentina's Dirty War against Human Rights and the United Nations* (Philadelphia: University of Pennsylvania Press, 1990).

an immunity against an extraterritorial authority punishing the perpetrators of these international crimes, but also overrides the interest that explains that immunity. Now, to claim that S lacks this immunity means only that at least some extraterritorial authority would hold the power to punish an offender.[59] It is not yet a full endorsement of universal jurisdiction, which means that every state holds the power to do so. This argument will have to wait until the next chapter.

The interest of, for example, the Germans in 1939 in a foreign body not punishing an offender for acts of genocide on German soil is not sufficiently important to warrant conferring upon Germany an immunity against a foreign body punishing the offender. The interests of the German Jews and other prosecuted minorities in such a criminal rule being in force in Germany is more important than the interest of their Aryan co-nationals in being left alone. If nothing else, the German Aryans would be able to lead a minimally flourishing life even without a right preventing foreign authorities from dictating criminal rules binding in Germany against widespread and systematic murder, whereas members of persecuted minorities would find it much harder to live a decent life in a state in which their rights not to be killed, tortured, and so on, are not protected by the criminal law system.

Let me clarify further the position hereby advocated in three relevant respects. First, under the account favoured here, international offences need *not* be committed exclusively by state officials or individuals acting under their control. Certain non-state actors can also perpetrate this type of offence. In fact, in contemporary warfare most of these crimes are committed by irregular forces.[60] In certain areas in Colombia, for example, guerrilla or paramilitary groups hold de facto a significant portion of the powers which are often associated with the state. They function as police officers, judges, administrative authorities, and they even collect 'taxes'.[61] As David Luban suggests,

> warlords are sometimes the closest thing in [the] neighbourhood to public authority, and nationalist gangsters may actually have a valid revolutionary or irredentist political program.[62]

They also perpetrate a significant number of offences such as kidnapping and murdering political and military opponents, and even sympathizers.[63] As in the Argentine situation above, individuals living in the zones controlled by these non-state actors will not consider, either, that there is a criminal rule in force against being kidnapped or killed by these groups, that is, really binding upon their

[59] On this, see Chapter 1.

[60] Mary Kaldor, *New and Old Wars: Organized Violence in a Global Era* (Stanford: Stanford University Press, 2007).

[61] See Mauricio García Vilegas, *Jueces sin Estado: La justicia Colombiana en zonas de conflicto armado* (Bogotá: Siglo del Hombre, 2008), ch 3. A similar position may be held by Hamas in Gaza. On this see, Human Rights Watch, 'Under Cover of War. Hamas Political Violence in Gaza' (April 2009).

[62] David Luban, 'War Crimes. The Law of Hell' in Larry May (ed), *War: Essays in Political Philosophy* (Cambridge: Cambridge University Press, 2008), 280.

[63] On the situation in Colombia and how the state has been unable to deal with these groups even by using drastic emergency penality measures, see Manuel A Iturralde, *Castigo y liberalismo autoritario: la justicia penal de excepción en Colombia* (Bogotá: Siglo del Hombre, 2009).

members. At least when such acts are widespread or performed as a matter of policy, the fact that the Colombian state provides a criminal rule against members of these groups performing such acts does not contribute in any meaningful way to the sense of dignity and security of individuals living in these areas. As a result, individuals living in those territories would have a fundamental interest in these rules being in force that overrides their interest in the Colombian state holding an immunity against a foreign body punishing those responsible for these offences.[64]

The second relevant point of clarification is that not every wrong committed in a territorial state on a widespread or systematic scale would entail that this state lacks an immunity against an extraterritorial authority punishing those responsible for it. In short, systematic and widespread traffic violations or bicycle theft perpetrated on S do not amount, under the scheme advocated here, to international offences. The reason for this is, arguably, that individuals in S do not have a fundamental interest in these traffic regulations being in force that is sufficiently important to override their general interest in S being a self-governed entity. Only violations of fundamental rights such as the right not to be tortured, killed, or raped, would be sufficiently important. This, then, clarifies the role that moral egregiousness or enormity plays in defining international offences. It would be, of course, hard to decide where to draw the line. Yet the purpose of this chapter is only to explain in general terms why certain offences warrant conferring upon an extraterritorial authority the power to punish an offender, while others do not.

Third, and related, not simply anyone can carry out an international offence. Take genocide for example. In the vast majority of cases, when genocide is carried out in S, S's officials would be responsible for perpetrating, instigating, or allowing it, or be simply unable to do anything about it. Therefore, if a criminal rule against genocide is to be in force in S, S must lack a prima facie immunity against an extraterritorial body punishing those responsible for conducting that genocide. Genocide, then, should generally be considered an international offence. However, this might not always be the case. An instance of genocide might be perpetrated by an individual acting alone. David Luban illustrates this with the strange case of Abba Kovner, a poet and a survivor of the Shoah, who in 1945 attempted to poison the Hamburg water supply. Kovner claimed—it is reported—that his ultimate goal was to kill six million Germans.[65] An implication of the theory developed here is that, although his act may qualify as genocide, it is not an international offence in the jurisdictional sense advocated here. And this would be the case even if Kovner had succeeded. The German criminal law prohibiting this kind of behaviour does not require other states holding the power to punish an individual responsible for such an act for this criminal prohibition to be in force.

This example allows us to make some important points. It follows from it that although the theory advanced in this chapter claims significant explanatory power

[64] Admittedly, it may be questioned whether it really is the case that if an extraterritorial body had the power to punish an offender it would contribute to the rule against, eg, systematic torture being in force in a given state. This issue will be tackled in some detail in the following chapter.

[65] Luban, 'A Theory of Crimes against Humanity', citing Tom Segev, *The Seventh Million: The Israelis and the Holocaust* (1993), 14–16.

of how international crimes are regulated as a matter of international law, it is not committed to accommodating every instance of them. The purpose of this enquiry is evaluative, and as such it challenges certain aspects of the existing legal framework. The argument hereby provided ultimately advocates a less rigid understanding of international crimes, and one which is not based on the 'nature' of the crime as such. The Kovner example also shows that although the heinousness of the crime is a necessary condition for conferring upon an extraterritorial authority the power to punish someone for an international crime, it is not a sufficient one. Finally, this example illustrates what ultimately does the justificatory work in the explanation of international crimes advocated here: that there are specific *territorial* considerations that impinge upon the reasons for making certain wrongs an international offence.

On the basis of the above argument, it may be argued that the crucial feature of international offences is not explained either simply by the moral enormity of these acts or by the *locus* of their commission. Nor does it come down to the fiction that they harm or violate humanity itself. Rather, the reason why they are international rather than municipal offences resides in the interest that normally explains a state's power to punish a particular offender. With this fact lie three significant advantages of the explanation offered here. First, it suggests that the justification for meting out legal punishment for both domestic and international offences rests on similar considerations. Secondly, it explains why the territorial state lacks an immunity against an extraterritorial body *punishing* the offender, and not simply a claim-right against it intervening militarily to stop the crimes. And finally, it does not collapse the distinction between international and domestic offences.

5. War Crimes and Extraterritorial Jurisdiction

The next step is to assess whether the conception of international crimes advocated here can accommodate standard cases of war crimes. War crimes present, it will be argued below, a particular set of problems for this approach. It is useful to start by succinctly considering what constitutes 'war crimes'. The definition section of the London Charter establishing the Nuremberg Tribunal defines war crimes as:

> violations of the laws and customs of war. Such violations shall include, but are not limited to, murder, ill-treatment or deportation to slave labour or for any other purpose of civilian population of or in occupied territory murder or ill-treatment of prisoners of war or persons on the seas, killing of hostages, plunder of public property, wanton destruction of cities, towns or villages, or devastation not justified by military necessity.[66]

Currently, the most comprehensive list of war crimes is contained in the Rome Statute of the ICC.[67] The law on war crimes is too complex to give a full account

[66] Art 6, cited in Leslie C Green, *The Contemporary Law of Armed Conflict* (3rd edn, Manchester: Manchester University Press, 2008), 324–5.

[67] It does not include, however, every offence arguably recognized in customary law.

of here. For present purposes, however, war crimes are a set of secondary rules that criminalize conduct in breach of certain primary rules provided for under the laws of armed conflict when there is good reason to confer upon an extraterritorial body the power to punish perpetrators.[68] As already suggested, my purpose is not to provide an argument for the specific criminalization of certain acts committed in war, but only to examine whether the jurisdictional conception of international crimes advocated here can accommodate core cases of war crimes. The issue is whether we can distinguish—from the point of view of the jurisdictional rules applicable to them—an act of murder or theft as an ordinary crime committed in the context of war from war crimes such as attacking civilians or pillage.

Let us take the war crime of 'intentionally directing an attack against a civilian population as such' (hereinafter 'attacking civilians').[69] Again, the claim is that a criminal rule against attacking civilians cannot really be in force unless the parties to an armed conflict lack an immunity against some extraterritorial body punishing an individual for this war crime. This claim, however, needs careful scrutiny. Unlike the case of crimes against humanity committed within the territorial state, these crimes typically involve two different states which could both claim the power to punish the perpetrator. Both belligerent powers holding criminal jurisdiction over such offences might suffice for the prohibition against attacking civilians being in force. Let us call them Attacking State and Defending State and let us assume that the offender is a pilot of the Attacking State air force directing an attack against civilians on the territory of the Defending State. Arguably, the fact that the Attacking State holds the normative power to punish this pilot for this offence would not suffice for the criminal rule prohibiting this kind of behaviour being in force in the Defending State. As in the case of crimes against humanity in the previous section, it is highly unlikely that the Attacking State will prosecute its own pilots for an act it ordered or allowed them to perform. But even if some prosecutions were to take place, the key point is that they would hardly suffice for individuals in the Defending State to consider that under realistic circumstances the pilots, or crucially perhaps, high-ranking officials in the Attacking State are really bound by such a rule.

However, would not the Defending State holding a concurrent power to punish this pilot (and high-ranking officials) provide its citizens with the (limited) sense of dignity and security that such a criminal rule being in force is normally able to provide? And if this is the case, would individuals in the Defending State not have an interest in their state deciding for itself when a soldier in the Attacking State violated this rule, thus holding itself a prima facie immunity against third-party states doing so? Not really. Although the Defending State would arguably be

[68] I do not distinguish here between war crimes and the system of 'grave breaches' to the Geneva Conventions and Additional Protocol I. Grave breaches are commonly understood as a subset of war crimes. For our purposes, it can be argued that they both warrant universal (extraterritorial) jurisdiction, which merely warrants a power and a liberty to punish perpetrators. The fact that grave breaches are subject to the more demanding requirement of *aut dedere aut judicare*, which also includes a duty, is irrelevant for the purposes of the present enquiry. For this distinction see eg Georges Abi-Saab, 'The Concept of "War Crimes"', 115.

[69] Arts 8.1 and 8.2.(b)(i) of the Rome Statute.

able to deter this kind of attack, it cannot provide its civilian population with the specific sense of dignity and security that a criminal law being in force provides. Put differently, the Defending State can deter pilots or high-ranking officials in the Attacking State by means of retaliation or military reprisals. It can also deploy some of its troops exclusively for the purposes of protecting its endangered civilian population. However, it is highly implausible that individuals in the Defending State or external observers will consider the Defending State's criminal prohibition *binding* on enemy pilots and, in particular, over those ultimately responsible for the military effort. In most circumstances it would be almost impossible for the Defending State even to seize the relevant accused. As a result, individuals in the Defending State will not have a plausible reason to consider its criminal rules binding on the Attacking State's officials, thereby enhancing their sense of dignity and security.

From the perspective of the Attacking State, its citizens also ultimately lack an interest sufficiently important to confer upon this state an immunity against third parties punishing a pilot for war crimes. On the one hand, they might have an interest in the Attacking State conducting warfare in accordance with international humanitarian law, if only to avoid being victims of reprisals and retaliation. For this purpose, it will certainly help that the Attacking State's high-ranking officials and soldiers consider themselves bound by, at least, an international prohibition on war crimes. And on the other hand, individuals in the Attacking State usually benefit from the legal prohibition of war crimes being in force, that is, being binding on the Defending State. As suggested above, this can only obtain, if it can obtain at all, if at least some third (extraterritorial) party holds the power to punish those responsible for war crimes.

Thus, both individuals in the Attacking State and in the Defending State share an interest in neither of them holding an immunity against a third party punishing war criminals. Note that the point made here is a purely negative one: the belligerent states holding exclusive jurisdiction over war criminals will *not* warrant the belief of individuals there (and of external observers) in the criminal rules prohibiting war crimes being binding on those conducting the war efforts. This is not yet to argue that some extraterritorial authority holding this power will make a difference in this respect.[70]

It might be suggested that the arguments above do not work in every plausible scenario. Individuals in superpower S might not be particularly concerned with individuals in developing country D on the other side of the world, with which S is at war, being able to commit war crimes against them. As a result, *their* sense of dignity and security would not be enhanced by stripping both S and D of their immunity against a third party prosecuting their service personnel for war crimes perpetrated against either state. This, however, would be too hasty as an analysis. US service personnel deployed in Afghanistan would certainly have an interest in Taleban fighters being bound by the criminal rules prohibiting the commission of war crimes against them. This would arguably contribute to their sense of dignity

[70] This claim will be defended in the following chapter.

and security. Moreover, even in the situation in which they themselves would not be at risk (eg because of high altitude bombing of unprotected cities or facilities that shield them), the interest of individuals in Afghanistan (ie, civilians) in these rules being in force would suffice to warrant conferring upon at least some third party the power to punish war crimes committed there. This interest should suffice as a matter of normative argument to conclude that both S and D lack the relevant immunity.

Admittedly, there may be other types of war crimes that are more resilient to this kind of argument. One example may be those war crimes committed against property or the environment. Larry May, for instance, does not deal with them in any detail in his book on war crimes and suggests that they are less central to a theory of international crimes such as his because they do not concern attacks on persons.[71] I believe, by contrast, that this is the reason why they create a pressing challenge to a normative account of war crimes. Consider pillage. The Rome Statute of the ICC prohibits '[p]illaging a town or place, even when taken by assault'.[72] Quite schematically, pillaging involves the appropriation of property for private or personal use (ie, not justified by military necessity) without the consent of the owner and in the context of an armed conflict of an international or not of an international character.[73]

Considering pillage a war crime in the jurisdictional sense advocated here is entirely consistent with the account of international crimes laid out in this chapter. A simple example would illustrate this point. Let us assume that service personnel of the Attacking State pillage small towns in a given province of the Defending State. As discussed above, individuals in the Defending State would not consider soldiers on its territory and military leaders in the Attacking State actually bound by this criminal prohibition unless some extraterritorial authority (besides the Attacking State) had jurisdiction over them. Moreover, their fundamental interest in this criminal rule being in force in their state would suffice to override any interest that individuals in the Attacking State have in that state having exclusive jurisdiction over these crimes. This is not as controversial as it appears, since conferring upon the Defending State this power on *territorial* grounds, that is, over crimes perpetrated there, would also require overriding such immunity.

It has been argued, however, that although '[p]illage is usually committed by combatants, ... the injunction embraces also civilians'.[74] This is not, per se, a problem for the account favoured here. As argued in the previous section, if this war crime is perpetrated by members of a state-like organization, holding significant authority or power over a given territory, it would fall squarely within the concept of international crimes defended here. If, by contrast, the case concerns individuals

[71] May, *War Crimes and Just War*, 19.

[72] Art 8(2)(b)(xvi). This conduct is also proscribed in armed conflicts not of an international character under Art 8(2)(e)(ix).

[73] See, the Elements of Crimes of the ICC Statute. It also requires that the perpetrator be aware of the factual circumstances that establish the existence of an armed conflict.

[74] See Yoram Dinstein, *The Conduct of Hostilities under the Law of International Armed Conflict* (Cambridge: Cambridge University Press, 2003), 214–15.

or neighbourhood gangs stealing or looting private property in a village in the midst of war, the position advocated here is that this need not be considered an international crime. It may be that this view is not entirely consistent with international law.[75] Yet there does not seem to be enough intuitive appeal in such an extension. The situation would be roughly the same as that obtaining in a failed state, or in the aftermath of a natural cataclysm, such as a devastating earthquake. In these contexts, conferring upon an extraterritorial body the power to punish these acts would arguably do very little in terms of grounding the belief of individuals in the existence of a criminal rule prohibiting looting, at least without a large-scale foreign military or police presence on the ground.[76] In fact, in these situations international law does not confer criminal jurisdiction over individual acts of looting upon an extraterritorial authority.

A more damaging objection against this account is arguably that under international law one single incident of pillage may be considered an international crime. The Rome Statute, for instance, provides that the ICC 'shall have jurisdiction in respect of war crimes *in particular* when committed as part of a plan or policy or as part of a large-scale commission of such crimes'.[77] The words 'in particular' seem to indicate that the ICC would also have jurisdiction over an act of pillage which is not part of a plan or policy, or perpetrated on a large-scale basis. This would conflict with the conception of international crimes advocated here by collapsing the distinction between a single act of theft and the war crime of pillage. However, the ICC itself has taken a narrow interpretation of this provision. While examining the situation of Jean-Pierre Bemba Gombo, Pre-Trial Chamber II argued that

> pillaging a town or place pursuant to article 8(2)(e)(v) of the [ICC] Statute entails a somewhat large-scale appropriation of all types of property ... which goes beyond mere sporadic acts of violation of property rights

Hence 'this means that cases of petty property expropriation may not fall under the scope of' pillage as defined under the ICC Statute.[78] Accordingly pillage as an

[75] Dinstein, eg, cites as an example of pillage the case of looters in the events following the overthrow of Saddam Hussein's regime in Iraq (ibid, 215).

[76] For a more careful treatment of this point, see Chapter 3.

[77] Art 8(1) (emphasis added). It has been suggested that the threshold identified in this provision does not entirely coincide with that provided for crimes against humanity (namely, widespread or systematic) advocated above (Robert Cryer et al, *An Introduction to International Criminal Law and Procedure* (Cambridge: Cambridge University Press, 2008), 241). This is immaterial for present purposes. As argued throughout, this chapter concerns explaining core cases of international crimes, not examining the precise boundaries between international and municipal ones.

[78] Decision Pursuant to Article 61(7)(a) and (b) of the Rome Statute on the Charges of the Prosecutor Against Jean-Pierre Bemba Gombo (ICC-01/05-01/08, 15 June 2009), para 317. See, similarly, the opinion of Pre-Trial Chamber I in the Warrant of Arrest for Omar Hassan Ahmad Al Bashir (ICC-02/05–01/09, 4 March 2009) and the distinction between widespread and systematic looting and isolated instances of vandalism in the 2008 conflict in South-Ossetia (Independent International Fact-Finding Mission on the Conflict in Georgia, 'EU Report—Volume II' (September 2009), 363). This whole point, however, concerns a difficult legal question. Guenael Mettraux argues that the jurisprudence of the ad hoc tribunals is contradictory on this particular point, but he seems to favour the approach advocated here (see his *International Crimes and the ad hoc Tribunals* (Oxford: Oxford University Press, 2005), 97–8). The International Committee of the Red Cross (ICRC) Commentary to the Additional Protocols, by contrast, suggests that pillage as a war crime also covers

international crime may include an isolated act of pillage but only if it is part of a large-scale appropriation of all types of property. Both interpretations would be compatible with the conception of international crimes defended here.[79]

This clarifies a further important aspect of the argument developed so far. The example discussed above implies that what explains the 'internationalization' of war crimes generally is not simply the fact that they are in some way connected to an armed conflict (the war *nexus* requirement). Rather, much of the explanation for their distinct jurisdictional regime is that they are committed as part of a plan or policy, or on a large-scale basis, and that they are serious enough to warrant overriding the belligerents' prima facie immunity against interference by extraterritorial bodies.[80] In effect, I have argued that international criminal rules are those which cannot be in force in a particular territory on the basis of the belligerent powers having *exclusive* criminal jurisdiction over them. This consideration allows us to make sense of the relevance of the armed conflict for making most war crimes into international offences: the existence of an armed conflict is often enough a condition of possibility for this kind of offence. War creates specific risks for participants and bystanders, and it empowers individuals in ways which would not be available to them in times of peace. This means that armed conflicts need specific regulation under a separate subset of rules in international criminal law. It may even mean that, under certain circumstances, we may have to relax the specific threshold for triggering extraterritorial jurisdiction.[81] But it does not attach the 'internationalization' of a crime to the bare existence of an armed conflict.

Finally, the normative consideration on which this argument rests accounts for three standard features of the law on war crimes. On the one hand, it allows us to accommodate without further argument the fact that certain crimes committed in the context of an armed conflict *not of an international character* are also international crimes. On the other hand, this explanation can easily account for the fact that under existing international law, war crimes cannot be committed by service personnel against their own military, something which none of the previous theories examined in this chapter would be able to explain.[82] And finally, it makes sense of the fact that not all violations of the laws of armed conflict involve war crimes. Many of them, for instance, can in fact be sanctioned by military codes for

'pillage resulting from isolated acts of indiscipline' (ICRC, *Commentary to the Geneva Convention IV*, 1376, para 4542). The argument here is not that this type of conduct should not be criminalized; rather, it is only that it does not constitute an international crime in the jurisdictional sense hereby advocated.

[79] Consideration of the laws on war crimes regarding pillage or destruction of cultural property is beyond the scope of this work.

[80] On this, see section 4 above, *in fine*.

[81] This allows for the suggestion that the requirements under Art 8(1) of the ICC Statute (part of a plan or policy or part of a large-scale commission) are less demanding than those provided for under Art 7(1) (widespread and systematic).

[82] See the cases of *Pliz*, Dutch Special Court of Cassation, and *Motosuke*, Temporary Court Martial of the Netherlands East Indies, at Amboina (cited in Cassese, *International Criminal Law*, 48).

disciplinary purposes.[83] Others, such as theft or the murder of a neighbour, would be proscribed by the domestic criminal laws of the relevant belligerent state.

6. Do We Need a Theory of International Crimes?

Altman and Wellman have argued against the project of defining certain categories of 'super crimes' which would provide compelling justification for overriding state sovereignty, and ground 'international criminal jurisdiction over moral wrongs that do not cross [state] borders'.[84] They call this project the 'received view' and propose a different way of thinking about international criminal law. The framework advocated here shares with theirs several of the critical points they make against standard accounts of international crimes available in the literature. It rejects, however, that any of these criticisms lead to the conclusion that the notion of international crimes is conceptually or normatively flawed. Their criticism relies on two basic points: they take issue with the 'heinousness' requirement that the received view attaches to international offences, and suggest that extraterritorial prosecutions should also potentially apply to ordinary or municipal crimes under certain circumstances. More precisely, they argue that international prosecutions should be warranted in failed or illegitimate states when an 'accumulation of separate criminal acts [are being] committed by individuals operating solo'.[85] From these two propositions it purportedly follows that the concept of an international offence should play no part in a theory of international criminal law.

Altman and Wellman provide an alternative explanation of when and why it is justified to 'pierce state sovereignty', which does not rely on the relevant offences being morally egregious. They argue that when states are unwilling or unable to prevent systematic or widespread violations of individual rights those states loose their right against third-party interference in what would otherwise be their domestic affairs.[86] The heinousness of the offences, then, purportedly plays no significant role in explaining extraterritorial jurisdiction over crime. But this seems too hasty a judgement. It seems implausible to suggest that widespread or systematic bicycle theft, or credit card fraud would suffice to 'pierce the sovereignty' of the territorial state. And the reason why one would reject this implication is precisely that bicycle theft and credit card fraud are not sufficiently heinous or egregious to override the considerations on which states' right to self-government is based. In short, Altman and Wellman seem to believe that the 'received view' cannot but rely on the unpersuasive argument that international crimes are simply those which are so morally egregious as to harm humanity itself.[87]

[83] Abi-Saab, 'The Concept of "War Crimes"', 112.

[84] Andrew Altman and Christopher Heath Wellman, 'A Defense of International Criminal Law', *Ethics* 115/1 (2004), 43. Their account has been updated, and somewhat revised in their *A Liberal Theory of International Justice* (Oxford: Oxford University Press, 2009), ch 4.

[85] Altman and Wellman, 'A Defense of International Criminal Law', 49.

[86] Ibid, 48. This threshold is confirmed in *A Liberal Theory of International Justice*, 80.

[87] Altman and Wellman, 'A Defense of International Criminal Law', 50.

But from the plausible claim that moral egregiousness cannot be the sole criterion that explains an extraterritorial body holding the power to punish the perpetrators of a given offence we should not jump to the conclusion that it should play no role at all.

The second critical point on which their attack of the notion of 'international crimes' is based is that, under certain circumstances such as a failed state or even an illegitimate state, an 'ordinary' offence perpetrated by an individual acting alone would also warrant conferring criminal jurisdiction upon an extraterritorial authority. Their position is based on a plausible criticism of the domestic analogy discussed in Chapter 1, namely, the position that states in the international sphere are analogous to individuals in the interpersonal realm.[88] States, they argue, have a moral responsibility towards their nationals, and this makes them more akin to parents *vis-à-vis* their children, than to individuals with respect to their self-regarding affairs.[89] The right to intervene in the territory of a failed or illegitimate state to stop or prevent human rights violations would thereby be analogous to interfering with an abusive parent.[90]

This analysis may seem appealing in light of the existing legal framework. If a foreign or international body militarily intervened and occupied the territory of a failed or illegitimate state, it would not only hold the power to punish serious offences perpetrated as part of a widespread or systematic attack, that is international crimes. It would also hold the power to punish offenders for ordinary crimes.[91] An occupying force could then, in principle, hold the power to punish a single theft committed for private reasons by an individual acting alone. But would the same hold for an extraterritorial authority (a foreign state or an international tribunal), that is, one that will not intervene militarily? This seems to be the critical question that international criminal law must answer.

Answering this question in the affirmative does not simply follow from the framework described above. Extraterritorial bodies differ from occupying powers, at least, in that they do not have any measure of control over the territory in which the offences have been perpetrated. Occupying powers, by contrast, exercise a certain number of the territorial state's functions. Accordingly, it seems to be the fact that occupying powers are in a position to replace or complement the failed or

[88] Altman and Wellman, *A Liberal Theory of International Justice*, 77–8. [89] Ibid, 77.

[90] Their argument here seems also to undermine their previous claim against the significance of the moral egregiousness of the crime. It is doubtful that widespread or systematic offences that do not reach a significant level of gravity would warrant giving an extraterritorial authority the *liberty* to occupy a failed state militarily. Although Altman and Wellman advocate an argument for humanitarian intervention that rejects that human rights violations in the targeted state should be the 'most egregious', they still require that it satisfy a requirement of proportionality. That is, humanitarian intervention against an illegitimate state would only be 'permissible if the risk to the safety and security of noncombatants is not disproportionate to the rights violations that one can reasonably expect to avert' (ibid, 103–4). Given the harm that military intervention almost invariably brings about, the moral threshold would still have to require significant gravity.

[91] Cf Fox, *Humanitarian Occupation*, ch 3. See also Yoram Dinstein, *The International Law of Belligerent Occupation* (Cambridge: Cambridge University Press, 2009), 137–40; Art 43 of the Hague Regulations annexed to the Hague Convention respecting the Laws and Customs of War on Land (No II of 1899 and No IV of 1907); and Art 64 of the Geneva Convention relative to the Protection of Civilian Persons in Time of War, 12 August 1949 (Geneva Convention IV).

illegitimate state's system of law enforcement that explains their having criminal jurisdiction over ordinary crimes perpetrated by individuals acting alone. This is why having effective control over the relevant territory is crucial for a foreign state to acquire the status (ie, the special responsibilities and special rights over individuals in the occupied territories) of an occupying power.[92] In fact, when an extraterritorial authority becomes an occupying power, its criminal jurisdiction becomes based on the territoriality principle, not on extraterritorial grounds (ie, universality).[93] This rationalization of the position of occupying powers is supported by the fact that even an *illegitimate* occupying power would be entitled validly to claim, at least under international law, the power to punish individuals for both international and ordinary offences perpetrated in the occupied territories.[94] It is also supported by the fact that as soon as the occupying power ceases to have an effective level of control over the relevant territory, it ceases to have criminal jurisdiction over domestic offences, yet not over international crimes.[95]

Altman and Wellman may object that these difficulties are irrelevant as a matter of normative argument, and would only show the need for legal reform. However, their difficulties do not seem to arise merely from this set of institutional arrangements, but rather are arguably connected with the underlying normative issue. A first problem with their account is that it seems to presuppose a kind of 'all or nothing' solution to the issue of extraterritorial criminal jurisdiction on failed or illegitimate states. Once the territorial state forfeits its right against interference, this would automatically provide extraterritorial bodies with the right to punish any offence perpetrated there. Yet it is not obvious why the fact that state S is violating the human rights of minority Y on a widespread and systematic basis would account for an extraterritorial authority holding the power to punish the homicide of an individual of minority Z perpetrated by a fellow member of Z. Put boldly, it seems unclear why it would be reasonable to place the kidnapping and subsequent torture of a left-wing sympathizer perpetrated by members of the Chilean armed forces under Pinochet, on a par with a crime of passion perpetrated in Santiago de Chile on the same night by an ex-lover. Such an approach would simply override the fact that in the former case individuals in Chile would not have reason to trust the state authorities to enforce the relevant criminal prohibition, whereas there would not be any reason why the Chilean state would not prosecute the individual responsible in the latter case. This distinction is not only part of

[92] Dinstein, *The International Law of Belligerent Occupation*, 42–5.

[93] See Sharon Weill, 'The Judicial Arm of the Occupation: The Israeli Military Courts in the Occupied Territories', *International Rev of the Red Cross* 89/866 (2007), 395–419. On the position of the Allied powers after the Second World War, see Madeleine Morris, 'High Crimes and Misconceptions: The ICC and Non-Party States', *Law and Contemporary Problems* 64/1 (2001), 13–66.

[94] Dinstein, *The International Law of Belligerent Occupation*, 3.

[95] Ibid, 283–4. This gap between a state's extraterritorial criminal jurisdiction and its powers as an occupying power are further illustrated by Art 77 of Geneva Convention IV, which provides that:

> Protected persons who have been accused of offences or convicted by the courts in occupied territory, shall be handed over at the close of occupation ... to the authorities of the liberated territory.

the account of international crimes favoured in this book; it is also implicit in the underlying reasoning why failed and illegitimate states in particular would lack the right against foreign interference.

But arguably this general point cuts deeper into Altman and Wellman's general argument. They rely on an analogy between failed or illegitimate states and abusive parents: just as the right to interfere with an abusive parent is explained by the interests of the child, the power of an extraterritorial authority to punish an offender must be explained by the interests of individuals in the territorial state. This analogy seems to be based on the capacity of the intervening agent to prevent or stop violations of the basic rights of those who are in a vulnerable position. Yet, as argued above in this chapter, the right to intervene in order to stop an actual attack confers upon the right-holder essentially a Hohfeldian liberty to use force in defence of potential victims. Moreover, while humanitarian intervention is purely prospective in nature, punishment is applied retrospectively. In other words, the right to intervene on humanitarian grounds can only be justified as long as widespread or systematic human rights violations are still being perpetrated in the territorial state. Accordingly, this argument would not be able to explain why an extraterritorial body should hold the power to punish offenders after the widespread or systematic crimes have ceased. This is particularly problematic in a world in which even regime change barely entails domestic prosecutions of crimes perpetrated in failed or illegitimate states.

These two implications of the argument ultimately lead to a more serious philosophical shortcoming. The crucial question both for Altman and Wellman and or the account favoured here is what the interest of individuals in the failed or illegitimate state is that justifies an extraterritorial body holding, in particular, a second order Hohfeldian power to punish offenders. Altman and Wellman do not provide an explicit answer to this question. As argued throughout this book, and as the previous paragraph illustrates, to infer such a power from the liberty to stop human rights violations is to reason on the basis of a *non sequitur*.

To conclude, then, Altman and Wellman's view of the scope of international criminal law seems ultimately unconvincing. This is partly because they reject the claim that the gravity of the crime has any role to play in the justification for extraterritorial prosecutions. Furthermore, their explanation of why a failed or illegitimate state would lack the right against third parties interfering by punishing (in particular) both standard international offences and ordinary crimes seems ultimately flawed. These two considerations should suffice to account for the need of a concept of international crimes in a general account of extraterritorial punishment. Our next task is to precise the jurisdictional rules applicable to this category of crimes.

5

Extraterritorial Jurisdiction for International Crimes

> There are also those who think that an act of cruelty committed, for example, at Constantinople may be punished at Paris for [the] abstracted reason that he who offends humanity should have enemies in all mankind ... as if judges were to be the knights errant of human nature in general, rather than guardians of particular conventions between men.[1]

1. Universal Criminal Jurisdiction

This chapter provides a philosophical argument for universal criminal jurisdiction over international crimes. It contends that both individual states and the International Criminal Court (ICC) should have the normative power to punish an offender for an international crime regardless of where the offence was committed, or of the nationality of both offender and victim.[2] The literature on universal jurisdiction is vast, even unmanageable. However, many specialists complain about its 'under-theorization'.[3] Universal jurisdiction is arguably the most difficult case for a theory of punishment such as mine, which is based mainly on territorial considerations. This is because it not only entails conferring criminal jurisdiction in the absence of any link or *nexus* between the prosecuting body and the crime. In addition, and crucially, it entails providing an argument that accounts for *every* state (and a particular international court created by some of them) holding the power to punish offenders extraterritorially.

The structure of the chapter is as follows. Section 2, provides a normative justification for universal jurisdiction, namely, it argues that the argument for legal punishment advocated fully supports the proposition that every state should hold

[1] Cesare Beccaria, *On Crimes and Punishments* (Indianapolis: Hackett, 1986).

[2] I shall not distinguish here conceptually between universal jurisdiction, commonly exercised by states, and international jurisdiction, normally claimed by international or internationalized tribunals. On this, see section 2 below.

[3] Leila Nadya Sadat, 'Redefining Universal Jurisdiction', *New England L Rev* 35/2 (2001) and Anthony Sammons, 'The "Under-Theorization" of Universal Jurisdiction: Implications for Legitimacy on Trials of War Criminals by National Courts', *Berkeley J of International Law* 21 (2003). See also Theodor Meron, 'International Criminalization of Internal Atrocities', *AJIL* 89/3 (1995), 563.

a power, universal in scope, to punish international offences.[4] Moreover, it suggests that this argument is better suited than alternative accounts to explain why states hold universal jurisdiction over international crimes, but also to reconcile this explanation with a more comprehensive account of the extraterritorial scope of their own domestic criminal laws. Section 3 examines the case for the jurisdictional scope of the ICC. It takes issue with the standard arguments that purportedly account for the scope of its power to punish, and argue that they are theoretically flawed. It will argue that under a more plausible normative account, the jurisdiction held by the ICC as a matter of law is unduly restricted at the bar of justice. Finally, section 4 will cover various objections raised against this 'pure' form of extraterritorial punishment. It will conclude that although some of these objections do raise doubts as to the ultimate moral value of the principle of universal criminal jurisdiction today, none of them is capable of rebutting the case made in the first two sections.

To the reader this way of organizing the argument might seem strange. Indeed, the previous chapter argued that international crimes are those for which at least *some* extraterritorial authority should have the power to punish their perpetrators. Would it not be natural to examine the case of a global criminal court holding this kind of power first? The case for individual states holding universal jurisdiction appears more difficult, and seems better left till last. The ICC, however, is not a global criminal court. It is a treaty body created in virtue of an agreement between a certain number of states. As a matter of law, treaties can only create rights and obligations for their parties.[5] As a matter of fact, three of the biggest powers in the international scene (the US, China, and Russia) are not only not parties to this treaty but largely see the ICC as a potential threat. Thus, it is far from clear that the argument provided in Chapter 4 would straightforwardly lead to the ICC holding universal jurisdiction to try an offender for an international crime. Rather, and according to the leading explanation available in the literature, the scope of the ICC's criminal jurisdiction is ultimately dependent on the jurisdictional scope of its parties.

2. The Case for States Holding Universal Criminal Jurisdiction

This section argues that under current non-ideal conditions individual states ought to be granted universal jurisdiction over international crimes. This is a normative claim and it is the main claim that will be advocated here. But first, a conceptual point is in order. Universal jurisdiction is defined here as the power of some entity (for example, state S) to punish an offender irrespective of where she perpetrated

[4] Provided it satisfies the conditions to claim itself legitimate authority. These conditions are set in Chapter 6.

[5] See, eg, Arts 26 and 34 of the Vienna Convention of the Law of Treaties; see also I Brownlie, *Principles of Public International Law* (Oxford: Oxford University Press, 2003), 592.

her offence, and of both her nationality and that of the victim.[6] Moreover, the crucial feature of the regime of universal jurisdiction is that *every* state can claim this power.

This take on universal jurisdiction is not without its difficulties. Ian Brownlie famously warns against conflating the proposition that every state holds a power to punish crimes under international law with the principle of universality. Universality, he claims, is only about individual states holding the power to punish certain crimes under their domestic law, for which international law recognizes every state's criminal jurisdiction.[7] Anne-Marie Slaughter clarifies his position as follows:

> The principle of universality ... is a *procedural* device by which international law grants all states jurisdiction to punish specified acts that are independently crimes under [their] national law.[8]

Piracy is allegedly the paradigmatic example because, they contend, it has traditionally been defined and prosecuted under domestic law.

This distinction seems to challenge the framework defended here. However, it does nothing of the kind. Rather, it is useful because it forces us to distinguish between conceptual and normative philosophical issues and these, in turn, from those concerning specific institutional arrangements. But let us deal with one thing at a time. It is necessary first to explain what we *mean* by universal jurisdiction. This is a conceptual issue. I suggested that universal jurisdiction consists in states holding the power to punish an offender irrespective of where she committed an offence and irrespective of her nationality or that of the victim. This definition is uncontroversial enough and is, in fact, consistent with Brownlie's position.

As a separate question we need to determine whether certain crimes, such as those covered in the previous chapter, warrant conferring upon states universal criminal jurisdiction. We could examine this issue either as a matter of normative argument or as a matter of international law, ie existing institutional arrangements. Brownlie and Slaughter's claim is that universal jurisdiction refers to offences provided under domestic criminal law *as a matter of law*. Accordingly, if we consider this proposition as a technical statement about a particular set of institutional arrangements, their position (whether it is right or wrong) is irrelevant for our purposes. Our concern is, rather, to explain why certain offences *should* warrant conferring upon states criminal jurisdiction on universality grounds as a matter of moral principle. This is a philosophical issue of a normative kind.

If, by contrast, we are to consider their statement as a philosophical claim about what moral powers states have at the bar of justice, they are both conflating

[6] See eg *Institute de Droit International*, 2005 Resolution, 'Universal Criminal Jurisdiction with Respect to the Crime of Genocide, Crimes against Humanity and War Crimes', available at <http://www.idi-iil.org/idiE/navig_chon2003.html> (last accessed 1 August 2010), para 1.

[7] Ibid, 303.

[8] Anne-Marie Slaughter, 'Defining the Limits: Universal Jurisdiction and National Courts' in Stephen Macedo, *Universal Jurisdiction: National Courts and the Prosecution of Serious Crimes under International Law* (Philadelphia: University of Pennsylvania Press, 2004), 169, 319, quoting Brownlie.

the conceptual question with the normative one, and begging the latter. Let me explain. By advocating such a restrictive conceptual definition of universal jurisdiction they rule out a normative possibility as a matter of definition. Yet they do not provide any normative argument as to why universal jurisdiction should apply only to crimes provided under states' domestic criminal laws. Their claim is not necessarily subject to this kind of criticism. But it follows from this point that their objection does not really undermine the conceptual framework advocated here, which stipulates that universal jurisdiction applies to international crimes as defined in the previous chapter.

In fact, the same criticism can be made against Bassiouni's exact opposite proposition that universal jurisdiction should not be conflated with the universal reach of extraterritorial *national* jurisdiction.[9] The concept of universal jurisdiction he advocates, which is contained in Principle 1 of the Princeton Principles on Universal Jurisdiction, is that of

> criminal jurisdiction based solely on the nature of the crime, without regard of where the crime was committed, the nationality of the alleged or convicted perpetrator, the nationality of the victim, or any other connection to the state exercising such jurisdiction.[10]

This definition is obviously quite close to the one advocated here. However, Bassiouni is also smuggling a normative point into a conceptual one. Whether universal jurisdiction is based solely on the nature of the crime is a normative claim for which he needs to argue, not part of its definition.[11]

2.1 An argument for individual states having universal jurisdiction over international crimes

As a matter of public international law, it may be argued that universal jurisdiction is probably, but not unambiguously, part of customary international law.[12] Judges

[9] Bassiouni, 'The History of Universal Jurisdiction and Its Place in International Law', in ibid, 42.

[10] Ibid.

[11] We should not conflate the question asked in this chapter with that regarding the distinction between the narrow notion of universal jurisdiction, which entails only that the state where the accused is in custody may try her (called *forum deprehensionis*), and a broad notion also called absolute or pure universality, which entails that a state can prosecute an offender even if she is not at the time in the forum state. This distinction should not be treated as a conceptual question but as a normative one. What is at issue is not what constitutes the meaning of universal jurisdiction, but rather what constitutes the scope of states' power to punish offenders, or the conditions under which an extraterritorial state is in a position to exercise this power legitimately.

[12] Bassiouni argues that it cannot be inferred solely from existing state practice and *opinio juris* that universal jurisdiction is part of customary international law, but he contends that the cumulative effect of state practice, *opinio juris*, general principles of law and opinion by publicists does in fact suffice to make it into a rule of customary international law (Bassiouni, 'Universal Jurisdiction for International Crimes: Historical Perspectives and Contemporary Practice', 148 – 9). Cassese for his part considers that universal jurisdiction is warranted for certain offences under customary international law (Cassese, *International Criminal Law*, 293 – 5). Higgins, states that 'International law permits the exercise of jurisdiction in respect of certain offences against the international community' (Rosalyn Higgins, *Problems and Process: International Law and How We Use It* (Oxford: Clarendon Press, 1994), 56). Cryer concludes that the 'level of support is sufficient to suggest that

Higgins, Kooijmans, and Buerghenthal's joint separate opinion in the *Arrest Warrant* case is famously one of the most authoritative statements on this. They argued that '[t]here are certain indications that a universal criminal jurisdiction for certain international crimes is clearly not regarded as unlawful'.[13] In effect, universal jurisdiction seems to be relatively uncontroversial in respect of certain offences such as genocide, war crimes, and crimes against humanity, even if there is also agreement that it is only seldom exercised.[14]

For our purposes, however, this basis of jurisdiction needs to be defended on very different grounds. This book argues that the extraterritorial scope of a state's power to punish must be explained by the reasons that justify conferring upon that particular state the power to punish offenders in the first place. Chapter 2 argued that the normative power to punish is based on the collective interest of individuals in a particular state in having a system of criminal laws in force. This is because, or so it was suggested, having a set of rules in force prohibiting murder, rape, etc contributes to their sense of dignity and security. Chapter 3, however, argued that this justification is, in principle, against the extraterritorial application of domestic criminal rules, except on the ground of protection.[15] First, individuals in the state on whose territory the crime was committed generally have an interest in this state being a self-governed entity that is sufficiently important to warrant conferring upon it a prima facie immunity against extraterritorial authorities punishing offences committed on its territory. Secondly, individuals in the state in which the offence was committed (state S) normally lack an interest in an extraterritorial state holding such a power because the extraterritorial state's domestic criminal laws cannot be in force on S's territory. And finally, individuals in the extraterritorial state normally lack an interest in their state punishing offences committed abroad.

As we saw in the previous chapter, there are certain criminal rules, that is, rules which provide for international crimes, which cannot be in force in the territory of a state unless at least some extraterritorial authority holds a concurrent power to punish those who violate them. The reason for this is that whenever one of these crimes is perpetrated, it will necessarily be the case that the state in which they

the customary case for universal jurisdiction over core crimes can be made' (Cryer, *Prosecuting International Crimes*, 93). Finally, the authors in *Oppenheim's International Law* recognize that '[t]here are now very few writers who deny absolutely the right of a state to punish aliens for crimes committed abroad.' However, that statement refers both to universal jurisdiction and also to certain cases in which jurisdiction is justified on the basis of the protective principle (Sir Arthur Watts and Sir Robert Jennings, *Oppenheim's International Law*, vol 1, *Peace* (Harlow: Longman, 1992), 467, and 469 on international crimes). For criticism of this general view see the letter from Department of State Legal Adviser, John B Bellinger III, and Department of Defense General Counsel, William J Haynes II, to the President of the International Committee of the Red Cross, Jakob Kellenberger, 3 November 2006, published in 866 *International Rev of the Red Cross* (2007), 443–71.

[13] See paras 45–6. It must be noted, though, that of the judges who addressed this matter in the *Arrest Warrant* case, four were against the existence of universal jurisdiction and five explicitly in favour, all in *obiter dicta*. This issue is at the core of the *Certain Criminal Proceedings in France* (*Republic of the Congo v France*) case before the International Court of Justice.

[14] See Slaughter, 'Defining the Limits: Universal Jurisdiction and National Courts' in Macedo, *Universal Jurisdiction*, 170.

[15] That is, when a particular crime affects the sovereignty, security, or important governmental functions of the state.

are committed is either responsible for perpetrating, instigating, or allowing it, or simply unable to do anything about it. As a result, the fact that the territorial state criminalizes this kind of act cannot really contribute to the sense of dignity and security of individuals in that state. These offences are international crimes. It is now suggested that, as a matter of normative argument, every state should have the power to punish an offender for an international crime irrespective of where the offence was committed, and irrespective of the nationality of both the offender and the victim.

Take acts of torture as part of a widespread or systematic attack. In Chapter 4 I argued that the territorial state would lack a prima facie immunity against extraterritorial authorities punishing an offender for an international crime committed on its territory. This is because individuals in that state have a fundamental interest in there being a criminal rule in force in that state against widespread and systematic acts of torture. This interest is not only incompatible with that state holding such a prima facie immunity; it overrides that particular interest. This explanation, however, does not yet amount to an argument for universal jurisdiction. What we need to explain is why every state would hold the power to punish such an offender.

Chapter 2 has identified the relevant interest that, it is argued, explains conferring upon a particular state the power to punish a given individual. It remains for me to argue who is the holder of that interest in the case of international crimes, and what the implications of this are for establishing who the holder must be of the relevant power to punish perpetrators of international crimes. In brief, there are a vast number of people in different parts of the world who share a collective interest in there being a system of criminal rules prohibiting, inter alia, acts of torture perpetrated as part of a widespread or systematic attack. This is hardly controversial. Furthermore, it is hereby suggested that their interest in the sense of dignity and security that this criminal rule being in force affords them is sufficiently important to warrant conferring upon *every* state the power to punish perpetrators of this crime against humanity extraterritorially. But let us go one step at a time.

This interest is initially shared by many individuals in the territorial state. If such a crime is perpetrated on a state's territory, individuals there would have an interest in the perpetrators being punished. That is, individuals in those states where international crimes are being perpetrated have a fundamental interest in the criminal rules that provide for these offences being in force. But so would individuals in other states in which similar international crimes are taking place. The fact that an offender is punished, for her offence in a given state S, by an authority expressly authorized by the international legal system would not only ground the belief that such a criminal rule is in force in S. It would similarly be able to ground the belief that this rule is also in force in S2 (where these crimes are also being perpetrated). This explains the usual claim that whether Pinochet was punished for widespread or systematic torture committed in Chile was not merely an issue that affected the interests of Chileans. Admittedly, the Chileans may have many reasons for claiming priority to try and punish Pinochet. Yet, whether or not he was punished arguably affected the interests of other people around the world.

In particular, it affected their interest in the existence of the international criminal rule prohibiting, for example, widespread and systematic torture being expressed and communicated by assessing his compliance with it.

This explanation also accounts for conferring the power to punish upon states in which individuals are not overly worried about becoming victims of widespread or systematic torture such as, for example, Switzerland. Admittedly, the Swiss will generally not be too concerned about becoming victims of these international crimes; but the argument hereby advocated nowhere requires such a demanding threshold. First, as long as there are certain individuals in Switzerland, such as refugees, who will themselves benefit from believing there is a legal rule in force against torture as part of a widespread or systematic attack, this will suffice to confer upon Switzerland in particular universal jurisdiction over these offences. Several criminal prohibitions protect only a portion of a state's population or protect people differently. The legal prohibition of certain sexual activity with children, for instance, protects children exclusively. This does not mean that children's interests in there being a rule in force against such sexual offences does not suffice to confer upon the state the power to punish those who carry out this type of conduct.

But even if there are no refugees or members of any minority who will clearly benefit from such a rule being in force, this would not be fatal to my argument. And this is because, as argued above, Switzerland's power to punish an offender does not need to rely solely on the interests of the Swiss. In fact, it need not be based on the interests of the Swiss at all. It can be explained exclusively on the basis of the interests of individuals in those states in which this kind of offence is being perpetrated. This joint interest, by itself, might be considered sufficiently important to warrant conferring upon every state (including Switzerland) a power—that is universal in scope—to punish an individual for these offences. There is nothing in the account of rights defended here that precludes assigning A a right on the basis of an interest held by B.[16] An example at the interpersonal level may clarify this point. A would normally be at liberty to stop B when she is trying to escape with C's purse. A's liberty in this example is arguably based exclusively on the interests of C. Moreover, C's interest warrants conferring this liberty not only on A, but arguably on everyone who is in a position to stop B (namely, D, F, G, etc). The same could be argued, *mutatis mutandis*, about an extraterritorial state's power to punish an individual for an international crime.

It could be objected, of course, that this need not be the case in the international society. Individuals in Chile might take issue with Spain prosecuting Pinochet. They would probably feel even more strongly about this if it were Bolivia or Argentina doing so. There are two lines of reply to this objection. First, that it does not really address the point in contention. That is, it does not really claim that individuals in Chile and in several other states lack an interest in there being a rule in force against widespread or systematic torture. It does not even argue that the interest that Chileans might have in Pinochet not being punished would override the former interest in that rule being in force. Rather, it points to the

[16] See Chapter 1.

question of whether a *particular* country should be put, for historical, cultural, or other reasons, under a disability to punish Pinochet. This is an issue that concerns the authority (or standing) of a particular state, not with the specific interest that justifies conferring upon it the power to punish. Chapter 6 below will argue that the question of the authority of the state to punish a criminal offender is unrelated to the extraterritorial scope of its power to punish.

Secondly, if Argentina were to prosecute Pinochet for a crime committed on its own territory against a Chilean national (such as the assassination of General Prats and his wife in Buenos Aires in 1974), individuals in Chile would probably take issue with it too. And yet, the fact that individuals in Chile take issue with Argentina punishing Pinochet would generally not be considered a sufficient reason to hold Argentina under a disability to do so. As this example shows, Argentina's power to punish rests on considerations which are independent from the opinion of Chilean nationals. In fact, the claim hereby advocated is that the power to punish Pinochet is not grounded exclusively on the interest of Chileans. As long as this suggestion is sound, it is unclear why *their* taking issue with an extraterritorial state punishing Pinochet would be of crucial normative relevance.[17]

There is an obvious qualification to the general position advocated thus far. It might be that under certain circumstances, as for instance in the case of an incumbent head of state or head of government, the interests of individuals in the territorial state are sufficiently important to confer upon the offender a prima facie immunity against an extraterritorial state holding the power to punish her. It might well be, also, that their interest would outweigh the interest of individuals in all the states where this kind of crime is being committed in the offender being punished. As a line of argument, this seems unpromising. Yet it illustrates well a particular strength of the interest-based theoretical framework advocated here. On the one hand, it can accommodate the concern raised by biased states by referring to the conditions that states should satisfy in order to have the authority to punish an offender. And on the other hand, it shows exactly where the difficulty lies in this type of case. Namely, that it depends on carefully examining the interest that explains a state's power to punish versus the interest that explains an offender being granted immunity from prosecution. Resolving that issue is beyond our possibilities here. However, showing the way in which this could be done should dispel any anxiety that the initial objection might still generate.

To conclude, it is hereby argued that the collective interest of (admittedly a given subset of) individuals in a rule being in force against torture perpetrated as part of a widespread or systematic attack warrants conferring upon *every state* the power to punish those who violate that rule. This is required, at least, if these criminal rules are to provide any meaningful sense of dignity and security to them. In the absence of a centralized mechanism of distribution of criminal competence for international crimes, universal jurisdiction provides us with the closest we can get to these rules having any real sense of bindingness.

[17] I use the Pinochet example here for ease of exposition.

2.2 Competing arguments for universal jurisdiction

It is also submitted that the argument developed in this book fares better as a normative explanation of universal jurisdiction and extraterritoriality in general than the available alternatives. Among the arguments most often relied upon are the claims that extraterritorial punishment is justified as a means of enhancing peace,[18] fighting against impunity by closing the gap in law enforcement[19] and thus eliminating any safe havens for the perpetrators of atrocities.[20] Several of these arguments barely resist careful philosophical scrutiny. To say that the justification for punishing an offender is to fight impunity is tautological. It is precisely why it is important to fight impunity that this argument needs to explain. Retributivists have been traditionally concerned with this problem. By contrast, other considerations in this list point towards deterrence. Ultimately it is the fact that eliminating safe havens would (allegedly) provide individuals with greater incentives to refrain from committing these offences that would be doing the normative work. I shall briefly address these two arguments below.

But first, let me consider the argument that purportedly explains the power of an extraterritorial state to punish an offender on universality grounds by reference to the enhancement of peace. There are at least two fundamental problems with this argument. The first is that it provides only a contingent justification for universal jurisdiction.[21] In situations in which criminal trials will not enhance peace, for example because peace has already been secured, advocates of this justification would have to argue against carrying them out. But this is largely unconvincing. Secondly, even if we expect the criminal law to have a deterrent effect, it does not follow that it would deter the continuation of ongoing hostilities (war) in themselves. International criminal law essentially prohibits certain forms of warfare, but it does not necessarily criminalize the use of military force per se, at least when it does not amount to aggression. Thus, even if its premise were correct, this argument fails to lead to its purported conclusion.

Anthony Sammons provides a more elaborate account of universal jurisdiction.[22] He suggests that the justification for universal jurisdiction is not merely a question of explaining a state's power to punish a particular offender. Indeed, '[m]any commentators and jurists incorrectly seek to divorce the assertion of universal jurisdiction from the principles of state sovereignty'.[23] He provides an account of universal jurisdiction tailored specifically to address this difficulty. On his view, universal jurisdiction is mainly an interference with another state's domestic jurisdiction which must, therefore, be explained by reference to the principle

[18] See, eg, Preamble of SC Resolution 827 by which the International Criminal Tribunal for the former Yugoslavia was created.

[19] Princeton Principles, Art 24.

[20] Bruce Broomhall, 'Towards the Development of an Effective System of Universal Jurisdiction for Crimes under International Law', *New England L Rev* 35 (2000–2001), 406; Kenneth Roth, 'The Case for Universal Jurisdiction', *Foreign Affairs* 80/5 (2001), 153.

[21] On the problem with contingent justifications for legal punishment, see Chapter 2.

[22] Sammons, 'The "Under-Theorization" of Universal Jurisdiction'.

[23] Ibid, 127.

of state sovereignty. Sammons sees sovereignty as largely analogous to private property: states have a bundle of rights over their territory, including the rights to political autonomy, non-interference, and territorial integrity. Among these rights, sovereignty includes the right to pass criminal laws, to enforce these laws, and to prosecute and punish those who violate them.[24] This analogy, he claims, is also useful for understanding that sovereignty is not unlimited, but rather presupposes a certain level of respect for neighbours and their equivalent rights within their own territories. It is a feature of his account that sovereignty can be transferred to other states or to the international community. This is how, for example, the Allied powers exercised some form of sovereignty over German territory after the Second World War, including the right to prosecute and punish certain criminal offences. Thus, Sammons's account of universal jurisdiction relies on explaining how it is that the territorial state's sovereignty is transferred, at least in part, to the international community.[25]

Sammons argues that the main reason why states have the right to make certain criminal rules subject to universal jurisdiction concerns the fact that the territorial state has become *terra nullius*.[26] This was the case with pirates, who acted beyond the reach of any single state's jurisdiction. Alternatively, this may be the result of a breakdown in the criminal law system or its lack of capacity to prosecute a particular type of crime or group of perpetrators. As an example, he cites the case of Rwanda which, after the events of 1994, appealed to the Security Council to create an international criminal tribunal because its government felt it did not itself have the capacity to deal with the situation.[27] Similarly, he contends that any state that derogates from certain essential norms such as the prohibition of genocide, torture, etc transfers a portion of its sovereignty to the international community as a whole.[28]

Sammons's account is complex and points to a relevant gap in the literature on universal jurisdiction. An important source of its appeal seems to rest on the fact that it allegedly explains why universal jurisdiction should be regarded as a subsidiary mechanism for certain types of very serious offences. Moreover, unlike other accounts Sammons explicitly addresses the challenges raised by the principle of state sovereignty. And yet, it is far from clear whether he can consistently maintain this subsidiary character; moreover, one may also wonder whether his sovereignty-based explanation suffices to justify an extraterritorial state holding a universal *power* to punish an offender.

But first, an jurisprudential point is in order. Sammons's explanation of the transfer of a portion of the sovereignty of the territorial state (S) to the international community is analytically problematic. To start with, we need to distinguish cases in which S authorizes an extraterritorial state to exercise its criminal jurisdiction on its territory from those in which extraterritorial punishment is exercised against S's will. In Chapter 3, I argued that the justification for S's power to punish also entails S holding a normative power to authorize a specific extraterritorial

[24] Ibid, 124. [25] Ibid, 125. [26] Ibid, 128.
[27] Ibid, 131. [28] Ibid, 137.

body to visit punishment on her.[29] But this is hardly a justification for universal jurisdiction. Universal jurisdiction, rather, entails an extraterritorial state punishing an individual for acts committed in S irrespective of any authorization from S, and usually against S's will. Thus, the fact that S has become *terra nullius* can only explain why S has forfeited its immunity against an extraterritorial body punishing an offender for a crime perpetrated in S, but not yet why a particular extraterritorial state would, itself, hold the power to do so. This point is not just a matter of analytical rigour; it has important normative implications.

In standard rights discourse, when X forfeits one of her rights, she can forfeit her right *in rem*, that is, against the world at large, or *in personam*, namely, against certain individuals or bodies.[30] According to the general understanding of the rules that apply on *terra nullius*, the territorial state would forfeit immunity only *in personam*. As discussed in Chapter 3, under the standard conception of *terra nullius*, it is not the case that *every* state has the power to punish individuals for offences committed there; only the state of nationality of the offender or that of the victim would be empowered to do so. Although I disagreed with this position, this is immaterial for present purposes.[31] The point is that even under the standard account regarding the laws applicable on *terra nullius*, not all states automatically earn a power to punish offences committed there on universality grounds. They need to be able to point, in particular, to an interest that justifies *their* holding the power to do so.[32] In the final analysis, Sammons makes a mistake which is the mirror image of the one he identifies in the literature. He discusses universal jurisdiction only with regard to the issue of sovereignty, failing to grasp that he needs, crucially, an argument that accounts for specific states holding the extraterritorial power to punish offences committed there.

Finally, it seems that Sammons's scheme commits him to more than he would willingly admit. His argument does not seem to be limited, necessarily, to the most serious offences such as genocide, crimes against humanity, aggression, slavery, etc.[33] The nature of these offences and the identity of their perpetrators would function, in his account, as a sort of threshold below which intervention by way of extraterritorial criminal jurisdiction would be unwarranted. Nevertheless, his argument does not lead to this conclusion. This is not what a state becoming *terra nullius* would entail. It might well be that whenever systematic rape, torture, or even genocide are perpetrated on the territory of S, this country becomes something similar to an empty island, or Antarctica in terms of its government lacking an immunity against extraterritorial states having criminal jurisdiction over it. Yet, when a certain territory becomes *terra nullius*, it lacks not only an immunity against foreign bodies punishing a genocide that occurred there, but also an immunity against it punishing any domestic offences perpetrated there, such as robberies,

[29] This allegedly explains why the Allies exercised jurisdiction in Germany after the Second World War (at least over domestic offences): it was because Germany in its capitulation had explicitly authorized them to do so. A similar case could be made, to some extent, with Rwanda.

[30] On this distinction, see Chapter 1.

[31] See Chapter 3.

[32] On this, see also Hirst, *Jurisdiction and the Ambit of the Criminal Law*, 217.

[33] Sammons, 'The "Under-Theorization" of Universal Jurisdiction', 132.

assaults, etc. In sum, the notion of *terra nullius* on which his argument heavily rests, can explain neither an extraterritorial state holding a power to punish that is universal in scope, nor can it limit universal jurisdiction to international crimes.[34]

Let us now focus on other available arguments. I have suggested throughout this book that the extraterritorial scope of a state's power to punish is dependent upon the reasons that justify *that state* holding this power in the first place. Allow me to bypass here deterrence as a general justification for universal jurisdiction. Most of the difficulties that deterrence faces in this context have been aired in previous chapters. Most relevantly, it may be argued that: (a) it would advocate summary executions rather than criminal trials, and (b) it would entail the prosecuting state having universal criminal jurisdiction for both international and domestic offences.[35] This last objection also holds for standard accounts of retributivism with the possible exception of Antony Duff's communitarian justification for legal punishment. We will now turn to his general account.

In Chapter 3, I argued that Duff's general argument faced certain difficulties with regards to the power to punish domestic offences committed abroad. It may be claimed now that the main shortcoming of his general justification for legal punishment is in the area of international crimes. Duff sees punishment as a secular penance the main purpose of which is to communicate censure to moral agents. He is therefore concerned with being able to reach the offender's moral conscience. One of the conditions for this to obtain is that the relevant state (S) needs to have the moral standing to censure the offender for that conduct. S should therefore have, first, the appropriate relationship to the offender or to her action. This implies that there is a political community on behalf of which punishment is imposed. And secondly, S must not have lost that standing as a result of some (wrongful) previous dealing with the offender. It is only the first condition that matters to us here.[36]

As suggested in Chapter 3, providing an answer to this question would depend on what, on Duff's account, constitutes a political community. If he makes the requirements too thin (ie, mutual recognition and protection of basic human rights) then he would have to admit that almost every state would have the moral standing to censure an offender and as a result he would end up advocating universal jurisdiction for both domestic and international offences. By contrast, if he uses a thick notion of political community, he seems committed to rejecting universal jurisdiction altogether. No community other than that to which the offender belongs would be able to communicate with the offender in the relevant sense.[37] The question of what suffices for a group of people to be a political community in

[34] This is, in fact, the gist of the argument by Altman and Wellman examined in the last section of Chapter 4.

[35] See Chapters 2 and 3, respectively.

[36] For a fuller explanation of Duff's position, see Chapter 3. This second condition will be examined in Chapter 6.

[37] This creates, I have suggested in Chapter 3, other issues concerning, eg, offences committed by foreigners on the territory of the forum state.

Duff's terms is one of the most controversial aspects of his account.[38] For us, what matters is that, depending on what constitutes a political community, his initial approach seems doomed to advocate either universal jurisdiction for any type of offence, or preclude universal jurisdiction completely.

His more recent approach to the issue may solve this initial inadequacy.[39] Duff elaborates on the idea of moral standing by resorting to a relational notion of criminal responsibility. He argues that an offender is responsible for her offence 'as a citizen to S'.[40] This approach, he concedes, would be incompatible with universal jurisdiction. Thus, he needs to explain how it is that this reasoning does not apply to other offences such as genocide, war crimes, or crimes against humanity. Or, better, why it is that an offender would be responsible for such offences simply as a moral agent and to the whole of humanity.

Duff contends that both on principled and pragmatic grounds state S, the political community to which the offender belongs, has the power (standing) to hold her to account for an international offence she perpetrated on its territory. This, as it stands, is broadly uncontroversial. What Duff needs to show is how he extends this power to an extraterritorial state. First, he claims that

> if the wrong is serious and persistent enough, and if the [territorial] state radically fails in its duty to prosecute and punish such wrongdoing, it may become in principle legitimate for others ... to intervene, and may become practicable for them to do so.[41]

I take it from Duff's argument that the seriousness of the offence and its persistence are both necessary and sufficient conditions for an extraterritorial state to intervene legitimately (provided that the territorial state fails to prosecute these crimes itself). This, however, hardly constitutes an explanation for conferring the power to punish this offender upon a state with no connection to the offender, the victim, or the crime (ie, on universality grounds). This argument seems to get its moral pull from the fact that it is both legitimate and practicable for states to stop or prevent these wrongs. But, as it has been repeatedly argued in this book, the power to punish an offender does not follow (neither logically nor normatively) from the liberty to defend or protect the victim. These two Hohfeldian incidents belong to different levels of argument. If based on the liberty to protect individuals in the territorial state, this 'right to intervene' would be contingent on serious wrongs still being committed (persisting) at the time of the intervention. This means that there would be no extraterritorial punishment for Barbie, Karadzic, and other similar offenders once the conflict has ended. This is not only unconvincing; it sits

[38] Most recently, von Hirsch and Ashworth, *Proportionate Sentencing: Exploring the Principles*, ch 7.

[39] Duff in his paper only considers the case of an international tribunal, not of individual states. His explanation for this is that individual states exercise universal jurisdiction as a way of 'filling the gap' left by the absence of an effective international criminal court (Duff, 'Criminal Responsibility, Municipal and International'). I will not take issue with this position. Most arguments for universal jurisdiction usually explain the power to punish an offender on universality grounds by claiming that it belongs to the international community as a whole, and then explain why it is that states are entitled to act, individually, on behalf of that community.

[40] See Chapter 3.

[41] Duff, 'Criminal Responsibility, Municipal and International', 18.

very uncomfortably with Duff's own justification for the power to punish, namely, providing the conditions for a secular penance.

Ultimately, Duff needs to explain why it is every state's business to punish an offender for, say, an act of genocide carried out extraterritorially. He presents two possible answers to this question. First, an extraterritorial state would act on behalf of the political community in the state on whose territory the genocide was committed.[42] Although he is not too clear about how convincing he himself finds this claim, this line of argument seems unpromising. He does not explain why it is that an extraterritorial state can have the standing (in his terms) to act on behalf of the political community in another state. This is particularly problematic for his account. If an extraterritorial state could simply act on behalf of the political community in the territorial state, this would completely undermine the necessary relationship he so carefully tries to build between the offender and the state with the power to punish her, and on which this state's own standing is based. Thus, this answer can be readily rejected.

His second answer is that an extraterritorial state should have 'jurisdiction over (and only over) those crimes whose perpetrators must answer not to this or that particular political community, but to humanity itself'.[43] This proposition makes his relational account of criminal responsibility compatible with universal jurisdiction only for certain offences. However, it is worth examining his argument more closely. Duff rejects any suggestion that these offences harm or victimize humanity 'as a whole'.[44] This position, he rightly contends, is too artificial: an individual living in Mexico would not be harmed or victimized himself in any meaningful way by a genocide committed in Korea. Rather, his account relies on the following analogy: in the same way we say that crimes are public wrongs, that is, that they are the kind of wrong that properly concern the political community as a whole, certain offences such as crimes against humanity are wrongs that properly concern the whole humanity as such.[45] Despite its intuitive force, this analogy begs two fundamental questions. First, it assumes that the reasons why a single homicide is the exclusive business of the political community to which both the offender and the victim belong are clear enough. And secondly, it assumes that these reasons similarly explain (by analogy) why an act of genocide is *not* the exclusive business of that political community but, rather, the business of humanity as a whole.

It is not entirely clear whether Duff can explain the former issue convincingly. In Chapter 3 I argued that Duff's citizenship-based explanation has difficulties in accounting for a state's power to punish foreigners who perpetrate an offence on its territory. Yet the latter proposition seems even more mysterious. If we are to consider an act of genocide the business of humanity as a whole, a further explanation is warranted. Duff admits that we should not try to portray humanity as a political community.[46] Rather, he sees humanity only as a moral community.

[42] Ibid, 20. [43] Ibid, 21. [44] Ibid, 21–2.

[45] Ibid, 22 (emphasis added).

[46] Antony Duff, 'Authority and Responsibility in International Criminal Law' in Samantha Besson and John Tasioulas (eds), *Philosophy of International Law* (Oxford: Oxford University Press, 2010).

He claims that these wrongs are everyone's business 'simply in virtue of our shared humanity with their victims (and with their perpetrators)'.[47] Yet, if we accept that we all belong to 'that broadest of human communities',[48] then one may wonder what precisely is the normative work that belonging to a political community—whatever that community may be—does in his explanation. Put differently, even if we accept that we share our human condition, the question subsists of how that makes it every state's business to punish someone for an act of genocide but not for a single homicide or rape committed extraterritorially. This, Duff does not explain, and it is precisely what he needs to explain.

The problem ultimately rests with the fact that Duff treats the question of a state's 'standing' as being analytically separate from the question regarding the reasons that justify that state visiting punishment upon an offender.[49] His relational notion of criminal responsibility is to a large extent theoretically independent from his normative justification for the power to punish. *Contra* Duff, it may be argued that whether the notion of responsibility, criminal or otherwise, is necessarily relational does not take us far enough in explaining the allocation and scope of states' power to punish. What we need to explain is the normative basis of this relationship. I have argued that citizenship as a normative consideration is unfit to account for that relational aspect in a number of situations. It seems, moreover, that the theoretical question about the relational character of criminal liability and about the justification for legal punishment cannot be so easily separated and that, in fact, it is the latter issue which was doing the explanatory work all along. Take an example of Duff's discussed previously: university X has itself the power to sanction one of its lecturers (L) for neglecting her classes because the members of X have an interest in the classes being up to the required standard that is sufficiently important to warrant conferring upon X disciplinary powers over L. By contrast, university Y lacks the power also to sanction L because the interest that its own members have in lectures being up to a given standard is not important enough to give Y that power. This same reasoning would arguably apply to states and their criminal laws.[50]

3. The Jurisdiction of the International Criminal Court

It is time to examine the ICC's jurisdictional scope. The ICC, you will recall, is not a global criminal court. It is a treaty body created as a result of an agreement between certain states.[51] As the international law on treaties makes clear, treaties create rights and obligations only *vis-à-vis* their parties. Under the Rome Statute, the ICC has jurisdiction over an offender if either the state on whose territory the offence was committed or the state of which the offender is a national are a party to the Statute, or if either of the two explicitly accepts its jurisdiction in a

[47] Duff, 'Criminal Responsibility, Municipal and International,' 22. [48] Ibid, 21.

[49] Interestingly, he explicitly admits that 'it bears directly on [it]' (ibid, 14).

[50] On states' 'moral standing' see Chapter 6.

[51] Rome Statute of the ICC (hereinafter Rome Statute or ICC Statute).

particular case.[52] Moreover, the ICC can have jurisdiction over an offence irrespective of where it was committed or of the nationality of both the offender and the victim, for example on universality grounds, if it is referred to the Prosecutor by the Security Council acting under Chapter VII of the UN Charter.[53] Finally, jurisdiction of the ICC over an offence is 'complementary' to domestic criminal jurisdiction.[54] This means that the ICC's jurisdiction will be triggered only if 'the [s]tate which has jurisdiction over it ... is unwilling or unable genuinely to carry out the investigation or prosecution'.[55] As it stands, the jurisdiction of the ICC may seem unduly restricted. In effect, the scope of its power to punish is narrower than that of individual states.[56]

The leading framework to explain this jurisdictional scope relies on the idea that '[j]urisdiction is given to the ICC by a delegation of traditional Westphalian jurisdiction by the member states'.[57] According to this view, which we may term the 'delegation argument', the ICC is not a state and therefore has no 'interests' of its own.[58] What justifies its power to punish an offender is the consent of states which authorized it to exercise jurisdiction over certain offences when committed on their territory or by one of their nationals (ie, when they themselves have jurisdiction over the relevant crime). This section will argue that this framework is inadequate to explain both the jurisdiction the ICC actually has as a matter of law, and the jurisdiction it ought to have as a matter of normative argument.

But before examining this issue, we need to consider an objection famously put forward by the US government, and defended by some prominent officials and academics.[59] They suggest that scope of the ICC's power to punish, as it stands, is illegitimately broad. More precisely, they argue that the ICC should lack the power to punish nationals of non-party states, even if their offence is committed on the territory of a state party, or a state which consented to the jurisdiction of the court

[52] Art 12 ICC Statute.

[53] Art 13 ICC Statute. See also SC Res 1593 (2005) referring to the ICC the situation in Darfur, Sudan. Under the same provisions, the Security Council can also prevent the ICC from investigating or prosecuting an offence temporarily (see Art 16 ICC Statute).

[54] Preamble and Art 1 ICC Statute.

[55] See Art 17(1)(a), (b), and (c) ICC Statute.

[56] Yet some of the offences included in the Rome Statute, arguably, do not warrant universal jurisdiction for individual states under international law. On this, Madeline Morris, 'High Crimes and Misconceptions: The ICC and Non-Party States', *Law and Contemporary Problems* 64/1 (2001). For a conflicting view see Michael P Scharf, 'The ICC's Jurisdiction over Nationals of Non-Party States: A Critique of the US Position', *Law and Contemporary Problems* 64/1 (2001), 79–80.

[57] Kontorovich, 'The Piracy Analogy', 200. See also Diane F Orentlicher, 'The Future of Universal Jurisdiction in the New Architecture of Transnational Justice' in Macedo, *Universal Jurisdiction*, 217; Diane F Orentlicher, 'Politics by Other Means: The Law of the International Criminal Court', *Cornell International LJ* 32 (1999); and Scharf, 'The ICC's Jurisdiction over Nationals of Non-Party States'. Accepting this framework but arguing that the delegation argument cannot legally ground the provisions on jurisdiction contained in Art 12 of the Rome Statute, see Morris, 'High Crimes and Misconceptions'.

[58] Morris, 'High Crimes and Misconceptions', 49.

[59] See ibid and David Scheffer, 'Opening Address at the Universal Jurisdiction Conference at the New England School of Law', *New England L Rev* 35/2 (2001). For a more political version of this position, see William K Lietzau, 'International Criminal Law after Rome: Concerns from a US Military Perspective', *Law and Contemporary Problems* 64/1 (2001).

on an ad hoc basis. This is mainly a legal claim. But the argument on which it is grounded is in part a normative one.[60]

The claim is that the ICC's jurisdiction over nationals of non-party states is incompatible with the theory of delegation of powers. States cannot delegate to an international tribunal either their universal or their territorial power to punish offenders. Madeline Morris presents the most elaborate version of this argument. She first argues that because there are significant differences between national courts and an international tribunal, we cannot assume from the fact that universal jurisdiction can be exercised by the former, that it can automatically be delegated to the latter.[61] Her problem with this delegation is that the ICC Statute purports to bind non-party states.[62] Some scholars flatly reject this claim. The ICC Statute, they suggest, does not impose any obligation upon states; it only binds individuals.[63] But Morris finds this rebuttal unconvincing. The ICC would not simply assess the individual culpability of a particular defendant; quite often it would have to adjudicate on the lawfulness of official acts of states.[64]

This, in itself, does not suffice as an argument for her position. She needs to explain why it is that states cannot delegate a power they unquestionably hold *to the ICC*. To do this, Morris draws on principles related to the legal institution of assignments. In a nutshell, she argues that as a matter of principle state S can delegate to the ICC a right it has against state T if and only if this does not prejudice T's position.[65] As a matter of fact, she submits, delegating the power to punish nationals of a non-party state to an international tribunal would prejudice the position of that non-party state. This assertion is based on three claims. First, the ICC, unlike an individual state, can only provide 'a diminished availability of compromise outcomes in interstate disputes'.[66] Secondly, its verdicts would have a higher political impact on the state of which the offender is a national than those reached by a foreign national court. And finally, its decisions would have a much greater role in shaping the law, and would create impediments for the diplomatic protection of nationals.[67] On this basis, she concludes, states lack the power to delegate to the ICC their territorial or universal jurisdiction over nationals of non-party states.[68]

Michael Scharf has responded to this argument by claiming that states simply lack the right (a Hohfeldian immunity) against the ICC (or other states) deciding on the lawfulness of acts committed by their officials extraterritorially.[69] He does not provide any explanation for why this is so, but this proposition is on the right track. For state S to hold an immunity against the ICC punishing one of its

[60] The legal argument has already been addressed in the relevant literature. See, Orentlicher, 'Politics by Other Means' and Scharf, 'The ICC's Jurisdiction over Nationals of Non-Party States'. I shall concentrate here on its normative force.

[61] Morris, 'High Crimes and Misconceptions', 29 and ff.

[62] Ibid, 14.

[63] Orentlicher, 'Politics by Other Means', 490; Scharf, 'The ICC's Jurisdiction over Nationals of Non-Party States', 75.

[64] Morris, 'High Crimes and Misconceptions', 14.

[65] Ibid, 51.

[66] Ibid, 45.

[67] Ibid.

[68] Analytically, the argument should be that non-party states have an *immunity* against parties to the ICC delegating their power. The relevance of this analytical point will become clear in the next paragraphs.

[69] Scharf, 'The ICC's Jurisdiction over Nationals of Non-Party States', 75.

nationals, individuals in S would have to have an interest sufficiently important to warrant putting the ICC in particular under a disability to do so. I have argued that quite the opposite is true. Individuals in S would normally have a collective interest in a system of international criminal rules prohibiting, inter alia, genocide, war crimes, and crimes against humanity being in force in S. But even if they lacked such an interest (because, *arguendo*, it would not contribute to *their* sense of dignity and security) individuals in other states in which these types of crimes are being, or have recently been, perpetrated have a fundamental interest in these rules being in force. For these rules to be binding also upon S's state officials, it is necessary that extraterritorial authorities have the power to punish those who violate them. And this certainly covers the ICC.

Put differently, the reasons why Morris holds that state S's position would be prejudiced by the ICC having jurisdiction over acts committed by its nationals may well be reasons for which individuals in S, and crucially, in other states would have an interest in prioritizing the ICC exercising its criminal jurisdiction over individual states. The ICC would not try to find a negotiated outcome; it would generally decide on the offender's culpability or lack thereof. It would not accept diplomatic protection of nationals and it would probably have a bigger impact on S's domestic politics and on the development of international criminal law. These considerations seem to provide individuals with stronger reasons to believe that international criminal laws are in force than the imposition of legal punishment by an individual extraterritorial state. The complementarity regime, which essentially gives priority to individual states over the ICC, does not seem to challenge this view at all. It rather indicates that the ICC simply lacks the capacity and resources to deal with all these cases as the first point of call.

Someone may argue that my answer here begs the relevant question. Would not individuals in non-party state S, which is involved in an air campaign against a terrorist group in state T, have an interest in the actions of S being immune from the jurisdiction of the ICC? If they want their national security enhanced, for example, they may want their government officials to act free from the threat of being prosecuted by the ICC. The obvious response to this question is that the interest individuals in S may have in their collective security is not sufficiently important to confer on S a Hohfeldian liberty to perpetrate war crimes while doing so. In fairness, defenders of this immunity against the ICC do not advocate that S should be able to do anything it considers that fits its own interests in order to pursue their military goals; rather, their contention is that extraterritorial authorities, and in particular the ICC, should not have the power to decide whether the chosen course of action was lawful.[70]

The problem with this approach is that it considers these two matters as separate, unrelated questions when, in fact, they are nothing of the kind. If officials of state S are to be considered bound in any meaningful sense by the rules of international criminal law, it is not enough that S alone holds the power to prosecute and punish them. Rather, if individuals (in S, T, and elsewhere) are to believe that these rules

[70] Morris, 'High Crimes and Misconceptions', 53.

are in force at all, at least some extraterritorial body would need to have jurisdiction over them. As Morris suggests, the ICC would then be in a privileged position to claim this power. In other words, one cannot consistently argue at the same time that S's personnel should be bound by the rules of international criminal law and that S should have an immunity against the ICC exercising jurisdiction over acts of its nationals. If this proposition is correct, it must therefore follow that states can validly delegate their territorial jurisdiction (and their universal jurisdiction) to the ICC.

Nevertheless, we may arguably take issue with the whole 'delegation' framework. Admittedly, this approach would seem generally compatible with the normative claims made so far. As argued in Chapter 3, the interest that individuals in state S have in there being a system of criminal laws in force in the territory of S warrants conferring upon S the normative power not only to punish an offender for a crime she committed there, but also to authorize an extraterritorial body to do so. This would include authorizing both foreign states and an international criminal tribunal. Earlier in this chapter, I argued that individual states hold a normative power to punish an offender for an international crime that is universal in scope. As with their territorial jurisdiction, states would then hold the normative power to authorize the ICC to exercise universal jurisdiction for international offences on their behalf.

This delegation framework would successfully explain most aspects of the jurisdictional scope the ICC has as a matter of law. States would be able to delegate their territorial criminal jurisdiction to the ICC, and they would also be entitled to delegate their universal jurisdiction. Furthermore, because it is *their* powers they are delegating, they have the power to authorize the ICC to exercise them under certain conditions. This would explain the ICC having universal jurisdiction only upon the condition of the UN Security Council referring the case to the Prosecutor, and would also be able to account for the principle of complementarity. There is, however, an exception to this general compatibility. Defenders of the delegation theory would have difficulty explaining the jurisdiction over nationals of state parties to the ICC for offences committed on the territory of non-party states—that is, jurisdiction based on the nationality principle. If the argument put forward in Chapter 3 holds water, a consistent account would have to admit that states lack the power to delegate the power to punish a national of theirs for offences she committed outside their territory. To this extent, the rule provided in Article 12(b) of the Rome Statute would be unwarranted.

Nevertheless, the problems with the delegation framework as a normative explanation for the scope of the ICC's power to punish cut deeper. To put it boldly, the delegation argument wrongly identifies those whose interests ultimately explain the ICC's power to punish certain offenders. Take the power of the ICC to punish an offender for an international crime perpetrated on a non-party state by a national of a non-party state. For the delegation argument to be justified, the power held by the ICC would have to rely on the power held individually by the state parties. Chapter 3, for instance, argued that state S could delegate to state T an extraterritorial power to punish an offender for a crime she perpetrated in S. That delegation was needed to empower T because the reason for conferring upon S the power to punish such offender does not itself warrant conferring upon T a concurrent power to do so. Individuals in T lack an interest in T punishing an offender for a crime she committed in S, and the interest of individuals in S in having a system of criminal rules in force does not, per se, warrant conferring upon T the power to do so. In fact, they have an interest in S holding a prima facie immunity against this type of intervention. Delegation, then, is crucial for T to hold the power to punish that offender under those circumstances.

This does not obtain in the case of the ICC. Rather, the collective interest that justifies each individual state holding universal jurisdiction over international crimes *also* warrants conferring this power upon the ICC. The delegation argument seems to rely heavily on the claim that, unlike states, the ICC has no interests of its own.[71] But as we saw, the power of a state to punish an offence committed on its territory is grounded on a specific collective interest of individuals in that state. It is not grounded on an interest of the state itself. Just as the ICC, under the collective view of group rights defended in this book, states have no interests of their own either.[72] We talk about the interests of the UK or of Sri Lanka only as a shortcut to refer to the interests (usually of a collective nature) of individuals in the UK and Sri Lanka respectively. It is ultimately individuals' interests (taken singly or collectively) and their well-being that matter morally. The delegation argument simply obscures this important fact.

By contrast, section 2.1 above argued that individuals in different parts of the world have a collective interest in there being a legal system in force prohibiting international crimes such as genocide, crimes against humanity, and war crimes. For this to obtain, it is necessary that states have universal jurisdiction over these crimes. Thus, it is the collective interest of these individuals that warrants conferring upon every individual state the power to punish an offender irrespective of where she perpetrated the offence and irrespective of the nationality of both the offender and the victim. This same collective interest warrants conferring universal jurisdiction upon the ICC.

This alternative explanation is less controversial than it may initially appear. For example, despite being an advocate of the 'delegation argument', Scharf explicitly recognizes that

> the drafters [at the Rome Diplomatic Conference] did not view the consent of the state ... as necessary ... to confer jurisdiction on the court. Rather, they adopted the consent regime as a limit to the exercise of the court's inherent jurisdiction as a politically expedient concession to the sovereignty of states in order to garner broad support.[73]

[71] See text at n 58 above. [72] On this, see Chapter 1.

[73] Scharf, 'The ICC's Jurisdiction over Nationals of Non-Party States', 77, citing Philippe Kirsch and John T Holmes, 'The Rome Conference on an International Criminal Court: The Negotiating Process', *AJIL* 93/2 (1999).

It may well be that this concession was politically necessary for the establishment of the ICC.[74] Yet we may still argue that the delegation argument does no normative work in the justification for the scope of the ICC's power to punish.

In any event, if the jurisdiction of the ICC is grounded on the collective interest of certain individuals worldwide in there being a system of international criminal laws in force, then there are reasons to criticize the scope of this jurisdiction for not being broad enough. That is, if we take seriously the interests of individuals worldwide and we admit that millions of individuals living in different parts of the globe share an interest in there being a criminal law system in force that prohibits, inter alia, genocide, war crimes, and crimes against humanity, then it must follow that the ICC should have the normative power to punish individuals responsible for any of these crimes irrespective of whether the Security Council refers the situation to the Prosecutor acting under Chapter VII of the UN Charter.[75] A finding by the Security Council that a given situation constitutes a threat to international peace and security adds nothing to this straightforward proposition.[76] Accordingly, this institutional arrangement must be explained as a necessary political concession for the creation of the Court, that is, as a matter of institutionalization; but it is simply irrelevant as a matter of normative argument.

4. Objections to Universal Jurisdiction

It has been argued so far that both individual states and the ICC should have, at the bar of justice, criminal jurisdiction over international crimes irrespective of where they are perpetrated or of the nationality of the offenders and victims. In this last section I will tackle three objections which may be raised against this position, namely, that universal criminal jurisdiction criminalizes political decision-making, that it is a tool against political adversaries, and that it is ultimately an expensive taste for western elites.[77]

4.1 Universal jurisdiction criminalizes political decision-making

Henry Kissinger has famously complained that universal jurisdiction means submitting international politics to criminal procedures. Heads of state and senior public officials, he suggests, should not be equated with pirates, hijackers, and

[74] See Elizabeth Wilmshurst, 'Jurisdiction of the Court' in Roy S Lee (ed), *The International Criminal Court, Issues, Negotiations, Results* (The Hague: Kluwer, 1999) 127, 132–3; and Claus Kress, 'Jurisdiction and Cooperation in the Statute of the International Criminal Court: Principles and Compromises', *Yearbook of International Humanitarian Law* (1999) 2, 154–5.

[75] This position was favoured by certain countries in Rome, such as Germany (see the Proposal of Germany, A/AC.249/1998/DP.2).

[76] In fact, it seems to take us back to the unpromising notion that international crimes are those which ultimately cross international borders. On criticism of this view see Chapter 4.

[77] Some of the arguments commonly flagged against universal criminal jurisdiction, such as charges of victor's justice, 'clean hands', trials *in absentia*, and so on will be examined in Chapter 6. This is because they arguably challenge the authority of a given state to punish an offender, rather than the reasons that justify it holding the power to do so.

other similar outlaws.[78] This argument ultimately points to the complicated debate regarding the relationship between criminal liability and politically motivated behaviour. The distinction between crime and politics is a tough one, and beyond the scope of this enquiry.[79] Far from trying to untangle the intricacies of this issue here it may suffice to note, rather, that this objection has a logical flaw.

The issue it raises is whether a particular instance of conduct (eg, systematic torture of alleged terrorists) should be criminalized or, by contrast, considered merely a political decision. This is ultimately an issue concerning the criminalization of such behaviour. Unfortunately, we cannot enter that debate in any depth here. My point rather is that general questions about criminalization of particular conduct should not be conflated with the issue of *who* should have the power to punish an offender for them. Kissinger conflates these two separate questions and reasons on the basis of a *non sequitur*. From a premise that ultimately objects to torture being criminalized *simpliciter* when ordered by certain state officials, he concludes that an extraterritorial authority should lack the power to punish torturers on universality grounds. However, if his premise is convincing it must follow that neither the state on whose territory the offence was perpetrated, nor the state that employs the offender should have the power to punish her for these acts. It seems dubious that Kissinger would be really committed to the view that, for example, the US under Barack Obama would lack the power to punish acts of torture committed by its own troops in Abu Graib or even on American soil as part of the so-called 'war on terror'. But even if he were, his is not an argument against an extraterritorial state exercising *universal* criminal jurisdiction over the offender.

4.2 Universal jurisdiction risks becoming a tool against political adversaries

Another common ground of criticism stems from the possibility of states using criminal trials as foreign policy tools to prosecute adversaries or advance their national interest.[80] In Kissinger's words

> The Pinochet precedent, if literally applied, would permit the two sides in the Arab-Israeli conflict, or those in any other passionate international controversy, to project their battles into the various national courts by pursuing adversaries with extradition requests.[81]

This, some add, would be particularly problematic due to the lack of judicial independence in many countries.[82]

This argument has significant normative pull. However, I suggest it is ultimately unconvincing. First, this objection is liable to the flaw of contingency. Namely, it takes issue with certain states (ie, political adversaries) exercising extraterritorial

[78] Kissinger, 'The Pitfalls of Universal Jurisdiction', 87.

[79] For a brief discussion of some of the issues that arise from this discussion see Stanley Cohen, 'Crime and Politics: Spot the Difference', *British J of Sociology* 47/1 (1996), 1.

[80] Madeline Morris, 'Universal Jurisdiction in a Divided World: Conference Remarks', *New England L Rev* 35/2 (2001), 354.

[81] Kissinger, 'The Pitfalls of Universal Jurisdiction', 92.

[82] Morris, 'Universal Jurisdiction in a Divided World', 353.

jurisdiction over an offender, not every state. Accordingly, it fails adequately to account for the fact that states regard this type of prosecution as unacceptable even when the prosecuting state is not a political adversary. The protests against the arrest warrants issued by UK courts *vis-à-vis* high-ranking Israeli officials for allegations of war crimes illustrate this well.[83] Furthermore, it is not always the case—and it may be doubted how plausible the premise is as a descriptive proposition in international relations—that states have tried to take international political conflicts before their own domestic criminal courts. Criminal trials are slow, costly, burdensome, and arguably unsatisfying in the context of heated political disputes. The typically public character of such proceedings renders them uncomfortable fora to discuss delicate issues of foreign policy. Negotiations, reprisals, and ultimately war have proven far more popular. Thus, the risk they actually create seems largely overstated.

Secondly, and more importantly perhaps, this objection ultimately fails to address extraterritoriality per se: it would undermine both a territorial and an extraterritorial state exercising their criminal jurisdiction against a political adversary. That is, it would not only undermine Iran's power to punish Israeli soldiers for alleged international crimes perpetrated in the Gaza Strip; it would similarly undermine Syria's power to punish offences committed by Israeli soldiers *on Syrian territory*, or Dubai's intention to prosecute high-ranking Israeli officials for the assassination of a senior member of Hamas's military wing perpetrated on its territory.[84] Ultimately, the charge of potential abuse affects not the interest on which the justification for punishing extraterritorial offences on universality grounds rests, but the conditions that any given body should allegedly satisfy in order to hold the power to do so (its authority). In the next chapter, I argue that countries with corrupt or unreliable judiciaries, or carrying out biased prosecutions against political adversaries lack, as a matter of normative argument, the authority to punish political or military opponents. But more importantly for our purposes, it is argued that the considerations on which this authority rests are unrelated to the *extraterritorial* scope of the power to punish an offender.

4.3 Universal jurisdiction is just an expensive taste for elites

Arguably, the most damaging objection to extraterritorial punishment on grounds of universality advanced in this book is the supposedly negligible effect it has on the lives of the very individuals whose interests seem to ground this power. As Luban boldly puts it,

> the enterprise of occasionally putting perpetrators on trial—even leaders like Milosevic and Kambanda—seems more like a publicity stunt than a commitment to humanitarian legal values.[85]

[83] See, eg, 'Israel fury at UK attempt to arrest Tzipi Livni', BBC News, 15 December 2009, available at <http://news.bbc.co.uk/2/hi/middle_east/8413234.stm> (last accessed 1 August 2010), and the reported attempts to arrest former military chief Moshe Yaalon, and former head of Israeli forces in the Gaza Strip, General Doron Almog.

[84] The issue of jurisdiction is, of course, entirely separate from whether those responsible for the killing could legitimately claim a defence under international law.

[85] Luban, 'A Theory of Crimes against Humanity', 130.

This objection implies that, as a matter of fact, it is unrealistic to believe that a system of international criminal rules will meaningfully contribute to individual's well-being. No such system can succeed unless states are willing to yield some of their most treasured attributes. Most people would argue that the US are not willing to have alleged misdeeds of its military and civil leaders defined by people with no interest in the turmoil an arraignment would cause in the American political system. But, as Alfred Rubin suggests, would any state be willing to do so?[86] This not only applies to state officials:

> when people are willing to die for a cause, send their children to die for it, and pay for the effort in supplies and other ways, the notion that international supervision will limit atrocities is unrealistic in the absence of the full panoply of world government.[87]

In Chapter 2, I expressed my sympathy if this objection were viewed in terms of the capacity of extraterritorial punishment to *deter* future offences.[88] Yet the putative strength of a system of international criminal laws as a deterrent of atrocities is not a matter that should concern us, for deterrence plays virtually no part in the justification hereby advocated. This objection, however, does challenge the view defended here, though in a different way. It claims that international criminal laws cannot meaningfully contribute to the dignity and security of individuals worldwide. This would be very damaging for my position. Chapter 3 argued that because France, for example, holding the power to punish an offender for a robbery she committed in Cuba can contribute neither to the sense of dignity and security of individuals in France nor in Cuba, France lacks that particular power.[89] If this objection is sound, one must reject the claim that both individual states and the ICC should have universal jurisdiction.

However, this would be a rush to judgement. Conferring upon an extraterritorial authority the power to punish an offender is capable of contributing to the sense of dignity and security that *international* criminal rules provide to individuals worldwide and, for this to obtain, both individual states and the ICC must have universal jurisdiction over international crimes. This might seem somewhat unwarranted today. But let me clarify exactly what is the submitted position. It has been argued in this chapter that if a system of international criminal law is in force, it would contribute to the sense of dignity and security of millions of individuals worldwide, including those on the territory of the states in which these crimes have been perpetrated. The claim that not many people on earth currently feel any extra sense of dignity or security stemming from international criminal rules being in force does not undermine this argument entirely.

First, we should not take this proposition at face value. There seems to be some empirical evidence that in practice the fact that an extraterritorial authority claims

[86] Rubin, 'The International Criminal Court: Possibilities for Prosecutorial Abuse', 164.

[87] Ibid, 157.

[88] In fact, despite the fact that there are no empirical studies to prove this claim the literature seems confident in that its deterrent effects are negligible. See eg Sloane, 'The Expressive Capacity of International Punishment', 71–5; Drumbl, *Atrocity, Punishment, and International Law*, 169–73; and Tallgren, 'The Sensibility and Sense of International Criminal Law', 569–79.

[89] See Chapter 3, sections 3 and 4.

criminal jurisdiction in a given conflict can have a non-negligible impact on the ground. The likelihood of accountability, albeit extraterritorial, seems capable of having some effects. When Colombia threatened the guerrilla forces and drug-trafficking cartels with extradition to the US to face charges, this generated a bloody wave of terrorist attacks, kidnappings, etc, designed to make the Colombian Government step back.[90] Similarly, the ICC merely announcing the analysis of the situation in the country made a significant difference for all the relevant actors: guerrilla forces, paramilitaries, and certain state authorities and members of the armed forces. This was seen in the debate on the Peace and Justice Bill in Congress, as well as in certain developments of the jurisprudence of the relevant courts.[91] But more tellingly, it was allegedly mentioned by the relevant actors themselves.[92] For them it made a huge difference whether they would be prosecuted for any of these crimes, and whether they would be put in prison in Colombia or abroad. But it also made a big difference for those being targeted by those groups.[93] There have been some indications that the ICC opening an investigation has changed things on the ground *vis-à-vis* both those responsible for international offences and the vulnerable, targeted minorities in Sudan, Uganda, and the Democratic Republic of the Congo.[94] Moreover, there might be some clear exceptions to this general objection such as the situation of prisoners of war in *certain* armed conflicts. Albeit anecdotally, these examples show that the empirical assumption on which this objection rests is far less certain than its advocates are willing to admit.

Finally, it is not even clear that if this objection were empirically accurate today it would lead to rejecting universal jurisdiction altogether. The fact that individuals do not have a sense of being right-bearers, and that the criminal law protects their rights might not be so much a consequence of the impossibility of this system achieving anything meaningful for them, but rather a result of it not yet being fully in force. International criminal law is arguably still in its infancy, and few people will deny that it has a long way to go before becoming established as an institution in both international and domestic life.

The objector, however, may push the point further by suggesting that international criminal law will never be able to provide the benefits that domestic criminal law systems create for individuals. I will have to concede that much. An extraterritorial state would usually have difficulties in investigating or obtaining custody of the offender. Moreover, the territorial state will often refuse to collaborate with these investigations by, among other things, not disclosing information, refusing access

[90] As one may imagine, their privileges (which in some cases amounted to escaping from prison) would have been rather different.

[91] Interview with a law professor in Colombia.

[92] Interviews with public officials, NGOs, and IGOs staff, and academics in Colombia.

[93] See eg the fight by victims associations and NGOs (such as the Comisión Colombiana de Juristas, or the Colectivo de Abogados José Alvear Restrepo) in favour of the involvement of the ICC in Colombia.

[94] See Suliman Baldo, *The Impact of the ICC in the Sudan and DRC* and 'Pursuing Justice in Ongoing Conflict: A Discussion of Current Practice', Report of the International Center for Transitional Justice both at <http://www.peace-justice-conference.info/documents.asp> (last accessed 19 August 2010). On Uganda see, eg, William Schabas, 'Complementarity in Practice: Some Uncomplimentary Thoughts' *Crim Law Forum* 19 (2008), 19–20.

to witnesses, facilities, and victims, not extraditing defendants, and so on. It would be pointless to reason on different assumptions. Nevertheless, this does not mean that a system of international criminal law can achieve nothing. Even if the level of convictions would be low, and even if it faces difficulties and limitations, many individuals would arguably benefit from a system of international criminal laws coming of age. Such a system of criminal law would provide them with some additional sense of possessing legal rights against widespread or systematic acts of torture, rape, murder, and so on, and that these rights are taken seriously and protected by criminal laws irrespective of the capacity or willingness of the government under which they live. This kind of sense of dignity and security, many domestic systems of criminal law are simply unable to provide.[95]

[95] Sloane, 'The Expressive Capacity of International Punishment', 85 and Drumbl, *Atrocity, Punishment, and International Law*, 176.

6

Legitimate Authority and Extraterritorial Punishment

1. The Argument for Authority and the Power to Punish

To close this account of extraterritorial punishment it is necessary to provide a sound explanation of the legitimate authority of courts. The question in this book so far has been about when a particular extraterritorial body is normatively justified in meting out legal punishment to a given offender. Chapters 3 and 5 explained, respectively, how the interest-based justification for the power to punish advocated here accounts for different extraterritorial bodies holding the power to punish a particular individual for domestic and international offences. However, identifying an interest that is sufficiently important to confer upon a particular body this normative power does not suffice as a complete explanation for the allocation of this right. This body would normally also have to fulfil certain conditions such as, quite plausibly, not to decide a defendant's culpability on the basis of a confession extracted by torture. In other words, for a given body to have the power to punish a particular offender, it is not sufficient that someone's interest would be served by the conferral of that power; this body must also have the authority to do so.

Chapter 1 illustrated this point by way of a simple example: A needs prescribed drug D to fight her illness, and B knows about this illness, and knows that drug D would be appropriate, but he is not a doctor. Arguably, although B would be *justified* in prescribing D to A, he would not have the normative power to do so. This is not, or so it was claimed, because A lacks the relevant interest in getting the drug, or B lacks the relevant interest in prescribing it for her, but rather because B lacks the *authority* to do so. The same can be argued, *mutatis mutandis*, in respect of any given state or international tribunal: for it to claim the power to punish a particular offender, it must satisfy certain conditions that render its decision authoritative. This chapter provides a philosophical account of these conditions.

Although this is obviously an important question for any theory of legal punishment, it may seem of particular importance for an account of extraterritoriality. In this context, defendants, victims, and third parties characteristically tend to question the authority of the court deciding the case based on several popular challenges. The authority of the International Military Tribunals at Nuremberg and Tokyo, for instance, was objected to on the basis that it was nothing more than victor's justice, and that the Allies had also committed war crimes during the war (*tu quoque*). Other proceedings bear the charge of being 'show trials' or 'trials by ambush'. In its case against former Chilean dictator Augusto Pinochet, Spain's standing was questioned on the ground that it had failed to prosecute the crimes of the Franco era. Italy and France, for their part, have often been criticized for trying offenders *in absentia*. Finally, sometimes offenders are brought before the court after being abducted abroad (Eichmann) or illegally transferred.

This chapter examines each of these charges and assesses their force and implications for the normative account hereby advocated. In particular, it will do two things. Sections 2, 3, and 4 will provide a general account of when a particular body satisfies the minimum requirements to hold, itself, legitimate authority to punish a defendant. Sections 5 and 6, for their part, will examine some of the challenges illustrated above against extraterritorial prosecutions in the light of this account, and argue that none of them are connected with the issue of extraterritoriality. Before proceeding, however, a caveat is in order. We must not conflate the question of what conditions state S must satisfy in order to have, itself, the authority to punish a particular offender, with the justification for the need to confer upon some authority the power to punish that offender. While the former question concerns what gives S (in particular) authority over a certain issue, the latter justifies the need for having *some* sort of centralized authority to deal with it. These questions are analytically independent of each other: regardless of whether we consider that we need a centralized authority or that we should allow individuals to decide for themselves whether an offender should be punished, we might still require that they both satisfy certain conditions in order to exercise that prerogative authoritatively.

Admittedly, few would argue that we would be better off if each individual, rather than the state, held the power to punish offenders. But it is worth clarifying why this is so. The obvious objection to vigilante jurisdiction is the risk of potential abuse.[1] However, that risk could be rendered marginal by imposing strict conditions for the exercise of that power. We may require that trials remain public, provision for defence counsel is adequate, stringent rules of evidence are adhered to, sentencing guidelines are provided, etc. These limitations are perfectly compatible with conferring upon any interested party the power to punish an offender. Quite possibly vigilante jurisdiction will still be resisted on the grounds that 'it is unreasonable for Men to be Judges in their own Cases'.[2] Yet this claim does not, or not as yet, argue in favour of having a centralized authority to resolve these matters; rather, it suggests that *victims* should not be allowed to try their alleged offenders themselves.

[1] See, eg, Luban, 'A Theory of Crimes against Humanity', 106; Locke, *Two Treatises of Government* (Cambridge: Cambridge University Press, 1988), Second Treatise, §13, 275; and J Gardner, 'Crime: in Proportion and in Perspective' in Andrew Ashworth and Martin Wasik (eds), *Fundamentals of Sentencing Theory: Essays in Honour of Andrew von Hirsch* (Oxford: Oxford University Press, 1998).

[2] Locke, *Two Treatises of Government*, 275.

By contrast, the main reason why there should be a *centralized* authority is the need for coordination and cost reduction.[3] I cannot offer here a full defence of this claim; however it should suffice to note that it would be too onerous for individuals themselves to bear the costs of investigating, prosecuting, and sentencing offenders. All this position assumes, in any event, is the need for centralization; the more difficult philosophical question at stake in this chapter is what confers upon that centralized body a legitimate authority to punish an offender.[4]

2. The Service Conception of Authority

Joseph Raz's service conception of authority may help us to tackle the issue at hand. This conception of authority has not only been highly influential in the philosophical literature, but it is also arguably the best suited to account for the legitimate authority of courts in the context of adjudication of criminal cases.[5] The main reason for this is that it links the conferral of authority to a body having a certain epistemic advantage. It thereby captures the fundamental insight that courts are in a much better position than individuals generally to decide a particular case due to their better knowledge of the facts and the applicable law. These considerations are, under most accounts, a central aspect of the criminal process.[6]

As Raz argues, the issue of authority presents us with both a normative and a theoretical question.[7] The normative question is, ultimately, on what grounds we can justify subjecting one's judgement to that of another person, in our case by allowing *her* to decide, for instance, whether a particular defendant should be punished. The theoretical question concerns the implications of recognizing A as an authority on a given matter, that is, how the existence of an authoritative decision affects the reasoning or decision-making of others.[8] Raz's service conception rests on three central theses, the first two of which provide an answer to the normative question, and the third, to the theoretical one. The Normal Justification Thesis (NJT) argues that the normal reason why a person ought to subject his will to that of another person is that he

> is likely better to [conform] with reasons which apply to him (other than the alleged authoritative directives) if he accepts the directives of the alleged authority as authoritatively

[3] See, eg, Raz, *Practical Reason and Norms*, 159 or Raz, *The Morality of Freedom*, 30–1.

[4] This argument is entirely independent of the particular justification for the right to punish advocated in this book. It is therefore compatible with other standard justifications, such as deterrence, retributivism, etc.

[5] For a good introduction to the issue of authority and a good example of the relevance of Raz's version of the service conception in current debates see S J Shapiro, 'Authority' in Scott Shapiro and Jules L Coleman, *The Oxford Handbook of Jurisprudence and Philosophy of Law* (Oxford: Oxford University Press, 2002).

[6] By narrowing the conception of authority to that of criminal courts, this account bypasses one of the main sources of resistance the service conception has met, namely, its lack of interest in democratic procedures. See eg Thomas Christiano, 'The Authority of Democracy', *J of Political Philosophy* 12/3 (2004) and Shapiro, 'Authority', 431–9.

[7] Joseph Raz, 'The Problem of Authority', *Minnesota L Rev* 90 (2006).

[8] Joseph Raz, 'Authority and Justification', *Philosophy and Public Affairs* 14/1 (1985), 3.

binding and tries to follow them, rather than by trying to follow reasons which apply to him directly.[9]

This normative claim has a limit built into it: the Dependence Thesis states that in order for directives to be authoritative, they 'should be based on reasons which already independently apply to the subjects of the directives and are relevant to their action in the circumstances covered by the directive'.[10] Finally, the Pre-emption Thesis (PT) provides an answer to the theoretical question identified above; it maintains that

> the fact that an authority requires performance of an action is a reason for its performance which is not to be added to all other relevant reasons when assessing what to do, but should exclude and take the place of some of them.[11]

As discussed below, the answers to the moral and the theoretical questions are deeply interconnected.

But let us start at the beginning. The service conception rests on a particular understanding of practical reason.[12] It suggests that in any given circumstance individuals ought to act on reasons that apply objectively to them. Regardless of whether Alice is driving, playing chess, or adjudicating in a criminal case the reasons she may have for not speeding, avoiding loosing her rook, or convicting a given defendant only if he is proven guilty beyond reasonable doubt would apply to Alice independently of her will, or her perception of these reasons. With this in mind, it is only natural that the normal reason why a person ought to subject his will to that of another person is that he is likely to conform better with reasons which apply to him if he accepts the directives issued by that authority rather than if he tries to follow these reasons directly (NJT). When playing chess, one would do better to listen to Kasparov's advice than to try to work out the right move for oneself. And this is precisely why we recognize Kasparov as an authority on chess. Accordingly, the service conception suggests that the normal function of legitimate authority is to mediate between people and the right reasons that apply objectively (and independently of the authoritative directives) to them, and enhance their conformity with those reasons. Authority is therefore ultimately grounded on epistemic advantage.[13]

This dissolves one of the traditional concerns with accepting an authority. Authorities are not an arbitrary denial of one's capacity for rational action, but rather a device through which one can achieve that aim more effectively.[14] In Raz's words, 'the primary value of our general ability to act by our own judgment derives from the concern to conform to reasons, and that concern can be met in a variety of ways.'[15]

[9] Raz, *The Morality of Freedom*, 53; Raz, 'The Problem of Authority', 1014.
[10] Raz, *The Morality of Freedom*, 47 and *Ethics in the Public Domain*, 214.
[11] Raz, *The Morality of Freedom*, 46.
[12] Again, providing a defence of this approach is beyond the scope of this enquiry. For critical remarks see Heidi M Hurd, *Moral Combat* (Cambridge: Cambridge University Press, 1999).
[13] Raz, *Ethics in the Public Domain*, 214.
[14] Raz, 'The Problem of Authority', 1018.
[15] Ibid, 1017.

It has been often objected, however, that the NJT provides only a prudential reason for accepting someone's authority, and does not yet explain why we are *bound* to do so. The standard example goes: even if as patients we would comply better with reasons that apply to us by following the doctor's advice than by relying on our own judgement, this does not entail per se that we are bound to follow her advice (or that the doctor has authority over us).[16] This proposition, however, is only partially correct. For while it is true that doctors lack authority to oblige patients to follow certain medical treatment, they do have authority to prescribe (or not to prescribe) certain medications. Admittedly, the NJT cannot explain this difference of treatment; in both situations we would comply better with the reasons that objectively apply to us by following the doctor's advice than by following reason directly. However, it is not initially clear that the NJT should provide such an explanation. The difference seems to lie in the type of decision involved, and which one should be left for an authority to decide.[17] Thus the fact that A satisfies the NJT does not entail that we are bound by her decision. We are only bound to accept an authoritative directive

> where a substantial good is at stake, a good that we have moral reasons to secure for ourselves and for others but that can in the circumstances be best secured by yielding to a coordinating authority.[18]

This objection seems to misunderstand the normative work that the NJT does within the service conception. The NJT explains only why we recognize doctors as the relevant authority to prescribe certain drugs or engineers as authorities regarding whether we can build certain buildings. The *bindingness* of their decisions, by contrast, rests on other considerations, which are contained in Raz's answer but which it pays to clarify further. First, this bindingness is explained by the fact that there are things we have an interest in, an interest which is important enough to warrant the protection of a right; and secondly, that the best way to serve this interest is to empower a centralized authority. It is only when these two conditions *and* the NJT are satisfied that we have a moral case for considering the decisions of A binding. Two of the multiple activities that would satisfy these conditions may well be the regulation of certain pharmaceutical products or the imposition of legal punishment.

[16] Kenneth Einar Himma, 'Just 'Cause You're Smarter Than Me Doesn't Give You a Right to Tell Me What to Do: Legitimate Authority and the Normal Justification Thesis', *OJLS* 27/1 (2007), 124.

[17] Raz argues that authorities are also limited by the kind of acts they can or cannot regulate ('Authority and Justification', 14). Moreover, in his latest restatement of the service conception, he places significant emphasis on what he calls the Independence Condition, ie, that 'the matters regarding which the [NJT] is met are such that with respect to them it is better to conform to reason than to decide for oneself, unaided by authority' (Raz, 'The Problem of Authority', 1014). This chapter works on the assumption that empowering an authority to decide whether a defendant should be punished or not (and if she is, how much) poses 'no threat to the authenticity of one's life, or to one's ability to lead a self-reliant and self-fulfilling life' (id, 1016) and that, as a result, it satisfies the Independence Condition.

[18] Raz, 'The Problem of Authority', 1016. See, similarly, Raz, *The Morality of Freedom*, 100.

Before moving on to the theoretical question identified at the outset, that is, what are the implications of recognizing A as an authority on a given matter, two further points are in order. First, under the service conception, for a certain body to hold legitimate authority it must have some de facto authority. In Raz's words,

> in most cases the normal justification cannot be established unless the putative authority enjoys some measure of recognition and exercises power over its subjects.[19]

Simply put, if A's authority relies on the fact that it is capable of solving certain coordination problems, and of providing a particular good, it must have some degree of recognition from its peers and obedience from those subject to it. This helps to explain why states are natural candidates to claim the authority to punish offenders, and it provides a sensible evaluative threshold for extraterritorial authorities, such as governments in exile or international tribunals, and for domestic non-state institutions such as tribal authorities, belligerent movements, etc.[20] In the remainder of this chapter we may assume that the relevant body satisfies that requirement.

Secondly, A's authority is limited by the kind of reasons on which she may or may not rely in making a decision. To repeat: in order to be binding, directives must be based on reasons which already apply independently to the subjects of those directives and are relevant to the subjects' action in the circumstances covered by the directives (Dependence Thesis). This is a moral thesis on how authorities must use their powers. It follows from it that in order for a decision reached by a given state S (or one of its organs) to be authoritative, it must be based on the reasons that apply to individuals whose interest explains conferring upon that particular body the power to punish her. This point allows us to link the service conception with the particular justification for legal punishment advocated in this book. Namely, individuals in S have an interest in legal rules being in force prohibiting murder, theft, and also war crimes and crimes against humanity sufficiently important to confer upon certain bodies the power to punish those who perpetrate them.[21] Accordingly, decisions reached primarily for other reasons, such as political expedience, economic interest of a certain kind, vindictiveness, hate, etc cannot claim authoritative force.[22] This explains why a verdict reached through bribery or threats to jurors can claim no authoritative force even if it is factually accurate.

[19] Raz, *The Morality of Freedom*, 56.

[20] This position commits this account to the view that, under certain circumstances, a body different from the state would be able to hold the power to punish an offender if, at least, it is authorized by the state, like the Gacaca in Rwanda, or if that body acts de facto as the state (on Gacaca courts, see, William A Schabas, 'Genocide Trials and Gacaca Courts', *J of International Crim Justice* 3 (2005), 896 and E Daly, 'Between Punitive and Reconstructive Justice: The Gacaca Courts in Rwanda', *NYU J of International Law and Politics* 34 (2002), 355). However, this commitment holds only insofar as that body satisfies the relevant conditions outlined below. This seems in fact compatible with international law (see eg Sandesh Sivakumaran, 'Courts of Armed Opposition Groups: Fair Trials or Summary Justice?', *J of International Crim Justice* 7/3 (2009), 497).

[21] This does not mean they are, as a matter of fact, guilty. For a detailed explanation of this proposition see Chapter 2.

[22] See, eg, Duff, *Answering for Crime*, 186, and cases cited in fns 143 and 144.

As suggested above, the answer to the theoretical question identified at the outset, namely, what are the implications of saying that S has legitimate authority to try a particular offender, rests with the PT:

> the fact that an authority requires performance of an action is a reason for its performance which is not to be added to all other relevant reasons when assessing what to do, but should exclude and take the place of some of them.[23]

Thus, Raz argues that authoritative decisions work as second order reasons that pre-empt the subject from relying on the first order, background reasons which apply to her independently. The reason for excluding other background reasons is that an authority cannot succeed in improving our conformity with reason and solving coordination problems if it does not pre-empt our background reasons, if individuals have to rely on their own judgement of the merits.[24]

3. The Service Conception and the Legitimate Authority of Criminal Courts

We turn now to see how the service conception accounts for the authority of criminal courts. As argued in Chapter 2, the existence of a legal system prohibiting certain kinds of wrongdoing is a good we have reasons to secure for ourselves and for others. The collective interest of individuals in this system being in force is sufficiently weighty to warrant conferring a normative power to punish those who violate these rules. Furthermore, the best way to comply with these background reasons is to empower some form of centralized authority to investigate and try criminal offences. This is mainly due to better coordination and cost reduction. This authority would normally be territorial or extraterritorial depending on whether the relevant offence is municipal or international.[25] The bulk of this chapter is therefore concerned with identifying when such institutions satisfy the NJT, that is, when individuals are likely to conform better with reasons which (independently) apply to them by accepting its directives rather than by trying to follow these reasons directly.

Following Ashworth and Redmayne, a plausible answer to this question is that a given court satisfies the NJT when it seeks 'accurately to determine whether or not a person has committed a particular criminal offence and does so fairly'.[26] In

[23] Raz, *The Morality of Freedom*, 46. This is arguably one of the most controversial aspects of Raz's service conception. For a review on some of the criticisms, see Shapiro, 'Authority', 411–13.

[24] Raz, *The Morality of Freedom*, 47–8; Raz, 'The Problem of Authority', 1019.

[25] To remind the reader, Chapter 2 argues that individuals in state S have an interest that warrants conferring upon S in particular the normative power to punish offences committed on its territory or against its sovereignty, security, or important governmental functions even if committed abroad. Chapters 3 and 4 argue that both the International Criminal Court (ICC) and extraterritorial states hold the power to punish international offences regardless of where they were perpetrated, and of the nationality of both the offender and the victim.

[26] Andrew Ashworth and Mike Redmayne, *The Criminal Process* (Oxford: Oxford University Press, 2005), 22.

other words, the *normal* reason why individuals should recognize the authority of a given court to decide a particular criminal case concerns its greater knowledge of the facts of the case and the relevant law, and its careful consideration of the conflicting viewpoints on the matter. This response certainly has much intuitive appeal. However, there are at least three issues that require further elaboration.

First, although the accuracy requirement captures the epistemic advantage that courts normally offer, it raises the question as to why accuracy actually matters. According to the NJT, an authority's epistemic advantage must be connected to the reasons which independently apply to us, and to which it helps us better to conform. Ashworth and Redmayne's answer to this question is therefore consistent with the rationale for legal punishment they endorse, namely, retribution. If state S's power to punish is based on the fact that the offender deserves to be punished, it is only natural that the criminal procedure is intended to determine, as accurately as possible, whether she is guilty. Retributivism has been criticized in previous chapters for being incompatible with the interest theory of rights, and for leading to unacceptable positions when faced with the issue of extraterritoriality.[27] However, if accuracy is to be an element of the NJT under the account hereby advocated, it is necessary to explain why it would also be required by the argument for legal punishment advanced in this book.

The position is that state S's power to punish an offender is based on the collective interest of individuals in S in there being a rule in force against murder, robbery, systematic torture, etc. For that criminal rule to be in force, those who violate it must be punished; they must be punished by an authority expressly authorized by the relevant legal system; and they must be punished *because they violated this rule*. Only when all these conditions are met would punishing this offender send the right message to individuals that the rule is in force.[28] Accordingly, we need to ensure as far as possible that only the guilty are convicted. Punishing innocent people *qua* innocent will not do for the simple reason that it would ultimately undermine the credibility of the criminal law system and, with it, the sense of dignity and security that it brings to individuals living under it.[29]

Secondly, we need to clarify what it means to try someone fairly and explain why this would also be required by the NJT. The former question is perhaps simpler to answer than the latter. Fairness in this context is normally connected with respect for certain rights. It is beyond the scope of this account to provide a complete list of the rights that a fair criminal process must respect. A sensible option, in any event, is to look at the different incidents that embody the right to a fair trial as provided in the relevant international human rights instruments. Article 14 of the International Covenant on Civil and Political Rights, for example, establishes that 'everyone shall be entitled to a fair and public hearing by a competent, independent and impartial tribunal established by law'; 'shall have the right to be presumed innocent until proved guilty'; and shall be entitled to several minimum guarantees,

[27] See Chapters 2 and 3, respectively. [28] See Chapter 2.

[29] I do admit, however, that a given decision might be authoritative even if in a specific case the defendant is wrongly acquitted or wrongly convicted. On this, see below.

such as, 'to be informed promptly and in detail in a language which he understands of the nature and cause of the charge against him'; 'to have adequate time and facilities for the preparation of his defence and to communicate with counsel of his own choosing'; and so on.[30] There are certainly other rights that the criminal process should respect, which are not normally covered by the right to a fair trial as such. Among them, one could mention the right to privacy, to personal liberty, to freedom from torture, etc.[31]

Far more difficult is to explain why fairness is required by the NJT, that is, why accuracy is not enough. Is not the NJT based on the notion of epistemic advantage, and is not the epistemic advantage linked to whether we have sufficient evidence that the defendant is guilty of wrongdoing? Ashworth and Redmayne suggest that accuracy and fairness are twin, concomitant aims. They even resist the idea that individual rights work as mere side-constraints in the pursuit of truth. For them the criminal process 'is not just a diagnostic procedure, of which the sole purpose is to establish as accurately as possible ... what happened'; they insist that respect for rights should be seen as an objective to be attained while pursuing that end.[32] However, this proposition fails to explain why a violation of the right to a fair trial would undermine the authority of a given state when the illegally obtained incriminatory evidence is overwhelming and reliable, and it seems to take for granted that accuracy and fairness will never collide.

There are two main positions in the literature regarding this specific issue. On the one hand, the 'separation thesis' suggests that 'each part of the criminal justice process should be considered independently', that is, that if a wrong was committed during the investigation, the police officers who carried it out should themselves be punished, but this should have no bearing on the situation of the defendant.[33] On the other hand, the 'integrity thesis' claims that a breach of, for instance, someone's right not to be tortured during the criminal process would undermine the authority

[30] These provisions are fairly standard and contained in a large number of sources. See further Art 8 of the American Convention on Human Rights, Art 6 of the European Convention on Human Rights, Art 7 of the African Charter on Human and People's Rights; also Art 21 of the Statute of the International Criminal Tribunal for the former Yugoslavia (ICTY), Art 20 of the Statute of the International Criminal Tribunal for Rwanda (ICTR), and the more detailed provisions in Arts 55, 63, 66, and 67 of the Rome Statute. See complementary rights and provisions in the UN Convention on the Rights of the Child, and the Charter of Fundamental Rights approved by the European Union in 2000. Finally, see common Art 3 to the Geneva Conventions, and Arts 84 and 105 of Geneva Convention (III) Relative to the Treatment of Prisoners of War, Art 75 of Additional Protocol I, and Art 6 of Additional Protocol II. Even if it has been suggested that the level of protection may be somewhat lowered due to the intensity of the conflict, it has also been suggested that fair trial guarantees, at least those provided for in Art 6 of Additional Protocol II, are largely based on the International Covenant on Civil and Political Rights (ICRC Commentary on the Additional Protocols of 8 June 1977 to the Geneva Conventions of 12 August 1949 (Geneva: ICRC, 1987), at mn 4597). On this see *Hamdan v Rumsfeld, Secretary of Defence et al* 548 US 557 (2006), per Stevens J at 69 and ff.

[31] Some of the particulars of these rights would be jurisdictionally specific (eg, the right to have legal advice when questioned at a police station). Ultimately the argument here rests on a more basic catalogue of rights (eg, the right to an adequate defence), the different forms of institutionalization of which are immaterial for present purposes.

[32] Ashworth and Redmayne, *The Criminal Process*, 24 and 45 respectively (emphasis added).

[33] As described by Duff *et al*, *The Trial on Trial*, vol 3, 226.

of the state to punish a defendant.[34] Ashworth and Redmayne take sides with the integrity thesis and this seems to be the right choice.[35] Yet the difficulty lies in providing a convincing account for this position.

A possible reason to endorse the integrity thesis is that fairness is a condition for accuracy. Accordingly, it has been argued that matters such as coerced confessions are generally unreliable.[36] This is the reason why most breaches of the rules of fair process undermine the state's authority. However, why should we not admit such a confession when it led to a very specific piece of incriminatory evidence that could not have been invented, and which confirms the defendant's culpability? Lack of reliability, thus, does not take us far enough.

Ashworth and Redmayne advocate a stringent version of the integrity thesis which they call protective or remedial. Ultimately, they argue that the only way to give significant force to a person's right not to be tortured is to exclude the evidence obtained in violation of this right, and that it is much more important to uphold this right than to convict a guilty defendant in such a case.[37] Their position, however, seems to rest on slippery ground. First, its premise is far from uncontroversial, since there are other ways of upholding an offender's right which do not involve excluding illegally obtained, but otherwise accurate and reliable, evidence. Most notably, and as the separation thesis advocate would argue, the officials who tortured an offender could be punished, and the offender could receive reparations for the harm she suffered. Ashworth and Redmayne could still suggest that 'the *ideal* remedy for breach of a right is normally (at least) restoration of the victim to the position he would have been in had the right not been violated'.[38] However, this would still fail to explain the exclusion of evidence when it is the right of a third party (eg, a co-defendant) that has been violated, and not that of the relevant defendant herself.[39] Secondly, their position would face a significant challenge in cases of trials for international crimes, when excluding this evidence would lead to the defendant's acquittal. Unless one is dealing with extreme situations such as torture, it might not be apparent why symbolically upholding someone's right, for example, not to be compelled to testify against himself would be more important than punishing an offender in instances such as

[34] See, generally, ibid, Chapter 8, and A Ashworth, 'Exploring the Integrity Principle in Evidence and Procedure' in Peter Mirfield and Roger Nov Smith, *Essays for Colin Tapper* (London: LexisNexis, 2003).

[35] A note of caution is in order here. This does not mean that under certain circumstances the state officials should not *also* be punished. It only means that their wrong is not entirely unrelated to the state's authority to punish the particular offender.

[36] See, eg, Sivakumaran, 'Courts of Armed Opposition Groups', 493. Interestingly, some 'coerced' interrogation techniques used at Guantanamo Bay were allegedly used by the Chinese during the Korean War to obtain confessions from American prisoners, most of them false (S Shane, 'China Inspired Interrogations at Guantánamo', *New York Times*, 2 July 2008).

[37] Ashworth and Redmayne, *The Criminal Process*, 330–1.

[38] As put by Duff et al, *The Trial on Trial*, vol 3, 230, 235 (emphasis added).

[39] This is why Duff et al seek to complement this account, which they call integrity as integration, with the principle of integrity as moral standing. On the relevance of moral standing, see below.

the indictment of key political or military figures responsible for mass atrocities in ongoing conflicts.[40]

By contrast, I suggest that the reason why fairness matters is ultimately connected to the NJT in a more fundamental way. The NJT rests on the reasons that objectively apply to us, and those are for our purposes the reasons that justify punishing an offender. If the infliction of punishment is to convey the message that the violated criminal rule is in force, it is vital that individuals see it as credibly meted out for that reason. Yet when an offender is punished after her rights to a fair trial are ostensibly violated, this raises doubts as to whether the reason that she is being punished is that she violated a criminal prohibition. And this would be true, most likely, even if there was strong evidence that indicates that she is guilty. Fairness is a necessary condition for credibility, and credibility is crucial for the existence of a system of criminal rules that confers rights on individuals and takes their protection seriously.[41]

Credibility here does not simply mean reliability as to whether the defendant, as a matter of fact, committed the offence. Rather, the submission is that it is crucial that the court is credibly seen as convicting or acquitting her for the right reasons. The trial is a means of communication with the public at large (including both the defendant and the victim).[42] Some degree of public confidence in courts satisfying this requirement is therefore necessary to convey the correct message. This confidence is not exclusively a product of the factual accuracy or reliability of the verdict.[43] Trials that are legitimately *perceived* as biased are problematic even if they convict the guilty or acquit the innocent.

This explains why the way in which the tribunal was established, its impartiality, and the publicity of the proceedings are widely endorsed considerations which account for any court's authority even when those considerations are not necessarily instrumental in reaching more accurate decisions. Secret trials or trials in which a defendant is not given access to incriminatory evidence are suspicious, and therefore unacceptable, even if the verdict happens to be accurate.[44] Similarly,

[40] This might well also apply in cases of serial killers such as Harold Shipman, serial rapists, and so on. See Adrian A Zuckerman, 'Illegally-Obtained Evidence—Discretion as a Guardian of Legitimacy', *Current Legal Problems* 40 (1987), 57.

[41] See below, the examination of 'show trials'.

[42] I H Dennis, 'Reconstructing the Law of Criminal Evidence', *Current Legal Problems* 42 (1989), 35.

[43] Duff et al, *The Trial on Trial*, vol 3, 88. The Canadian Constitution, eg, provides:

> Where ... a court concludes that evidence was obtained in a manner that infringed or denied any rights or freedoms guaranteed by this Charter, the evidence shall be excluded if it is established that ... the admission of it in the proceedings would bring the administration of justice into disrepute.

[44] As Bancaud writes in reference to the trials of Leon Blum and others under Vichy:

> the use of closed proceedings ... has the drawback of cancelling what justified recourse to the legal system, viz. the benefits of a process that promises to shed 'full light' and to show that the accusers have nothing to hide. (A Bancaud, *Une exception ordinaire: La magistrature en France 1930–1950* (Paris: Gallimard, 2002), 396, cited in Jon Elster, *Closing the Books: Transitional Justice in Historical Perspective* (Cambridge: Cambridge University Press, 2004), 89.)

irregularly created courts, or those which do not provide sufficient safeguards for defendants would lack legitimate authority under international law.[45] The House of Lords' decision in *Pinochet I* was quashed not because it was incorrect, not even because it was biased. As Lord Browne-Wilkinson put it,

> Senator Pinochet does not allege that Lord Hoffmann was in fact biased. The contention is that there was a real danger or reasonable apprehension or suspicion that Lord Hoffmann might have been biased, that is to say it is alleged that there is an appearance of bias not actual bias.[46]

This was considered sufficient to undermine the authority of the decision. Similarly, although it is being argued that, in practice, Military Commissions created in the US to try detainees linked to the 'war on terror' have overall been procedurally fair, their authority may have been severely (if not fatally) undermined by the treatment detainees suffered and the sustained efforts made to keep proceedings away from public scrutiny.[47]

To sum up, a court satisfies the NJT if and only if it *both* seeks to reach an accurate and reliable verdict, and it does so fairly. It is therefore not true that according to a generally instrumental conception of the criminal process

> the unreliability of the means by which [the decision] was arrived at, or the fortuitousness of its truth, gives us grounds to criticise those who arrived at it, but do not undermine its instrumental value.[48]

Under the version of the service conception defended here the justice of the outcome is not wholly independent of the justice of the procedures.

Interestingly, the service conception might be liable to the opposite charge. It may have to recognize the binding character of a credible wrong conviction or a mistaken acquittal.[49] Indeed, the Dependence Thesis does not require that authoritative decisions *correctly* reflect the balance of reasons on which they depend. This proposition is a necessary implication of the conception of authority advocated here, and a relatively salient one. Since the justification of legitimate authority relies on its capacity to resolve coordination problems, there is no point in having authorities unless their determinations are binding even if mistaken. This might seem hard to swallow. Yet the difficulty it creates should not be overstated.

First, we can devise rules to help us to minimize certain types of mistakes. For instance, states tend (and should) prefer to let a guilty person go free than

[45] See common Art 3 to the Geneva Conventions (and Art 75(4) of Additional Protocol I to the Geneva Conventions), requiring that sentence be passed by a 'regularly constituted court'.

[46] See *R v Bow Street Metropolitan Stipendiary Magistrate and others, ex parte Pinochet Ugarte (No 2)* [1999] UKHL 1; [1999] 1 All ER 577 (HL).

[47] *Hamdan v Rumsfeld* 548 US 557 (2006), 69. See, eg, Jennifer Trahan, 'Military Commission Trials at Guantanamo Bay, Cuba: Do they Satisfy International and Constitutional Law?', *Fordham International LJ* 30 (2006–2007), 780–835. On claims that proceedings have actually been overall fair, see, eg, Michael J Newton, 'Some Observations on the Future of US Military Commissions', *Case Western Reserve J of International Law*, 42/1 & 2 (2009), 151–70. These proceedings are also liable to the charges of *tu quoque* or 'clean hands', examined below.

[48] Duff et al, *The Trial on Trial*, vol 3, 88.

[49] Raz, 'Authority and Justification', 15.

punish an innocent one, and this explains why they require proof beyond reasonable doubt for conviction, and not merely on the balance of probabilities. In principle, it is commonly accepted, the latter standard would secure a greater degree of accuracy. Secondly, clear mistakes would disqualify the authority of a decision.[50] This means that the UK would not be bound by state S's decision to punish a particular defendant if it has clear and reliable information that he is entirely innocent of the offence. This would obtain, for example, if at the same time the defendant allegedly perpetrated a robbery in S, he was playing football in the Premier League. Under these circumstances the UK would be entitled not to extradite him to S. Finally, accepting the authority of a mistaken decision is far less problematic than one would initially think. When a court of law finds an individual guilty after a fair process, and on the basis of what seems reasonably accurate and reliable information, we normally accept its decision as binding. And rightly so: we would rather have this occur than have everyone trying to make up their own minds about whether to comply with the decision.

There is, however, a particular kind of mistake that should be accorded a different treatment. As Raz points out, the only mistakes that make an otherwise authoritative decision void are mistakes over jurisdiction.[51] Yet he does not give any reason why this would be so. It may be possible to submit that the fact that mistakes over jurisdiction undermine state S's authority to punish a particular offender concern neither S failing to meet the NJT nor the DT. Rather, the problem in such cases would be that S has no valid *reason* to punish the offender which are sufficiently important to confer upon it the power to do so. As explained in Chapter 3, the reason why Paraguay lacks jurisdiction to punish O for a robbery she committed in Spain (when it is not an offence against Paraguay's sovereignty, national security, or important governmental functions) is that individuals in Paraguay lack an interest important enough to merit conferring upon *it* such a power. Accordingly, states which mistakenly assert jurisdiction over offences committed extraterritorially cannot validly effect a normative change in the offender's moral rights, let alone do so with binding effect.

Finally, it is worth explicating further the theoretical implications of the conception of authority advocated here. Simply put, the PT accounts for the difference between saying that state S is justified in punishing offender O (as per Chapters 3 to 5) and claiming that S has the authority to do so. The former proposition means that someone has an interest which is sufficiently important to put O under a liability to have punishment inflicted upon her; the latter means that S's decision on this matter should be treated as binding by others.[52] Accordingly, individuals in S must abide by the court's decision. That is, they are not supposed to go to the local Mob asking for justice after the state sentenced the defendants

[50] Raz, *The Morality of Freedom*, 62. [51] Ibid.

[52] As explained above, the former proposition is one of the conditions that must be satisfied in order to claim that a given body has legitimate authority to punish an offender.

too leniently.[53] But also other states should consider that decision as authoritative, that is, they would lack a valid reason to reject it.[54]

We may be inclined at this juncture to distinguish between the authority of convictions and acquittals. Indeed, although a guilty verdict means that a particular defendant was found guilty beyond reasonable doubt, acquittals do not establish innocence but rather indicate that the guilty threshold was not reached. One could then suggest that acquittals should not then carry the same authority as convictions, and therefore that they need not be considered binding, particularly by other states. Accordingly, the fact that a defendant was acquitted in Uganda should not entail that she cannot be tried again (and convicted) in South Africa. But this conflates two different things. The reason why we might consider S an authority (ie, that it satisfies the NJT) is not what explains its decision pre-empting other authorities from deciding the case again. As suggested above, the PT is not grounded on Uganda making a more accurate decision than South Africa, but rather on the need for coordination and cost reduction. It would be deeply problematic for the purposes of the criminal law system to have conflicting decisions as to whether a particular defendant is innocent or guilty. Hence, the fact that Uganda's courts have acquitted an offender after a fair trial based on reliable evidence would render South Africa's conviction suspicious, at least if it was not grounded on new evidence. This would undermine the whole purpose of punishing her, for it will not convey a clear message that the rule she allegedly violated is in force.[55] To conclude, then, a defendant's acquittal does carry as much authority as her conviction (in the restricted sense of the PT), even if it arguably has an entirely different meaning.

4. Authority as 'Moral Standing'

There is a competing view that sees in a state's moral standing the main (though perhaps not the only) condition grounding legitimate authority to punish an offender. This position relies on a conceptual point, namely, that a

> complete account of the legitimacy of any authority must include an explanation of how the authority acquires the moral standing to hold others accountable, as well as an explanation of how it imposes genuine obligations.[56]

[53] Prudential reasons might also indicate likewise, as one may hear as a chilling reply:

> Some day, and that day may never come, I will call upon you to do a service for me. Until that day accept this justice as a gift on my daughter's wedding day. (Mario Puzo, *The Godfather* (New York: New American Library, 2002), 33.)

[54] *A contrario*, if a state fails to satisfy these conditions its decision cannot claim authoritative force.

[55] I cannot examine here whether states should have the power to try a defendant again on new evidence (for these purposes it is immaterial whether she is tried in a court in the same state or a different one). The majority of states seem to have rules against this kind of proceeding, called the safeguard against double jeopardy or *ne bis in idem*. The UK is one of the few states which allows a new prosecution under quite strict conditions (see Criminal Justice Act 2003, ss 75–81).

[56] Scott Hershovitz, 'Accountability and Political Authority' (2008), 5 (manuscript cited with permission from the author).

Crucially, state S's moral standing to hold someone (O) accountable for a breach of its rules is explained by the relationship between S and O. This is a plausible position to hold in several contexts. For instance, the objection goes, moral philosophers are not entitled to discipline any child they happen to see committing a misdeed on the street; that power is generally grounded in the parent-child relationship.

In this light, the service conception would be unsatisfactory as a full account of legitimate authority precisely because it is unable to provide a plausible explanation of how state S acquired the moral standing to hold a particular offender accountable. For Raz, 'remedies for breaches of the law [such as damages for acts of defamation] ... can be morally justified even if applied to those who are not subject to the authority of the government and its laws'; the 'importance of the law in such matters is in creating a centre of power which makes it possible to enforce moral duties'.[57] Thus, this objection claims, the service conception, and the predominantly instrumental justification it advocates only explain why the state is *competent* to hold the tortfeasor to account, but it cannot explain why it has the *standing* to do so. Competence does not (necessarily) warrant authority.[58]

The damage this criticism does to the service conception is hardly as significant as its proponents suggest. Its intuitive appeal seems to come from the fact that it misrepresents the service conception, and the normative work that the NJT does within it. The charge is that the NJT cannot explain why we are bound to obey a particular authority. In Hershovitz words, '[t]he normal justification thesis appears to tell us whether someone would make a good authority, not whether someone possesses it.'[59] Hershovitz himself admits that under the service conception, satisfying the NJT is not enough to hold legitimate authority over someone. However, he seems incorrectly to identify what explains S holding legitimate authority under it. He argues that what accounts for S possessing authority over O is that it has de facto authority over her.[60] His more plausible charge against the service conception is then that the fact that S has de facto authority over O, and that it satisfies the NJT does not entail that O is accountable to S. In effect, the fact that a particular offender is arrested in Chile, and that courts in Chile satisfy the NJT does not automatically entail that Chile has the normative power to punish O for theft. Chile would lack that power, for example, if she perpetrated that offence in Iran.

But this criticism seems wholly misplaced. State S satisfying the NJT and having de facto authority are simply necessary conditions for S to have authority over a defendant on a given matter. What explains the scope of its justified power is, by contrast, the fact that individuals in Iran (and not in Chile) have an interest in her in particular being punished that is sufficiently important to warrant conferring upon Iran (in particular) such power. As Raz puts it, a central aspect of the service conception is that it separates the issues of the authority of the state and the scope of its justified power.[61] As argued in previous chapters, no particular

[57] Ibid. [58] Ibid, 5. [59] Ibid, 18. [60] Ibid, 18–19.
[61] Raz, *The Morality of Freedom*, 104.

relationship between state S and a given offender is necessary for individuals in S to have an interest in the offender being punished. The moral standing theorist needs some sort of relationship between the state and the relevant offender because she fails to see that what explains state S being justified in punishing an offender is also a necessary condition for S possessing the authority to do so. Namely, that individuals in state S have an interest in a particular offender being punished which is sufficiently important to warrant the protection of a right, and reasons to empower an authority to do so.

Antony Duff et al take the moral standing line of argument further in a direction relevant for our enquiry. They provide a normative account of the criminal trial that 'takes as its starting point the ordinary social practice whereby one person calls another to answer in the light of evidence of serious wrongdoing'.[62] They illustrate their view by way of the following example:

> I think you have been spreading gossip about me at work. I call you to answer. I outline the reasons that I think this, and if they are good reasons, it seems that there is a legitimate demand that you answer.... This seems right even if you are in fact innocent of spreading gossip about me.[63]

In order to call someone to answer, and eventually hold her accountable for what she did, they argue, one needs to have the appropriate moral standing, namely, the right to assess the moral nature of their conduct.[64] What explains a particular state S's moral standing to hold an individual accountable is the notion of citizenship. Citizenship, they suggest, involves a network of responsibilities, obligations, and rights that structure relationships between citizens, and between citizens and the polity.[65] As a result of these relationships, defendants have the responsibility to answer to the charge based on the fact that they are citizens of S.[66] The criminal trial should then be 'normatively understood as a process in and through which citizens are summoned to answer to their fellow citizens for their alleged public wrongs'.[67]

However, this is too hasty. As Mike Redmayne has suggested, their example involves acquaintances, and the moral obligations between citizens may well be different. For instance, if someone on the street falsely accuses me of scratching her car, it is far from clear that as a matter of justice I am under a duty to answer to her, or that she has any right to call me to account.[68] The crucial point is, nevertheless, that no matter whether one takes Duff or Redmayne's side, it certainly does not seem to make any difference whether the person calling me to account is in fact a co-national, a tourist, or someone calling on the phone from the other side of the globe who has never set a foot in S. Put differently, it is not that X lacks the

[62] Duff et al, *The Trial on Trial*, vol 3, 223. [63] Ibid, 209.

[64] Ibid, 155–6. [65] Ibid, 140. [66] Ibid.

[67] Ibid, 165. This is also consistent with Duff's own justification for legal punishment in that for punishment to reach an offender's moral conscience it is necessary that the relevant authority has the appropriate moral standing to censure her for her wrong. On a broader analysis of this theory see Chapters 2 and 3.

[68] Mike Redmayne, 'Theorizing the Criminal Trial', *New Crim L Rev* 12 (2009), 287–313.

authority to call us to account because we are not answerable to X; we are not answerable to X because X has no authority.[69]

The more interesting proposition is that we must appeal to the fact that an offender is a citizen of S to explain why it is S and not some other state, which might be similarly well suited to the task (or even better suited), that has the standing to punish her.[70] This statement shows precisely where my disagreement with this position lies. Making S's authority over an offender dependent on whether she is a citizen of S creates far more problems than it actually solves. First, this position sits very uncomfortably with the core intuition that foreign visitors are bound by S's criminal laws while on its territory. Though Duff et al explicitly state that S's right to call to account applies to them, they fail to give any reason as to why this would be the case.[71] Secondly, their position would not be able to explain some standard cases of how criminal jurisdiction is currently distributed as a matter of international law. For instance, it would fail to explain why Scotland had the power to punish anyone (at least, anyone who is not a Scottish national) for the Lockerbie incident,[72] or why Uruguay would have the power to punish offences committed by foreigners in France against its sovereignty, security, or important governmental functions. After all, there seems to be no nationality or citizenship bond between the relevant offenders and these states. Finally, by requiring this kind of relationship between the state and the offender, they would have trouble explaining why states have extraterritorial jurisdiction to try international offences committed abroad on grounds of universality unless, of course, the relevant relationship is rendered so thin that it would be hard to see what normative work it is actually doing.[73]

To conclude, then, the specific claim hereby advocated is not that state S should lack a certain moral standing in order legitimately to claim the authority to punish an offender. Rather, my position is that this moral standing does not rely on any special relationship between the offender and S, and in particular, not on the relationship of citizenship. This completes our general account of authority. In the following sections, this account will be tested against some common arguments often (though not exclusively) raised against the authority of extraterritorial courts.

5. Show Trials, 'Clean Hands', and the Problem of Victor's Justice

Prosecutions for international crimes have often been subject, legitimately or not, to the charge of being show trials. This charge was explicitly raised by Hess in the Nuremberg trial, by Milosevic before the ICTY, by Saddam Hussein before the

[69] Joseph Raz, 'On Respect, Authority, and Neutrality: A Response', *Ethics* 120/2 (2010), 301.

[70] This claim is also made by Hershovitz, 'Accountability and Political Authority', 21.

[71] Duff et al, *The Trial on Trial*, vol 3, 135–6.

[72] See *Her Majesty's Advocate v Al Megrahi* (High Ct Justiciary at Camp Zeist), verdict upheld on appeal (*Al Megrahi v HM Advocate*, 2002 SCCR 509).

[73] My critique of Duff's position is mainly developed in Chapters 3 and 5.

Iraqi High Tribunal, and can be inferred in the statements by Justice Rutledge of the US Supreme Court on the trial of General Yamashita, and Justice Pal at Tokyo.[74] There seems to be no agreement in the literature on what makes a particular criminal proceeding a 'show trial'.[75] But some instances hardly need elaboration. Meir Cotic recounts that in the Prague proceedings, Regulation of 25 January 1950 stated

> The court must inform the Prosecutor in advance of the judgement it is about to hand down and get his opinion whether the judgement is correct ... the Prosecutor's opinion is binding on the Court.[76]
>
> [D]ress rehearsals were conducted prior to these trials and these rehearsals were taped so that if a defendant deviated from the script, the microphone was switched off and the tape would begin playing the defendant's pre-recorded responses.[77]

There is little doubt that this type of judicial proceeding is illegitimate, and that a relevant state conducting this type of process would lack legitimate authority to punish those who are convicted. The more interesting question is why exactly this is so.

Saddam Hussein faced trial before the Iraqi High Tribunal (IHT) for a number of offences related to killings perpetrated in the town of Dujail in 1982. He was sentenced to death and hanged on 30 December 2006. During the proceedings, he robustly questioned the authority of the IHT: 'I do not respond to this so-called court ... what is built on illegitimacy is illegitimate';[78] and he specifically raised the show trial charge: 'this is all theatre by Bush'.[79] If he was right in that the legitimacy of the court was tainted, as many suggest he was, where does the normative force of his claim lie? The central problem with the IHT, and the Dujail trial in particular, is not necessarily that the verdict was inaccurate, but rather that it failed to provide the defendants with a fair trial. Among its main reported shortcomings are severe political interference, breaches to concrete fair trial standards, and serious evidentiary and analytical gaps. It is reported that the Higher National De-Baathification Commission repeatedly intervened in the Tribunal's appointments and removals and functioned as a 'sword over [its] work'.[80] Moreover, defence counsel had limited access to important evidence and the IHT denied defendants the full opportunity to contest evidence presented against them. There was a failure to gather and disclose exculpatory evidence which, in turn, impaired the opportunity to confront and cross-examine witnesses. Due to the fact that the trial was held amidst intense conflict, it was impossible for the defence to conduct its own investigations, particularly in al-Dujail village.[81]

[74] Gerry Simpson, *Law, War and Crime* (London: Polity Press, 2007), 108.

[75] For a recent attempt, see Jeremy Peterson, 'Unpacking Show Trials: Situating the Trial of Saddam Hussein', *Harvard International LJ* 48/1 (2007).

[76] Cited in Simpson, *Law, War and Crime*, 130. [77] Ibid. [78] Ibid, 105.

[79] S Tisdall, 'A Chance for Justice, but Will It Be Seized?', *The Guardian*, 19 October 2005.

[80] Miranda Sissons and Ari S Bassin, 'Was the Dujail Trial Fair?', *J of International Crim Justice* 5 (2007), 277. [81] Ibid.

Saddam's trial shows the explanatory power of the service conception of authority while at the same time capturing what it is that we find objectionable about 'show trials'. According to the NJT, the IHT's authority must rely on it improving the conformity to reasons which independently apply to the relevant individuals. The reason which justifies the IHT having the power to punish Saddam (inter alia) is that individuals in Iraq (and possibly elsewhere) have an interest in a criminal rule against mass killings being in force. For this type of criminal rule to be in force, Saddam must be punished, by an authority expressly authorized by the relevant legal system, and for having violated this criminal rule. Now, the fact that he was subjected to an unfair trial can hardly ground the perception that he was punished for violating such rule. Fairness is crucial to credibility. This holds even if most people believed that Saddam was in any event guilty as charged. That is, lack of fairness harms the authority of any given body to try a particular offender in much the same way as lack of reliable evidence.[82]

But we can re-state this position in more general terms. Novelist Hilary Mantel has suggested, while discussing the trial of Louis XVI, that the problem in that instance was that Louis was in fact condemned before he walked into court.[83] The trial was perceived merely 'as window-dressing, as a curtain or blind held up to mask the operation of political will'.[84] Put differently, the problem with show trials is that they are little more than 'a polite assassination ... with the ritual trappings of the law'; they do not constitute a careful and fair evaluation of the conformity of the defendant's actions with the law, an assessment of her actual wrongdoing.[85] As a result, even if the defendant is convicted and punished, show trials do not convey the message that the violated rule is in force.

One may of course object that show trials are as a matter of fact capable of delivering public order. After all, Stalin used them in 1937–8 with considerable success to bring support to his 'kulak operation', which consisted in nothing other than mass killings ('smashing the enemies of the people').[86] However, this would be completely to misunderstand what the interest is that justifies having the power to punish offenders, and to turn it into a pure consequentialist argument based on conformity with any kind of rule. The Stalinist-type of public order is not based on the belief that certain criminal rules are in force and, what is more important, on these rules contributing to the sense of individuals being right-holders, and of these rights being warranted by the legal system. Rather, this type of public order is generally grounded on a 'who's next?'-type of concern.[87] In Findlay's words

[82] See, eg, Martha Minow, *Between Vengeance and Forgiveness: Facing History after Genocide and Mass Violence* (Boston: Beacon Press, 1998), 50.

[83] See also Jon Elster, *Closing the Books*, 85.

[84] 'Rules of Evidence' lecture given by Hilary Mantel at the LSE, 10 November 2009.

[85] Ibid.

[86] Michael Ellman, 'The Soviet 1937–1938 Provincial Show Trials Revisited', *Europe-Asia Studies* 55/8 (2003).

[87] Mark Findlay, 'Show Trials in China: After Tiananmen Square', *J of Law and Society* 16/3 (1989), 356.

exposing the harsher and more arbitrary operations of the criminal sanction to wide public scrutiny may not appear as a re-establishing of justice, but rather as a reactivation of power.[88]

A second thing to note in the Dujail trial is that the issue of extraterritoriality did not have any significant bearing on the legitimacy of the IHT's authority to punish Saddam. The character of the IHT as a territorial, extraterritorial, or hybrid institution is a complex philosophical, legal, and political issue in its own right. On its website, one could read that '[t]he IHT is purely a national tribunal and this is beyond discussion'. However, its creation was authorized by the Coalition Provisional Authority,[89] its statute was reportedly drafted by US officials, and its personnel and judges were selected by the US-appointed Iraqi Governing Council.[90] Admittedly, reports from people on the ground seem to emphasize how keen the Iraqis were in running the show their way. Charles Garraway has commented that the defiance of due process standards that characterized the Dujail trial contravened the explicit 'advice' of the occupying powers, and was probably a symbolic form of claiming sovereignty over the proceedings.[91] In any event, my contention is precisely that the illegitimacy of Saddam's trial had nothing to do with it being connected with an extraterritorial authority, but rather stemmed directly from the lack of fairness of the procedure and impartiality of the court. In fact, it may well be the case that the only way for a court to satisfy the requirements set out by the service conception of authority would have been for Saddam to be tried extraterritorially by, for example, Sweden, or the ICC, or a special International Tribunal as some advocated at the time.[92]

It may be objected that the fact that the new Iraqi government relied so heavily on US military support would have undermined the legitimacy of the trial anyway. But this is not to argue on the basis of the show trials charge. If anything, this claim receives its moral traction from the charge of 'victor's justice'. This charge is at least as popular as the 'show trials' charge when addressing extraterritorial prosecutions for international crimes. Underlying it, however, there is a simple question that proves difficult to answer: how does the fact that state S *won* the war disqualify it from punishing an enemy war criminal? Rather, it seems to be the fact that S *participated* in the conflict that might undermine its authority to punish

[88] Ibid, 354. See also, D Brown and D Neal, 'Show Trials: The media and the Gang of Twelve' in Mark Findlay and Peter Duff, *The Jury under Attack* (London: Butterworths, 1988).

[89] Order 48, 'Delegation of Authority Regarding an Iraqi Special Tribunal', issued on 10 December 2003.

[90] Moreover, the US contributed some $128 million to its funding, a sum which dwarfs the Tribunal's own budget, and facilitated extensive security arrangements for the Tribunal and associated personnel. Most IHT functions, such as analytical, logistical, and investigative support, relied heavily on the Regime Crimes Liaison Office (RCLO), based at the US Embassy. Bassin, 'Was the Dujail Trial Fair?'. See, more generally, Michael P Scharf, *Saddam on Trial: Understanding and Debating the Iraqi High Tribunal* (Durham, NC: Carolina Academic Press, 2006).

[91] Kevin Heller and Charles Garraway (Public Lecture, 'A Poisoned Chalice: The Substantive and Procedural Defects of the Iraqi High Tribunal', 13 November 2007, LSE).

[92] See International Center for Transitional Justice, 'Creation and First Trial of the Supreme Iraqi Criminal Tribunal' (October 2005).

enemy combatants. The charge of victor's justice seems only to acknowledge, uninterestingly, that the losing side is rarely able to try its enemies.[93]

The only way of making sense of this broader claim is to suggest that a certain state's authority would be undermined by the fact that it would be deciding its own case. It might be argued in this type of case that the courts of state S lack impartiality and, as a result, legitimate authority to try an enemy war criminal. This, however, would be too stringent a requirement to sustain. First, it would lead, *a contrario*, to the implausible proposition that the states involved in an armed conflict would also lack authority to try their own combatants for war crimes because of the risk of prosecutions ending up in 'partial' acquittals. Moreover, this line of argument would also make very little sense in a domestic setting. This would mean, *mutatis mutandis*, that the Spanish courts would lack the authority to try foreigners for the Atocha bombings in Madrid. This is hardly a limitation most people would accept.

Ultimately, it seems that this charge once again stands on a mistaken analogy between states and individuals.[94] Most rules guarding the impartiality of courts normally make reference to the impartiality of specific judges, or jurors, but not to that of the judicial or political system itself. Moreover, rules on this issue are normally more stringent than this argument presupposes. It is the fact that judge J is the sister of victim V, not merely a co-national, that would undermine her authority to try V's attacker. In short, then, provided that the court complies with the conditions of the NJT and the DT set out above, the fact that the state to which it belongs participated in a given conflict is not a sufficient reason to hold that it would lack legitimate authority to try its own soldiers, as well as enemy ones.

This leaves us with the charge of *tu quoque* or, as I prefer to call it, the issue of 'clean hands'. This kind of argument was the speciality of Jacques Vergès, who is best known perhaps for defending Klaus Barbie, and who argued the case brought by the Democratic Republic of the Congo (DRC) against France for certain (extraterritorial) criminal proceedings before the International Court of Justice. His approach suggests that 'the real battle lay[s] ... in achieving control of the historical and didactic aspects of the' proceedings.[95] On that occasion, he argued that France had no standing to try the DRC's Minister of the Interior based on the nature of French colonial rule, the failure of the French authorities to indict President Chirac for alleged acts of corruption, and the racial bias underlying the French judicial system.[96]

A first version of the 'clean hands' objection suggests that, for example, Spain did not have the standing to try Pinochet, because it had been unable or unwilling to prosecute Spaniards for crimes against humanity committed in Spain during

[93] Hersch Lauterpacht, 'The Law of Nations and the Punishment of War Crimes', BYIL 21 (1944), 68.

[94] On the meaning and plausibility of the domestic analogy, see Chapter 1.

[95] Martti Koskenniemi, 'Between Impunity and Show Trials', 6 *Max Planck UNYB* (2002), 30.

[96] *Certain Criminal Proceedings in France (Republic of the Congo v France)* 2003, ICJ, oral proceedings, audience of 29 April 2003, available at <http://www.icj-cij.org/docket/index.php?p1=3&p2=3&k=d2&case=129&code=cof&p3=2> (last accessed 2 August 2010). See also, Simpson, *Law, War and Crime*, 106.

the Franco era. This allegedly shows some sort of moral hypocrisy, or at least double standards. This charge seems to imply—incorrectly in my view—that trials for crimes against humanity must start at home. Under the service conception of authority advocated here there would have been no significant problem with allowing Spain to try Pinochet, as long as he had been tried by competent judges, after a thorough investigation, and his procedural rights respected. Accordingly, this version of the clean hands objection does not seem to conflict with the argument for authority advocated here.

In fact, the charge of moral hypocrisy seems wholly misplaced. It has been argued above that international offences are those criminal rules that cannot contribute in any meaningful way to the sense of dignity and security of individuals in the territorial state unless at least some extraterritorial authority holds the power to punish offenders for them. This is because whenever this type of offence is committed on the territorial state it is the case that this state is either responsible for perpetrating, instigating, or allowing them, or simply unable to do anything about them.[97] Even in cases of regime change it is unlikely that the new regime will have the political power, or even the will to bring to account those members of the previous regime who are allegedly responsible for international offences. Chile and Spain are both standard examples of this. For instance, a request for the investigation of crimes committed during the Franco era in Spain has recently been sumbitted in Argentina.[98] Accordingly, the justification for extraterritorial prosecutions is based precisely on the ground that the territorial state would *not* normally prosecute offenders itself.

A second version of the 'clean hands' challenge would go: what if the actual regime is *itself* responsible for some international offence? Would this not undermine its authority to try enemy offenders? Surely a criminal state cannot legitimately claim this kind of authority. Had the Nazis won the war, is the argument advocated here committed to recognizing them as a legitimate authority to try the Allies for war crimes? One may say, of course, that it is unlikely that such a regime would satisfy the NJT. Iraqi law under Saddam, for instance, allowed for 'the admissibility of coerced confessions, the exclusion of Defence Counsel during some investigations, and some proceedings to be closed to the general pubic'.[99] In other cases blatant interference from the executive branch, or admissibility of evidence obtained through torture, would disqualify a state's claim for authority. Yet even if the Nazis had wanted to try Allied personnel for war crimes fairly, they would arguably still have lacked the legitimate authority to do so. This is not because the court itself would have necessarily failed to comply with the NJT, or the DT. Rather, the reason is that Germany punishing enemy offenders would not bring about the benefits of having a system of criminal laws in force. Individuals living under

[97] On this, see Chapter 3.

[98] See, eg, 'Presentan la primera demanda contra el franquismo en la Argentina', *La Nación*, 14 April 2010, available at <http://www.lanacion.com.ar/nota.asp?nota_id=1254162> (last accessed 2 August 2010). It is, admittedly, unlikely that it will actually proceed.

[99] Jose E Alvarez, 'Trying Hussein: Between Hubris and Hegemony', *J of International Crim Justice* 2 (2004), 324.

such a regime would not consider their fundamental rights protected by such laws; they would not consider a criminal state such as the Nazi regime bound by any of these laws.

The last and perhaps most difficult case is that of a state which, though perhaps being decent overall, has entered the war unjustly or failed to fight it in accordance with the laws of war.[100] This was arguably the position of the US and the UK after the Second World War where their authority to carry out war crimes trials was challenged on the grounds of their own behaviour in the Dresden and Hiroshima bombings. This charge points to the uneasy relationship between the categories of *jus ad bellum*, *jus in bello*, and *jus post bellum*. Whether they are logically and normatively interconnected is in itself a highly complex and controversial question that cannot be addressed here.[101] Still the conception of authority advocated here may provide a convincing answer in this type of case.

According to the service conception, insofar as the court satisfies the NJT and the DT, and is justified in punishing an offender, there is no good reason to disqualify its authority to try that offender. Few would argue that the US lacks the authority to try offenders domestically because of what it might have done in Abu Graib, Guantanamo Bay, or elsewhere. Whether it has the authority to punish a murderer in Minnesota ultimately depends on whether the competent court fulfils the requirements set out by the service conception.[102] Yet there might be no inconsistency in claiming that, for example, Israel has the moral standing to punish an offender domestically but lacks the standing to punish a member of Hezbollah. And the reason for this would be that although Israel has committed no crimes against its own people, it allegedly may have perpetrated some against the Lebanese.

This case is harder to make than one would initially think. The first thing that should be noted is that the charge of 'clean hands' consists in the claim that Israel lacks the authority to punish Hezbollah fighter O, not because of any crime against *her*, but rather for crimes it perpetrated in, say, Lebanon and against some of O's fellow nationals. Accordingly, we need to explain what the precise grounds of this charge would be. This objection cannot be simply grounded on nationality. The fact that some people who might have been unlawfully killed by state S military personnel were of state S2's nationality would probably not disqualify S from trying a group of S2 terrorists for hijacking a vessel flying S's flag on the Mediterranean. Similarly, this objection does not seem to rely on territorial considerations alone,

[100] For a standard notion of decency in this respect see Rawls, *The Law of Peoples*, 64–8.

[101] On this see, eg, Christopher Greenwood, 'The Relationship between *ius ad bellum* and *ius in bello*', *Rev of International Studies* 9/4 (1983), 221–34 and Marco Sassoli '*Ius ad bellum* and *ius in bello*—the separation between the legality of the use of force and humanitarian rules to be respected in warfare: crucial or outdated' in Michael N Schmitt and Jelena Pejic (eds), *International Law and Armed Conflict: Exploring the Faultlines—Essays in Honour of Yoram Dinstein* (Leiden: Martinus Nijhoff, 2007), 241–64.

[102] Duff et al touch upon a related issue when they discuss whether a given state can claim authority to try an offender under unjust socio-economic conditions. Ultimately, they suggest that the criminal trial is not the appropriate forum for this kind of claim, but rather that they should be discussed in a political forum (Duff et al, *The Trial on Trial*, vol 3, 156). In other words, they plausibly submit that we can never expect perfect legitimacy.

that is, on the fact that Israel might have committed crimes on Lebanese soil. If that were the case it would follow from this that Israel would lack the authority to prosecute and punish a Turkish national who is counterfeiting Israeli currency or passports in Beirut.

Rather, the only situation in which state S would lack the authority to try an offender is when, because of its criminal wrongs, it will not be deemed to convict her *for having committed a crime* by the relevant stakeholders. In such situation, the interest that explains its power to punish this particular offender, that is, the interest in a criminal rule against some wrongdoing being in force, would not be served. An example might clarify this point. It might be the case that the US lacks the authority to try Iraqi insurgents for war crimes committed against the Iraqi-established authorities even if those acts constituted crimes under international law. This is because the US would arguably be seen neither by the Iraqi people, nor it seems by anyone with a concrete interest in this type of act being punished, as enforcing the relevant legal rule prohibiting this kind of act. Yet we must be careful not to overstate the scope of this argument. It entails neither that the US would lack the authority to try an Iraqi counterfeiting US currency in Morocco, nor that they would lack the authority to try war crimes committed by or against their own soldiers in Iraq.

To sum up, then, the position hereby advocated is that the fact that state S's military forces have committed war crimes in a conflict against state S2 fighters or civilians, does not per se undermine S's authority to try and punish S2 war criminals. This, insofar as S is a minimally decent state, and is seen by the relevant stakeholders as credibly punishing offenders for the right reasons. Admittedly, it would not be easy to set out a list of criteria for when a state stops being minimally decent and becomes criminal in the sense that the Nazi state was arguably criminal. Similarly, it would be hard to establish a clear test that would tell us when a particular state would not be deemed to convict a given defendant for the right reasons. However, the aim of the theory here defended is not to decide where to draw the line, but rather to account for standard cases and provide a clear and consistent explanation for them.

6. Trials *in absentia* and of Defendants Abducted Abroad

This last section deals with two further issues that can arise in the context of extraterritorial prosecutions: trials *in absentia* and trials of defendants who were abducted or illegally transferred to the forum state. These issues do not pertain exclusively to the domain of extraterritorial prosecutions. Yet they constitute a sensitive issue that no theory of extraterritorial punishment can ignore. Ultimately, I will argue that while trials *in absentia* undermine a state's authority to try and punish a given offender, the fact that she is present before a court as a result of having been abducted or illegally transferred does not.

Let us concentrate first on the issue of trials *in absentia*. The question here is whether a state can render an authoritative verdict if the defendant was not present at her trial. We need not examine borderline situations, such as when she flees or absconds during trial or just before sentencing, or if someone is summonsed in an airport while in transit to a different state. Our interest is in the core issue of principle, namely, with whether, for example, France had the authority to try and convict Alfredo Astiz *in absentia* for crimes committed in Argentina.[103]

Although Article 14(3)(d) of the International Covenant on Civil and Political Rights (ICCPR) explicitly establishes that all defendants have the right 'to be tried in [their] presence', the general understanding is that there is no clear prohibition of trials *in absentia* under current international law.[104] Even the Human Rights Committee in charge of ensuring the ICCPR's implementation, noted that this provision 'cannot be construed as invariably rendering proceedings *in absentia* inadmissible irrespective of the reasons for the accused person's absence'.[105] According to a recent survey, of 139 national constitutions examined, only 25 prohibited trials *in absentia*, and most of these provided for certain exceptions to that general prohibition.[106] These exceptions include, standardly, unequivocal waiver on the part of the defendant, her causing disruption during trial, and her absconding once the hearing has started. In this context, it seems, there is hardly any point in examining this charge.

However, the status of trials *in absentia* is far from being as straightforward as these considerations seem to indicate. There are at least three elements in the law that undermine a state's claiming legitimate authority to try an offender *in absentia*. First, under the framework of the European Convention on Human Rights, trials *in absentia* are acceptable only insofar as the person convicted can obtain a retrial simply by asking for it.[107] In addition, this type of trial is far less popular in cases of extraterritorial criminal jurisdiction. The ICC, ICTY, and ICTR bar them almost absolutely. That is, defendants cannot be tried *in absentia* even if they fled or absconded after the beginning of the trial, and even if they have unequivocally waived their right to be present.[108] Although some hybrid tribunals have admitted

[103] See Fiona McKay, 'Universal Jurisdiction in Europe', Redress Trust (1999), available at <http://www.redress.org/downloads/publications/UJEurope.pdf> (last accessed 2 August 2010).

[104] This right is also recognized, albeit implicitly, in Art 6(1) of the European Convention of Human Rights, and it is implied by the confrontation clause contained the sixth amendment to the US Constitution. On the compatibility of trials *in absentia* with international law see, eg, Stefan Trechsel and Sarah J Summers, *Human Rights in Criminal Proceedings* (Oxford: Oxford University Press, 2005), 254; Cassese, *International Criminal Law*, 402; Mark Thieroff and Edward A Amley Jr, 'Proceeding to Justice and Accountability in the Balkans: The International Criminal Tribunal for the Former Yugoslavia and Rule 61', *Yale J of International Law* 23 (1998), 261; and Paola Gaeta, 'To Be (Present) or Not to Be (Present): Trials in Absentia before the Special Tribunal for Lebanon', *J of International Crim Justice* 5 (2007), 1174.

[105] *Daniel Monguya Mbenge v Zaire*, UNHRC, No 16/1977, para 76. This type of trial is not uncommon in many civil law countries (see, eg, the French Criminal Procedure Code, art 639). Although common law countries have tended to be more reluctant, the US, eg, has increasingly admitted this practice domestically (James G Starkey, 'Trials in Absentia', *St John's L Rev* 53 (1979)).

[106] M Cherif Bassiouni, 'Human Rights in the Context of Criminal Justice: Identifying International Procedural Protections and Equivalent Protections in National Constitutions', *Duke J of Comparative & International Law* 3 (1993), 279–80.

[107] See, eg, *B v France* (ECtHR), Application 10291/83 (12 May 1986) and *Colozza v Italy* (ECtHR), Application 9024/80 (12 February 1985).

[108] See ICC Statute Art 63; ICTY Statute Art 21(4)(d) and ICTR Statute Art 20(4)(d).

trials *in absentia*, they too provide for the possibility of retrial when the decision is challenged by the defendant.[109] Finally, the established law on extradition shows that while many states are comfortable enforcing their own convictions *in absentia*, they are far less happy extraditing offenders who have been convicted *in absentia* abroad. Some jurisdictions require that the requesting state provides evidence sufficient to support at least an indictment, but many may require a retrial or reserve the right to refuse to extradite the offender.[110]

The theoretical framework advocated here can help us to make sense of these seemingly conflicting claims. There is little dispute that a defendant has a right to be 'tried in his presence', to use the language of Article 14 of the ICCPR. Much hinges, however, on the actual structure of this right. One way of construing this right is in terms of a Hohfeldian claim-right. In that sense, the fact that a defendant has a claim-right to be tried in her presence only means that the state is under a *duty* not to exclude her from the proceedings by, for instance, denying her physical access to the courtroom. This possibly also entails a duty to notify her about the hearings, etc. There is, of course, little doubt that this right amounts at least to this. But this is not what the charge of trials *in absentia* usually concerns.[111]

A more ambitious way of describing this right is as also containing an immunity. This immunity would entail that the state simply lacks the power to try a defendant *in absentia*. Yet this interpretation of the right to be tried in one's presence has little promise. One would have to demonstrate that the interest of a defendant in being present in court is sufficiently important to put the state under a disability to try her. Put differently, this interest would have to outweigh the collective interest that individuals in that state have in its system of criminal rules being in force. In light of both the modest contribution that these rules being in force arguably make to these individuals' sense of dignity and security, and the serious consequences that follow from a criminal conviction, one may be tempted to conclude that this individual interest does suffice to confer upon defendants such an immunity. But this would be a rush to judgement.

We must note that the charge is simply that she is absent, not that the court is biased, or convicting her on what is clearly insufficient evidence. Furthermore, we must take into consideration the real implications of her absence. Sometimes courts carrying out trials *in absentia* will provide defendants with appropriate defence counsel *ex officio*. What is more, in most criminal proceedings it is the fact that the

[109] See Art 22(1) of the Special Tribunal for Lebanon Statute, rule 60 of the Special Court for Sierra Leone, and Art 114 of the SOC Law (Kram on Criminal procedure (8 February 1993), applicable to the Extraordinary Chambers in the Courts of Cambodia).

[110] Commentary, 'Foreign Trials in Absentia: Due Process Objections to Unconditional Extradition', *Stanford L Rev* 13 (1961), 377. The same rule applies in the UK (see, eg, Extradition Act 1989, s 6(2)). Even a strong supporter of trials *in absentia* like France has followed this trend. In the *Bozano* case (judgment of 18 December 1986, Series A no 111), France was ultimately condemned by the ECtHR for deporting the defendant to Switzerland, where he was to be extradited to Italy, after France itself refused to extradite him on the ground that he had been convicted *in absentia*.

[111] See criticisms by the Inter-American Commission in its *Report on the Situation of Human Rights in Panama* on this particular basis (OEA/Ser.L/C/11.44, doc 38, rev 1, 1978, accessible at <http://www.cidh.org/countryrep/Panama78eng/chap.4.htm>, last accessed 19 August 2010).

defendant's counsel is present, not the fact that the defendant is present, that best serves the defendant's interest.[112] Provided this is the case, then, it seems that her interest in not being tried *in absentia* is not as weighty as we might have initially thought and that, ultimately, there are other ways of protecting that interest which do not amount to conferring this immunity on defendants.[113]

The fact that the right to be tried in one's presence cannot be conceptualized as an immunity, however, does not exhaust the challenge that trials *in absentia* represent for the authority of a criminal court. This charge may still undermine the specific considerations on which the court's *authority* rests. The fact that under several legal systems trials *in absentia* warrant a right to request a retrial seems to confirm that these trials are seen as affecting specifically the *bindingness* of their decision, rather than their content.[114] For one, trials *in absentia* could affect a court complying with the NJT because the trials may undermine the accuracy of the verdict.[115] This would be the case, for instance, when the defendant is innocent, or there is some mitigating circumstance, as the defendant would know best how to defend the case. Yet this argument does not take us far enough. In other cases the incriminating evidence may be so overwhelming that the defendant's presence would not make much difference in terms of the accuracy of the outcome. The instances of trials *in absentia* that are the subject matter of the present analysis are such that a particular defendant, probably knowing about the existence of the proceedings, has deliberately decided to stay at large. Accordingly, she cannot complain about the inaccuracy of the result in much the same way as if she decided not to give testimony or point to crucial exculpatory evidence at trial.

Ultimately, trials *in absentia* seem to undermine the state's authority because they taint the credibility, even more than the accuracy, of the verdict. As suggested above, the state's authority rests not only on the NJT (and the DT for that matter), but also on the reasons that justify it meting out legal punishment on offenders, namely, that it contributes to the system of criminal rules being in force. For this to obtain, offenders have to be punished *because they violated these rules*. Yet when the credibility of the proceedings is compromised, as is arguably the case when a defendant is convicted *in absentia*, the fact that she is sentenced and eventually punished does not convey the message that the reason she is being punished is that she violated a criminal rule. Put differently, the sense of spuriousness that trials *in absentia* bring about stems from the fact that it is ultimately crucial that the defendant has herself, or through counsel of her choosing, the opportunity to

[112] Legal counsel is generally more effective in presenting evidence and scrutinizing the case of the prosecution, will not be perceived as trying to subvert the process in the defendant's favour, and will be less emotionally engaged. Duff et al, *The Trial on Trial*, vol 3, 212.

[113] Interestingly, this right was clearly understood as an immunity ('it deprived the court of jurisdiction') at the time when defendants were required to defend themselves without the assistance of counsel. Starkey, 'Trials in Absentia', 723.

[114] See, eg, the decision by the ECtHR in *Colozza v Italy*, Application 9024/80 (12 February 1985), *Gallina v Fraser* in the US, 278 F2d 77 (2d Cir 1960), art 639 of France Code of Criminal Procedure, and Art 22(3) of the Statute of the Special Tribunal for Lebanon.

[115] See Cassese, *International Criminal Law*, 403.

challenge the accusation if the trial is to be perceived as fair. This is illustrated by the fact that states themselves normally take great pains to ensure that defendants are present throughout the trial even against their will, going as far as keeping them in detention, or making them liable to arrest in order to be brought to trial if necessary.[116] *Ex officio* defence counsel cannot ultimately convey the belief that a particular defendant's interests are being appropriately protected. It is therefore only natural that states are reluctant to extradite offenders convicted *in absentia*. Giving an offender convicted *in absentia* the right to a retrial seems the appropriate solution. Yet, this simply means rejecting the bindingness (authority) of that state's original decision.

It may be suggested that, all in all, given the policy goals advanced by extraterritorial prosecutions (particularly those carried out for international crimes), and the difficulties they will normally have to confront, trials *in absentia* are preferable to impunity.[117] This objection, however, misses the particular claim on which the argument against them stands. The argument advocated here is that insofar as trials *in absentia* undermine the credibility of the court, they do not serve the interest that justifies punishing offenders in the first place. That is, either because the offender would remain at large, or because the reason why she is being punished is perceived as spurious, a decision reached *in absentia* would not contribute to our sense that the criminal rule that has been violated is in force, and that we have certain rights which the law endorses and protects.

Let us finally examine cases in which the defendant was abducted from the territory of a given state, and transferred to that of the abducting state to face trial. Abductions arguably are the most extreme case of illegal transfer, but the argument hereby provided should also hold for defendants who have been transferred to an abducting state by stealth, fraud, or other illegal means. This is a matter of concern in international prosecutions. The trials of Eichmann, Barbie, Milosevic, and Nikolic were all preceded by abductions or transfers of questionable legality.[118] Moreover, this issue affects extraterritorial prosecutions for domestic offences with almost the same intensity, as the significant array of cases referred to below illustrates.

Before examining this issue, however, a final caveat is in order. The purpose of this section is to examine whether an abducting state would have jurisdiction to try a defendant, not whether jurisdiction should be exercised.[119] It might be that there are all sorts of prudential reasons why states should refrain from trying defendants

[116] This account is also compatible with the fact that in less serious cases, some jurisdictions do not require the presence of the defendant (see eg the UK's Magistrates' Courts Act 1980, ss 11–12). Indeed, when the consequences of the trial are potentially minor, as in a fine for a traffic violation, the sense of spuriousness dissipates.

[117] Stefania Negri in Michael Bohlander, *International Criminal Justice: A Critical Analysis of Institutions and Procedures* (London: Cameron May, 2007), 29; Daniel J Brown, 'The International Criminal Court and Trial in Absentia', *Brooklyn J of International Law* 24 (1998–9), 782.

[118] Simpson, *Law, War and Crime*, 116.

[119] F A Mann, 'Reflections on the Prosecution of Persons Abducted in Breach of International Law' in Yoram Dinstein, Mala Tabory, and Shabtai Rosenne, *International Law at a Time of Perplexity: Essays in Honour of Shabtai Rosenne* (Dordrecht: Martinus Nijhoff, 1989), 414.

who have been abducted abroad.[120] Yet the specific point in contention here is only whether a decision reached in these cases would be authoritative. To argue that a given state has the power to punish an abducted defendant in these situations is fully compatible with the proposition that it would be up to the abducting state, and only up to that state, to weigh the countervailing prudential reasons.

It goes without saying that a state which authorizes or conducts the abduction of a person from the territory of another state is responsible for a violation of public international law.[121] However, it does not automatically follow that it lacks jurisdiction to try her as a result of that violation. A further argument is needed. The traditional view is that an abducting state violates the victim state's claim-right to territorial integrity.[122] This violation purportedly entails the abducting state being barred from trying an abducted defendant. Under this view, a defendant would be entitled to raise this claim in court herself, but she would only have a 'derivative' standing to raise this violation as a bar to the exercise of jurisdiction.[123] This is because she allegedly suffered no greater deprivation than that which she would have endured through lawful extradition.[124]

This view, however, merits careful analysis. It would entail, for instance, that if the state from where the defendant was abducted consented to the abduction, even if given *ex post facto*, it would make the abduction unproblematic.[125] This is unconvincing. The fact that the victim state's authorities may have consented to the abduction of a particular defendant by officials of another state does very little to ease our central intuition that some moral wrong has been committed. Instead of considering that consent cancelled the moral wrong, we tend to see the state from where the defendant was abducted as an accomplice to that wrong.

Furthermore, this traditional view fails even if considered in its own terms. It is far from clear that even in cases where a state does *not* consent to the abduction, the necessary implication of the wrong is a bar to the abducting state's power to try a defendant. When abducting her, the state violated the other state's *claim-right* to its territorial integrity. This claim-right, as argued in Chapter 1, is explained by the interest of individuals in state S in foreign officials not physically enforcing

[120] Among the often-cited ones are the risk of international friction and the fact that states may sacrifice the recovery of many more criminals through regular means in order to obtain a few drug traffickers or terrorists. See Mann, 'Reflections on the Prosecution of Persons Abducted in Breach of International Law', 420; Geoff Gilbert, *Aspects of Extradition Law* (Dordrecht: Martinus Nijhoff, 1991), 185; and Richard Downing, 'The Domestic and International Legal Implications of the Abduction of Criminals from Foreign Soil', *Stanford J of International Law* 26 (1990), 592.

[121] See Mann, 'Reflections on the Prosecution of Persons Abducted in Breach of International Law', 405 and references in n 1 therein.

[122] The abducting state may also be said to violate its treaty obligations *vis-à-vis* the state from which the defendant was abducted when there is an extradition treaty in force between them.

[123] Rosemary Rayfuse, 'International Abduction and the United States Supreme Court: The Law of the Jungle Reigns', ICLQ 42 (1993), 886, citing *United States v Verdugo Urquidez* 939 F2d 1341 (CA9 1991).

[124] *Davis v Mueller* 643 F2d 521 (1981), cited in Mann, 'Reflections on the Prosecution of Persons Abducted in Breach of International Law', 418.

[125] See Art 16 of the Harvard Draft Convention on Extradition, which states that 'no state shall prosecute or punish [a defendant] ... without first obtaining the consent of the state or states whose rights have been violated' at *AJIL* 29 Supp (1935), 623.

their own laws on S's territory. It is unclear whether this particular interest extends to the abducting state lacking also the normative *power* to punish a defendant. These two Hohfeldian incidents belong to different levels. Thus, there seems to be no clear reason why compensation should be ruled out as the appropriate remedy for a breach of this claim-right. Or, put differently, there seems to be no reason why the only acceptable remedy for this breach would be the restitution of the defendant to the territory of the state from where she was abducted before she is tried. Ultimately, as Rayfuse suggests

> a claim by an offended State for a violation of its rights ... is a separate and distinct matter from the issue of whether an individual might be entitled to rely on that violation as a bar to the exercise of a domestic court's jurisdiction.[126]

To infer this bar from the former violation is to reason on the basis of a *non sequitur*.

A more promising line of argument is to see abduction as an infringement of some of an individual's rights. Arguably, these abductions violate the defendant's rights to personal liberty, and freedom from arbitrary arrest and detention.[127] The crucial question is, once more, whether these violations warrant conferring upon the abducting state a *disability* to try this defendant. This implication is far from straightforward. In the eloquent words of F A Mann,

> With rare unanimity and undeniable justification the courts of the world have held that the manner in which an accused has been brought before the court does not and, indeed, cannot deprive it of its jurisdiction, of its right to hear the case against the person standing before it.[128]

This is the central tenet of the famous US Supreme Court's *Ker-Frisbie* doctrine, and is illustrated by the old adage *mala captus bene detentus*.[129] Admittedly, the UK and New Zealand have stayed criminal proceedings on the ground that the defendants had been illegally abducted abroad.[130] However, these decisions were not based on the proposition that they lacked the power to try them. Rather, they were framed on them having discretion (the power) not to hear the case.[131]

[126] Rayfuse, 'International Abduction and the United States Supreme Court', 890.

[127] See, eg, Art 9 of the ICCPR, Art 5 of the European Convention on Human Rights and Art 7 of the American Convention of Human Rights.

[128] Mann, 'Reflections on the Prosecution of Persons Abducted in Breach of International Law', 414. For a list of papers both supportive and critical of this position see Jacques Semmelman, 'Due Process, International Law, and Jurisdiction over Criminal Defendants Abducted Extraterritorially: The Ker-Frisbie Doctrine Reexamined', *Columbia J of Transnational Law* 30 (1992), fns 20 and 21 respectively.

[129] Named after the series of cases by which it was established: see *Ker v Illinois* 119 US 436 (1886) and *Frisbie v Collins* 342 US 519 (1952). For a more recent application of this doctrine see *United States v Alvarez Machain* 504 US 655 (1992).

[130] *Connelly v DPP* [1964] AC 1254 and *R v Hartley* [1978] 2 NZLR 199, respectively.

[131] In *R v Horseferry Road Magistrates Court, ex parte Bennett* [1994] 1 AC 42, the House of Lords held that the judiciary had the power to 'oversee executive action and to refuse to countenance behaviour that threatens either basic human rights or the rule of law' (per Lord Griffiths at 150). Yet, as it has been correctly argued, this already assumes that UK courts have the power to hear the case (Rayfuse, 'International Abduction and the United States Supreme Court', 893–4). For a conflicting position see *S v Ebrahim*, 1991 (2) SA 553 (A) in South Africa and the Jacob-Salomon incident between

I want to argue that the fact that a defendant was abducted from a given state does not, per se, undermine the abducting state's authority to try that defendant. This may seem deeply counterintuitive,[132] but I suggest that this intuition is ultimately misplaced. Arguably, the abducting state's behaviour constitutes a violation of the *substantive* rule against abducting individuals. However, this does not necessarily affect any of the considerations on which its authority to punish her stands. The fact that a defendant was abducted abroad affects neither the NJT nor the DT. She can clearly be convicted (or acquitted) on the basis of accurate and reliable evidence, her procedural rights during the investigation and trial upheld, and the tribunal may ultimately decide on the basis of reasons which independently apply to individuals in the abducting state (whether she was innocent or guilty).[133] Finally, the credibility of the abducting state's courts in terms of the fact that this defendant is being punished *because she committed an offence* is not necessarily undermined by her abduction. At least trials of abducted defendants have never been criticized on these grounds. In that spirit, the US Supreme Court in *Alvarez-Machain* argued that the constitutional procedural safeguards of a fair trial were sufficient to satisfy the requirements of due process of law.[134]

Accordingly, the adequate response to the violation of the substantive rule prohibiting kidnapping is to punish its perpetrators. To put it differently, if the state of Virtuosia were to prosecute and punish also its own state officials who ordered and carried out the unlawful abduction (regardless of their position in government), or allow their extradition to the state in which the abduction took place, few people would still find it problematic that it claims the normative power to punish the defendant.

To support this case further, let me explain why the two main arguments on which the abducting state's disability is based fail. First, the question has been sometimes framed as a matter of extending the exclusionary rule beyond the suppression of evidence which has been illegally obtained to the suppression of defendants who have themselves been illegally seized and brought before the court.[135] The first thing to note is that the feasibility of this extension depends on the

Switzerland and Germany in the 1930s (in Lawrence Preuss, 'Kidnapping Fugitives from Justice on Foreign Territory', *AJIL* 29 (1935), 502–7; and his comment to the settlement reached by Switzerland and Germany in *AJIL* 30 (1936), 123–4). Yet the general position in South Africa seems to be compatible with the Ker-Frisbie doctrine (John Dugard, 'Abduction: Does the Appellate Division Care About International Law?', *South African J of Human Rights* 12/2 (1996), 324–8). Moreover, the authority of both South African courts under apartheid, and courts in Nazi Germany would be problematic under the account favoured here for other, and arguably more fundamental, reasons.

132 Many authors disagree with this claim. See, Duff, *Answering for Crime*, 182.

133 This distinction seems to be incorporated in the law of some countries. Interestingly, an individual who is abducted, or even illegally arrested, would be able to suppress statements or evidence provided during his illegal custody (see Robert M Pitler, '"The Fruit of the Poisonous Tree" Revisited and Shepardized', *California L Rev* 56 (1968), 601 and ff). The reason for this, I would suggest, has nothing to do with the fact that she was abducted per se, but with their lack of reliability.

134 On trial, the charges against Alvarez-Machain were dismissed on the basis of insufficient evidence (see, Rayfuse, 'International Abduction and the United States Supreme Court', 886–7).

135 Note, 'The Greening of a Poisonous Tree: The Exclusionary Rule and Federal Jurisdiction over Foreign Suspects Abducted by Government Agents', *NYU L Rev* 50 (1975), 682. See also Duff, *Answering for Crime*, 185–6.

rationale underlying the rule. This extension is normally based on the proposition that we exclude evidence obtained illegally to deter officials' misconduct during an investigation.[136] Accordingly, this rationale implies that we should also suppress the defendant's presence to deter abductions. This argument, however, fails to explain this purported implication in its own terms. Prosecuting and punishing the abducting state's officials themselves would have a much greater deterrent effect on abductions than simply returning the defendant to the state where they perpetrated the abduction. Moreover, maximization of the criminal law's deterrent effect would indicate that the abducting state should also seek to punish the defendant, instead of sending her back. Of course someone will object that, as a matter of fact, the deterrent effect of this state prosecuting its own officials would be very weak because it will normally be very reluctant to do so (let alone extradite them to the state in which they conducted the abduction). However, this is hardly a reason to advocate suppressing the defendant over punishing state officials. As most of the cases in this area show, states are as reluctant to suppress abducted defendants as they are to prosecute (or extradite) their own officials.

A further reason on which the abducted state's disability has been based is that its government should not be allowed to 'benefit' from infringing the defendant's rights. As the maxim says, *ex injuria jus not oritur*; that is, the abducting state should be barred from realizing the fruits of its unlawful act by bringing the accused to trial.[137] This argument, however, seems to be based again on a misuse of the domestic analogy. It implies that it is the government or state itself which benefits from the defendant being punished. This might be so in certain instances, but it is certainly not the reason why that state itself holds the power to punish the defendant. This power is essentially explained by the fact that it benefits the *individuals* who happen to live or be in its territory. Accordingly, insofar as it relies on the claim that it is the abducting state or its government which benefits from punishing the offender, this objection has a logical flaw. For it to work it should show that individuals in the abducting state lack an interest in the relevant defendant being punished by that state for her crime. Yet this interest seems to support the abducting state holding the normative power to punish both the abducted defendant *and* the officials who ordered and executed her abduction.

To conclude, it is submitted here that it would be mistaken to derive, *as a matter of principle*, that from a defendant's illegal abduction normatively follows a disability on the abducting state to put her to trial. Rather, the appropriate normative implication of this wrong is that the abducting state should also prosecute and punish those responsible for it. By doing this, it both enforces the belief in the

[136] Deterrence seems to be particularly popular with some American writers: see Pitler, '"The Fruit of the Poisonous Tree" Revisited and Shepardized', 580; Julie Philippe and Laurent Tristan, 'International Law, Extraterritorial Abductions and the Exercise of Criminal Jurisdiction in the United States', *Willamette J of International Law and Dispute Resolution* 11 (2004), 75. See also Judge Mansfield writing for the majority in *United States v Toscanino* 500 F2d 267 (2d Cir 1974). The US Supreme Court, however, has explicitly rejected this rationale with respect to the suppression of a defendant in *United States v Crews* 445 US 463 (1980).

[137] Mann, 'Reflections on the Prosecution of Persons Abducted in Breach of International Law', 415. See, also, Pitler, '"The Fruit of the Poisonous Tree" Revisited and Shepardized', 600.

rule against abductions being in force, and morally distances itself from the wrong suffered by the abducted defendant. By contrast, the appropriate remedy for the violation of her claim-rights is therefore a civil suit for damages, not her return to the state from where she was taken. This is also consistent with the claim that, as argued above, this state's consent to her abduction or its collusion with the abducting state's authorities should have no bearing on the latter's power or lack of it. That many would still feel uneasy with this proposed solution concerns the fact that few states would normally behave like Virtuosia. The US, for example, explicitly authorized the FBI to abduct foreign nationals subject to outstanding US arrest warrants currently residing abroad, and to bring them back to the US for trial.[138] Yet we should not misconstrue the implication of this fact. It might well be that the best way of *institutionalizing* the bundle of moral claim-rights, powers, and liabilities examined here is to put abducting states under a *legal* disability to punish defendants in this type of case. However, my point is that this solution would be based on expediency, not moral principle or analytical rigour.

7. Conclusion

This chapter closes the account of extraterritorial punishment. It advocates three main propositions. First, it argues that the question regarding the conditions that any body should meet in order to hold, itself, the power to punish a particular defendant is ultimately a question regarding whether it has the *authority* to do so. Secondly, it claims that Raz's version of the service conception of authority provides us with an insightful and convincing account of why (and when) we should recognize a given body's authority to punish a defendant, and what it means to consider its decisions authoritative. Finally, this chapter examines several charges usually raised against extraterritorial prosecutions such as the issues of show trials, 'clean hands', victor's justice, trials *in absentia*, and trials of individuals abducted or illegally transferred abroad. It argues both that, analytically, they are all arguments against some body X having the *authority* to punish a particular defendant D, not against it being justified in doing so; and that in every case whether X has the authority to punish D is unrelated to the issue of extraterritoriality.

[138] See Downing, 'The Domestic and International Legal Implications of the Abduction of Criminals from Foreign Soil'.

Bibliography

Abi-Saab, Georges, 'The Concept of "War Crimes"' in Sienho Yee and Wang Tieya (eds), *International Law in the Post-Cold War World: Essays in Memory of Li Haopei* (London: Routledge, 2001).

Akehurst, Michael, 'Jurisdiction in International Law', *BYIL* 46 (1972–1973), 145–257.

Alexy, Robert, *A Theory of Constitutional Rights* (Oxford: Oxford University Press, 2002).

Altman, Andrew, and Christopher Heath Wellman, 'A Defense of International Criminal Law', *Ethics* 115/1 (2004), 35–67.

—— *A Liberal Theory of International Justice* (Oxford: Oxford University Press, 2009).

Alvarez, Jose E, 'Trying Hussein: Between Hubris and Hegemony', *J of International Crim Justice* 2 (2004), 319–29.

American Law Institute, *Restatement (Third) of The Foreign Relations Law of the United States* (St Paul: American Law Institute Publishers, 1987).

Andenaes, Johannes, *Punishment and Deterrence* (Ann Arbor: University of Michigan Press, 1974).

Arendt, Hannah, *Eichmann in Jerusalem: A Report on the Banality of Evil* (New York: Penguin Books, 1994).

Arnell, P, 'The Case for Nationality Based Jurisdiction', *ICLQ* 50 (2001), 955–62.

Ashworth, Andrew, *Principles of Criminal Law* (5th edn, Oxford: Oxford University Press, 2006).

—— and Mike Redmayne, *The Criminal Process* (3rd edn, Oxford: Oxford University Press, 2005).

—— and Martin Wasik, *Fundamentals of Sentencing Theory: Essays in Honour of Andrew von Hirsch* (Oxford: Oxford University Press, 1998).

Baldo, Suliman, 'The Impact of the ICC in the Sudan and DRC' (2007) at <http://www.peace-justice-conference.info/documents.asp>.

Bancaud, A, *Une exception ordinaire: La magistrature en France 1930–1950* (Paris: Gallimard, 2002).

Bantekas, Ilias, 'Corruption as an International Crime and Crime against Humanity', *J of International Crim Justice* 4/3 (2006), 466–84.

Barry, Brian, *Culture & Equality* (Oxford: Polity Press, 2001).

Bassiouni, M Cherif, 'Human Rights in the Context of Criminal Justice: Identifying International Procedural Protections and Equivalent Protections in National Constitutions', *Duke J of Comparative & International Law* 3 (1993), 235–97.

—— *Crimes Against Humanity in International Criminal Law* (2nd edn, The Hague: Kluwer, 1999).

—— 'Universal Jurisdiction for International Crimes: Historical Perspectives and Contemporary Practice', *Virginia J of International Law* 42/1 (2001), 81–162.

Beale, Joseph H, 'The Jurisdiction of a Sovereign State', *Harvard L Rev* 36/3 (1923), 241–62.

Beccaria, Cesare, *On Crimes and Punishments* (Indianapolis: Hackett Pub Co, 1986).

Beitz, Charles, *Political Theory and International Relations* (1999 edn, Princeton: Princeton University Press, 1979).

Bentham, Jeremy, *The Rationale of Punishment* (London, 1830).

Berman, Mitchell N, 'Punishment and Justification', *Ethics* 118 (2008), 258–90.
Besson, Samantha and John Tasioulas (eds), *Philosophy of International Law* (Oxford: Oxford University Press, 2010).
Blakesley, Christopher L, 'A Conceptual Framework for Extradition and Jurisdiction over Extraterritorial Crimes', *Utah L Rev* 1984 (1984), 685–761.
—— 'Extraterritorial Jurisdiction' in M Cherif Bassiouni (ed), *International Criminal Law* (Ardsley: Transnational Publishers, 1998).
—— and Otto Lagodny, 'Finding Harmony Amidst Disagreement Over Extradition, Jurisdiction, The Role of Human Rights, and Issues of Extraterritoriality Under International Criminal Law', *Vanderbilt J of Transnational Law* 24/1 (1991), 1–73.
Bohlander, Michael, *International Criminal Justice: A Critical Analysis of Institutions and Procedures* (London: Cameron May, 2007).
Braithwaite, John, and Philip Pettit, *Not Just Deserts: A Republican Theory of Criminal Justice* (Oxford: Clarendon Press, 1990).
Brierley, James Leslie, 'The Lotus Case', *LQR* 44 (1928), 154.
Brooks, Thom (ed), *The Global Justice Reader* (Oxford: Blackwell, 2008).
Broomhall, Bruce, 'Towards the Development of an Effective System of Universal Jurisdiction for Crimes under International Law', *New England L Rev* 35 (2000–2001), 399–420.
Brown, Chris, *Political Restructuring in Europe: Ethical Perspectives* (London: Routledge, 1994).
Brown, Daniel J, 'The International Criminal Court and Trial in Absentia', *Brooklyn J of International Law* 24 (1998–9), 763–96.
Brownlie, Ian, *Principles of Public International Law* (6th edn, Oxford: Oxford University Press, 2003).
—— *Principles of Public International Law* (7th edn, Oxford: Oxford University Press, 2008).
Cafritz, Eric and Omer Tene, 'Article 113–7 of the French Penal Code: The Passive Personality Principle', *Columbia J of Transnational Law* 41 (2002–3), 585–99.
Caney, Simon, *Justice Beyond Borders: A Global Political Theory* (Oxford: Oxford University Press, 2005).
Carmichael, Stephanie, and Alex R Piquero, 'Sanctions, Perceived Anger, and Criminal Offending', *J of Quantitative Criminology* 20/4 (2004), 371–93.
Cassese, Antonio, *International Law in a Divided World* (Oxford: Clarendon Press, 1986).
—— *International Law* (Oxford: Oxford University Press, 2001; reprint 2003).
—— 'Terrorism is also Disrupting Some Crucial Legal Categories of International Law', *European J of International Law* 12/5 (2001), 993–1001.
—— *International Criminal Law* (Oxford: Oxford University Press, 2003).
Chander, Anupam, 'Globalization and Distrust', *Yale LJ* 114 (2005), 1193.
Christiano, Thomas, 'The Authority of Democracy', *J of Political Philosophy* 12/3 (2004), 266–90.
Cochrane, Alasdair, 'Moral Obligations to Non-Humans', LSE PhD dissertation, 2007 (unpublished).
Cohen, Stanley, 'Crime and Politics: Spot the Difference', *British J of Sociology* 47/1 (1996), 1–21.
Commentary, 'Foreign Trials in Absentia: Due Process Objections to Unconditional Extradition,' *Stanford L Rev* 13 (1961), 366–78.
Cooke, Walter Wheeler, 'The Application of the Criminal Law of a Country to Acts Committed by Foreigners Outside the Jurisdiction', *West Virginia LQ* XL/4 (1934), 303–29.

Cottingham, John, 'Varieties of Retribution', *Philosophical Quarterly* 29/116 (1979), 238–46.
Cowles, Willard B, 'Universality of Jurisdiction over War Crimes', *California L Rev* XXXIII/2 (1945), 177–218.
Cruft, Rowan, 'Rights: Beyond Interest Theory and Will Theory?', *Law and Philosophy* 23/4 (2004), 347–97.
Cryer, Robert, *Prosecuting International Crimes: Selectivity and the International Criminal Law Regime* (Cambridge: Cambridge University Press, 2005).
—— Hakan Friman, Darryl Robinson, and Elizabeth Wilmshurst, *An Introduction to International Criminal Law and Procedure* (Cambridge: Cambridge University Press, 2008).
Dagger, Richard. 'Punishment as Fair Play', *Res Publica* 14 (2008), 259–75.
Daly, E, 'Between Punitive and Reconstructive Justice: The Gacaca Courts in Rwanda', *NYU J of International Law and Politics* 34/2 (2002), 355–96.
Daniels, Norman, 'Wide Reflective Equilibrium and Theory Acceptance in Ethics', *J of Philosophy* 75/5 (1979), 256–82.
Darley, John M, and Paul H Robinson, 'Does Criminal Law Deter? A Behavioural Science Investigation', OJLS 24/2 (2004), 173–205.
Deen-Racsmány, Zsuzsanna, 'Modernizing the Nationality Exception: Is the Non-extradition of Residents a Better Rule?', *Nordic J of International Law* 75 (2006), 29–61.
Dennis, I H, 'Reconstructing the Law of Criminal Evidence', *Current Legal Problems* 42 (1989), 21–48.
Devlin, Patrick, *The Enforcement of Morals* (Oxford: Oxford University Press, 1965).
Dinstein, Yoram, *The Conduct of Hostilities under the Law of International Armed Conflict* (Cambridge: Cambridge University Press, 2003).
—— *The International Law of Belligerent Occupation* (Cambridge: Cambridge University Press, 2009).
—— and Mala Tabory (eds), *War Crimes in International Law* (Boston: Martinus Nijhoff, 1996).
—— and Shabtai Rosenne, *International Law at a Time of Perplexity: Essays in Honour of Shabtai Rosenne* (Dordrecht: Martinus Nijhoff, 1989).
Dolinko, David, 'Some Thoughts About Retributivism', *Ethics* 101/3 (1991), 537–59.
Donnedieu de Vabres, Henri, *Les Principes Modernes Du Droit Pénal International* (Paris, 1928).
Dorfman, Ariel, *Death and the Maiden* (London: Nick Hern, 1995).
Douzinas, Costas, *The End of Human Rights: Critical Legal Thought at the Turn of the Century* (Oxford: Hart, 2000).
Downing, Richard, 'The Domestic and International Legal Implications of the Abduction of Criminals from Foreign Soil', *Stanford J of International Law* 26 (1990), 573–99.
Drumbl, Mark A, 'Judging the 11 September Terrorist Attack', *Human Rights Quarterly* 24 (2002), 323–60.
—— *Atrocity, Punishment, and International Law* (Cambridge: Cambridge University Press, 2007).
Duff, Antony, *Punishment, Communication, and Community, Studies in Crime and Public Policy* (Oxford: Oxford University Press, 2001).
—— 'Criminal Responsibility, Municipal and International', 1–27. Unpublished manuscript (2006).
——— *Answering for Crime: Responsibility and Liability in the Criminal Law, Legal Theory Today* (Oxford: Hart, 2007).

Duff, Antony, Lindsay Farmer, Sandra Marshall, and Victor Tadros, *The Trial on Trial*, vol 3, *Towards a Normative Theory of the Criminal Trial* (Oxford: Hart, 2007).

Dugard, John, 'Abduction: Does the Appellate Division Care About International Law?', *South African J of Human Rights* 12/2 (1996), 324–8.

Dugard, John, and Christine Van den Wyngaert, 'Reconciling Extradition with Human Rights', *AJIL* 92 (1998), 187–212.

Dworkin, Ronald, *Taking Rights Seriously* (7th impression, London: Duckworth, 1994).

Ellman, Michael, 'The Soviet 1937–1938 Provincial Show Trials Revisited', *Europe-Asia Studies* 55/8 (2003), 1305–21.

Elster, Jon, *Closing the Books. Transitional Justice in Historical Perspective* (Cambridge: Cambridge University Press, 2004).

Evans, Malcolm D, *International Law* (2nd edn, Oxford: Oxford University Press, 2006).

Fabre, Cécile, *Social Rights under the Constitution: Government and the Decent Life* (Oxford: Oxford University Press, 2000).

—— *Whose Body Is It Anyway?: Justice and the Integrity of the Person* (New York: Oxford University Press, 2006).

—— 'Permissible Rescue Killings', *Proceedings of the Aristotelian Society* 109 (2009), 149–64.

Fassbender, Bardo, 'Reflections on the International Legality of the Special Tribunal for Lebanon', *J of International Crim Justice* 5/5: 1091–106.

Feinberg, Joel, *Doing & Deserving. Essays in the Theory of Responsibility* (Princeton: Princeton University Press, 1974).

—— *Rights, Justice and the Bounds of Liberty* (Princeton: Princeton University Press, 1980).

—— *The Moral Limits of the Criminal Law*, vol 1, *Harm to Others* (Oxford: Oxford University Press, 1984).

Fenrick, William J, 'Should Crimes against Humanity Replace War Crimes?', *Columbia J of Transnational Law* 37 (1998–1999), 767–85.

Findlay, Mark, 'Show Trials in China: After Tiananmen Square', *J of Law and Society* 16/3 (1989), 352–9.

—— and Peter Duff, *The Jury under Attack* (London: Butterworths, 1988).

Finnis, J M, *Natural Law and Natural Rights* (Clarendon Law Series) (2nd edn, Oxford: Clarendon Press, 2011).

Fletcher, George P, 'Against Universal Jurisdiction', *J of International Crim Justice* 1 (2003), 580–4.

Follath, Erich, 'New Evidence Points to Hezbollah in Hariri Murder', *Spiegel Online*, 23 May 2009, available at <http://www.spiegel.de/international/world/0,1518,626412,00.html>.

Fox, Gregory H, *Humanitarian Occupation* (Cambridge: Cambridge University Press, 2008).

Frey, R G, and Christopher W Morris, *Violence, Terrorism, and Justice* (Cambridge Studies in Philosophy and Public Policy) (Cambridge: Cambridge University Press, 1991).

Frossard, André, *Le crime contre l'humanité* (Paris: R Laffont, 1997).

Gaeta, Paola, 'To Be (Present) or Not to Be (Present): Trials in Absentia before the Special Tribunal for Lebanon', *J of International Crim Justice* 5 (2007), 1165–74.

García-Mora, Manuel R, 'Criminal Jurisdiction over Foreigners for Treason and Offences against the Safety of the State Committed Upon Foreign Territory', *U of Pittsburgh L Rev* 19/3 (1957–1958), 567–90.

García Vilegas, Mauricio, *Jueces sin Estado: La justicia Colombiana en zonas de conflicto armado* (Bogotá: Siglo del Hombre, 2008).

Garrard, Eve and Geoffrey Scarre, *Moral Philosophy and the Holocaust* (Aldershot: Ashgate, 2003).

George Jr, B J, 'Extraterritorial Application of Penal Legislation', *Michigan L Rev* 64/4 (1966), 609–38.

Geras, Norman, *The Contract of Mutual Indifference: Political Philosophy after the Holocaust* (London: Verso, 1998).

Gilbert, Geoff, *Aspects of Extradition Law* (Dordrecht: Martinus Nijhoff, 1991).

—— 'Crimes sans Frontières: Jurisdictional Problems in English Law', *BYIL* 63 (1992), 415–42.

—— *Responding to International Crime* (2nd edn, Leiden: Martinus Nijhoff, 2006).

Ginsburgs, George, and V N Kudriavtsev (eds), *The Nuremberg Trials and International Law* (London: Martinus Nijhoff, 1990).

Glenny, Misha, *Mcmafia: A Journey through the Global Criminal Underworld* (1st ed edn, New York: Knopf Books, 2008).

Green, Leslie C, *The Contemporary Law of Armed Conflict* (3rd edn, Manchester: Manchester University Press, 2008).

Greenwood, Christopher, 'The Relationship between *ius ad bellum* and *ius in bello*', *Rev of International Studies* 9/4 (1983), 221–34

Grisby, W E, 'Mixed Courts of Egypt', *LQR* 12/3 (1896), 252–9.

Guest, Iain, *Behind the Disappearances: Argentina's Dirty War against Human Rights and the United Nations, Pennsylvania Studies in Human Rights* (Philadelphia: University of Pennsylvania Press, 1990).

Hacker, P M S, and Joseph Raz, *Law, Morality and Society* (Oxford: Clarendon Press, 1977).

Haque, Adil Ahmed, 'Group Violence and Group Vengeance: Toward a Retributivist Theory of International Criminal Law', *Buffalo Crim L Rev* 9 (2005), 273–328.

Harris, D J, *Cases and Materials on International Law* (6th edn, London: Sweet & Maxwell, 2004).

Hart, H L A, *Law, Liberty and Morality* (Stanford: Stanford University Press, 1963).

—— *Punishment and Responsibility: Essays in the Philosophy of Law* (rev edn, Oxford: Clarendon Press, 1978).

—— 'Between Utility and Rights', *Columbia L Rev* 79/5 (1979), 828–46.

—— *Essays on Bentham* (Oxford: Oxford University Press, 1982; reprint 2001).

—— *The Concept of Law* (2nd edn, Oxford: Clarendon Press, 1997).

Harvard Research in International Law, 'The Law of Nationality', *AJIL* 23 Supp (1929).

—— 'Draft Convention on Extradition', AJIL 29 Supp (1935), 21–428.

—— 'Draft Convention on Jurisdiction with Respect to Crime', *AJIL* 29 Supp (1935), 435–651.

Held, David, 'Law of States, Law of Peoples', *Legal Theory* 8/2 (2002), 1–44.

Hershovitz, Scott, 'Accountability and Political Authority'. Unpublished paper (2008).

Higgins, Rosalyn, *Problems and Process: International Law and How We Use It* (Oxford: Clarendon Press, 1994).

Higgins, Rosalyn, and Maurice Flory (eds), *Terrorism and International Law* (London: Routledge, 1997).

Himma, Kenneth Einar, 'Just 'Cause You're Smarter Than Me Doesn't Give You a Right to Tell Me What to Do: Legitimate Authority and the Normal Justification Thesis', *OJLS* 27/1 (2007), 121–50.

Hinsley, Francis Harry, *Sovereignty* (1986 edn, Cambridge: Cambridge University Press, 1966).

Hirst, Michael, *Jurisdiction and the Ambit of the Criminal Law* (Oxford: Oxford University Press, 2003).

Hobbes, Thomas, *Leviathan* (Indianapolis: Hackett, 1994).

Hohfeld, Wesley, *Fundamental Legal Conceptions* (New Haven: Yale University Press, 1919).

Holmes, John T, and Philippe Kirsch, 'The Rome Conference on an International Criminal Court: The Negotiating Process', *AJIL* 93/2 (1999), 2–12.

Honderich, Ted, *Punishment: The Supposed Justifications* (rev ed edn, Harmondsworth: Pelican Books, 1984).

—— *Terrorism for Humanity: Inquiries in Political Philosophy* (rev edn, London/Sterling, VA: Pluto Press, 2003).

Human Rights Watch, 'Under Cover of War. Hamas Political Violence in Gaza'. April 2009.

Hurd, Heidi M, *Moral Combat, Cambridge Studies in Philosophy and Law* (Cambridge: Cambridge University Press, 1999).

Hwang, Phillis, 'Defining Crimes against Humanity in the Rome Statute of the International Criminal Court', *Fordham International LJ* 22 (1999), 457–504.

International Center for Transitional Justice, 'Creation and First Trial of the Supreme Iraqi Criminal Tribunal'. Briefing paper, October 2005.

Iturralde, Manuel A, *Castigo y liberalismo autoritario: la justicia penal de excepción en Colombia* (Bogotá: Siglo del Hombre, 2009).

Jessup, Philip C, *Transnational Law* (New Haven: Yale University Press, 1956).

Jones, Peter, *Rights* (London: Macmillan, 1994).

—— 'Group Rights and Group Oppression', *J of Political Philosophy* 7/4 (1999), 353–77.

Joyner, Christopher C, 'Arresting Impunity: The Case for Universal Jurisdiction in Bringing War Criminals to Accountability', *Law and Contemporary Problems* 59/4 (1996), 153–72.

Kaldor, Mary, *New and Old Wars: Organized Violence in a Global Era* (2nd edn, Stanford: Stanford University Press, 2007).

Kassan, Shalom, 'Extraterritorial Jurisdiction in the Ancient World', *AJIL* 29/2 (1935), 237–47.

Kennedy, David, *The Dark Sides of Virtue* (Princeton: Princeton University Press, 2004).

Kershaw, Ian, *The Nazi Dictatorship. Problems and Perspectives of Interpretation* (2nd edn, London: Edward Arnold, 1989).

Kissinger, Henry A, 'The Pitfalls of Universal Jurisdiction', *Foreign Affairs* 80/4 (2001), 86–96.

Kontorovich, Eugene, 'The Piracy Analogy: Modern Universal Jurisdiction's Hollow Foundation', *Harvard International LJ* 45/1 (2004), 183–237.

Koskenniemi, Martti, 'The Future of Statehood', *Harvard International LJ* 32/2 (1991), 397–410.

—— 'Between Impunity and Show Trials', 6 *Max Planck UNYB* (2002), 1–36.

Kramer, Matthew H, and Hillel Steiner, 'Theories of Rights: Is There a Third Way?', *OJLS* 27/2 (2007), 281–310.

—— N E Simmonds, and Hillel Steiner, *A Debate over Rights* (Oxford: Oxford University Press, 1998).

Krizek, Monika B, 'The Protective Principle of Extraterritorial Jurisdiction: A Brief History and an Application of the Principle to Espionage as an Illustration of Current United States Practice', *Boston U International LJ* 6 (1988), 337–59.

Lacey, Nicola, *State Punishment: Political Principles and Community Values* (London: Routledge, 1988).
Latter, A M, 'The Government of the Foreigners in China', *LQR* 19/3 (1903), 316–25.
Lauterpacht, Hersch, 'The Law of Nations and the Punishment of War Crimes', *BYIL* 21 (1944), 58–95.
Lietzau, William K, 'International Criminal Law after Rome: Concerns from a US Military Perspective', *Law and Contemporary Problems* 64/1 (2001), 119–40.
Locke, John, *Two Treatises of Government* (ed Peter Laslett) (Cambridge: Cambridge University Press, 1988).
Lowe, Vaughan, *Extraterritorial Jurisdiction: An Annotated Collection of Legal Materials* (Cambridge: Grotius, 1983).
—— '"Clear and Present Danger": Responses to Terrorism', *ICLQ* 54 (2005), 185–96.
Luban, David, 'A Theory of Crimes against Humanity', *Yale J of International Law* 29 (2004), 85–167.
MacCormick, Neil, *Legal Reasoning and Legal Theory* (Oxford: Oxford University Press, 1978).
Macedo, Stephen, *Universal Jurisdiction: National Courts and the Prosecution of Serious Crimes under International Law* (Philadelphia: University of Pennsylvania Press, 2004).
Mackie, John, 'Morality and the Retributive Emotions', *Crim Justice Ethics* 1/1 (1982), 3–10.
Malamud-Goti, Jaime, 'Transitional Governments in the Breach: Why Punish State Criminals', *Human Rights Quarterly* 12/1 (1990), 1–16.
—— *Game without End: State Terror and the Politics of Justice* (Norman: University of Oklahoma Press, 1996).
Mann, F A, 'Doctrine of International Jurisdiction' in *Further Studies in International Law* (Oxford: Clarendon Press, 1990).
Manton, Martin T, 'Extradition of Nationals', *Temple LQ* 19 (1935), 12–24.
Maogoto, Jackson Nyamuya, 'Countering Terrorism: From Wigged Judges to Helmeted Soldiers—Legal Perspectives on America's Counter-Terrorism Responses', *San Diego International LJ* 6 (2004–2005), 243–94.
Matravers, Matt, *Punishment and Political Theory* (Oxford: Hart, 1999).
May, Larry, *Crimes against Humanity: A Normative Account* (Cambridge: Cambridge University Press, 2005).
—— 'Humanity, International Crime, and the Rights of Defendants', *Ethics and International Affairs* 20/3 (2006), 373–82.
—— *War Crimes and Just War* (Cambridge: Cambridge University Press, 2007).
—— *War: Essays in Political Philosophy* (Cambridge: Cambridge University Press, 2008).
McCarthy, John G, 'The Passive Personality Principle and its Use in Combating International Terrorism', *Fordham International LJ* 13 (1989–90), 298–327.
McGoldrick, Dominic, Peter Rowe, and Eric Donnelly (eds), *The Permanent International Criminal Court: Legal and Policy Issues* (Oxford: Hart, 2004).
McDermott, Daniel, 'The Duty to Punish and Legitimate Government', *J of Political Philosophy* 7/2 (1999), 147–71.
—— 'The Permissibility of Punishment', *Law and Philosophy* 20 (2001), 403–32.
—— 'Debts to Society', *J of Political Philosophy* 10/4 (2002), 439–64.
McGinley, Gerald P, 'The Achille Lauro Affair—Implications for International Law', *Tennessee L Rev* 52 (1984–5), 691–738.
McKay, Fiona, 'Universal Jurisdiction in Europe' (Redress Trust, 1999).

McMahan, Jeff, 'The Ethics of Killing in War', *Ethics* 114 (2004), 693–733.

Mégret, Frédéric, 'The Politics of International Criminal Justice', *European J of International Law* 13/5 (2002), 1261–84.

Meisels, Tamar, *Territorial Rights* (Dordrecht: Springer, 2005).

Meron, Theodor, 'Non-Extradition of Israeli Nationals and Extraterritorial Jurisdiction: Reflections on Bill No 1306', *Israel L Rev* 13 (1978), 215–29.

—— 'International Criminalization of Internal Atrocities', *AJIL* 89/3 (1995), 554–77.

—— *War Crimes Law Comes of Age: Essays* (Oxford: Clarendon Press, 1998).

Miller, David, 'The Ethical Significance of Nationality', *Ethics* 98/4 (1988), 647–62.

—— *On Nationality, Oxford Political Theory* (Oxford: Oxford University Press, 1995).

Minow, Martha, *Between Vengeance and Forgiveness: Facing History after Genocide and Mass Violence* (Boston: Beacon Press, 1998).

Mirfield, Peter, and Roger Smith, *Essays for Colin Tapper* (London: LexisNexis, 2003).

Moore, Michael S, *Placing Blame: A Theory of Criminal Law* (Oxford: Clarendon Press, 1997).

Morris, Herbert, 'Persons and Punishment', *The Monist* 52 (1968), 475–501.

Morris, Madeline, 'High Crimes and Misconceptions: The ICC and Non-Party States', *Law and Contemporary Problems* 64/1 (2001), 13–66.

—— 'Universal Jurisdiction in a Divided World: Conference Remarks', *New England L Rev* 35/2 (2001), 337–61.

Murphy, Jeffrie, 'Marxism and Retribution' in *Retribution, Justice and Therapy* (Dordrecht: Reidel, 1979).

—— 'Does Kant Have a Theory of Punishment?', *Columbia L Rev* 87 (1987), 509–32.

Nadelmann, Ethan A, 'The Evolution of United States Involvement in the International Rendition of Fugitive Criminals', *NYU J of International Law & Politics* 25 (1993), 813–56.

Nagel, Thomas, 'The Problem of Global Justice', *Philosophy and Public Affairs* 33 (2005), 113–47.

Nagin, Daniel, 'Criminal Deterrence Research at the Outset of the Twenty-First Century' in *Crime and Justice: A Review of Research* (ed Michael Tonry) (Chicago: University of Chicago Press, 1998).

Narayan, Uma, 'Appropriate Responses and Preventive Benefits: Justifying Censure and Hard Treatment in Legal Punishment', *OJLS* 13/2 (1993), 166–82.

Newton, Michael J, 'Some Observations on the Future of US Military Commissions', *Case Western Reserve J of International Law*, 42/1 & 2 (2009), 151–70.

Nino, Carlos Santiago, *Radical Evil on Trial* (New Haven: Yale University Press, 1996).

Note, 'The Greening of a Poisonous Tree: The Exclusionary Rule and Federal Jurisdiction over Foreign Suspects Abducted by Government Agents', *NYU L Rev* 50 (1975), 681–714.

Novaro, Marcos, and Vicente Palermo, *La Dictadura Militar 1976/1983: Del Golpe de Estado a la Restauración Democrática* (Buenos Aires: Paidós, 2003).

Nozick, Robert, *Anarchy, State, and Utopia* (Oxford: Blackwell, 1974; reprint 2002).

—— *Philosophical Explanations* (Oxford: Clarendon Press, 1981).

O'Keefe, Michael P, and C A J Coady, *Terrorism and Justice: Moral Argument in a Threatened World* (Carlton South: Melbourne University Press, 2002).

Orentlicher, Diane F, 'Settling Accounts: The Duty to Prosecute Human Rights Violations of a Prior Regime', *Yale LJ* 100 (1991), 2537.

—— 'Politics by Other Means: The Law of the International Criminal Court', *Cornell International LJ* 32 (1999), 489–97.

Osiel, Mark J, 'Why Prosecute? Critics of Punishment for Mass Atrocity', *Human Rights Quarterly* 22 (2000), 118–47.

Peirce, Garreth, 'America's Non-Compliance', *London Review of Books* 32/9 (2010), 18–22.

Peterson, Jeremy, 'Unpacking Show Trials: Situating the Trial of Saddam Hussein', *Harvard International LJ* 48/1 (2007), 257–92.

Philippe, Julie, and Laurent Tristan, 'International Law, Extraterritorial Abductions and the Exercise of Criminal Jurisdiction in the United States', *Willamette J of International Law and Dispute Resolution* 11 (2004), 61–80.

Pitler, Robert M, ' "The Fruit of the Poisonous Tree" Revisited and Shepardized', *California L Rev* 56 (1968), 579–651.

Plachta, Michael, '(Non-)extradition of Nationals: A Neverending Story?', *Emory International L Rev* 13 (1999), 77–159.

Pogge, Thomas, *Global Justice* (Oxford: Blackwell, 2001).

Poland, James M, *Understanding Terrorism: Groups, Strategies, and Responses* (Englewood Cliffs: Prentice Hall, 1988).

Pollock, Frederick, and Frederic William Maitland, *The History of English Law*, 2 vols (2nd edn, Cambridge: Cambridge University Press, 1898 [1911]).

Powers, T, 'Black Arts', *New York Rev of Books* 52/8 (2005).

Preuss, Lawrence, 'Kidnapping Fugitives from Justice on Foreign Territory', *AJIL* 29 (1935), 502–7.

Primoratz, Igor, 'Punishment as Language', *Philosophy* 64 (1989), 187–205.

Pufendorf, Samuel, '*De jure Naturae et gentium*' in James Brown Scott (ed), *The Classics of International Law* (Oxford: Clarendon Press, trans C H and W A Oldfather, 1934 [1688]).

Puzo, Mario, *The Godfather* (New York: New American Library, 2002).

Radin, Max, 'International Crimes', *Iowa L Rev* 32 (1946–1947), 33–50.

Rawls, John, 'Two Concepts of Rules' in *Philosophy of Punishment* (ed Robert M Baird and Stuart E Rosenbaum) (New York: Prometheus Books, 1988).

—— *The Law of Peoples With 'The Idea of Public Reason Revisited'* (Cambridge, MA: Harvard University Press, 1999; 4th reprint 2002).

—— *A Theory of Justice* (rev edn, Cambridge, MA: Belknap Press of Harvard University Press, 1999).

Rayfuse, Rosemary, 'International Abduction and the United States Supreme Court: The Law of the Jungle Reigns', ICLQ 42 (1993), 882–97.

Raz, Joseph, *The Authority of Law* (Oxford: Oxford University Press, 1979).

—— 'Authority and Justification', *Philosophy and Public Affairs* 14/1 (1985), 2–29.

—— *The Morality of Freedom* (Oxford: Oxford University Press, 1988).

—— *Ethics in the Public Domain: Essays in the Morality of Law and Politics* (Oxford: Clarendon Press, 1994).

—— *Practical Reason and Norms* (Oxford: Oxford University Press, 1999).

—— 'The Problem of Authority', *Minnesota L Rev* 90 (2006), 1003–44.

—— 'Human Rights without Foundations' (Oxford Legal Studies Research Paper Series) WP 14/2007.

—— 'On Respect, Authority, and Neutrality: A Response', *Ethics* 120/2 (2010), 279–301.

Recent Developments, 'Protective Principle of Jurisdiction Applied to Uphold Statute Intended to Have Extra-Territorial Effect', *Columbia L Rev* 62/2 (1962), 371–75.

Redmayne, Mike, 'Theorizing the Criminal Trial', *New Crim L Rev* 12 (2009), 287–313.

Reisman, M, 'In Defence of Public Order', *AJIL* 95/4 (2001), 833.

Renzo, Massimo, 'A Criticism of the International Harm Principle', *Crim Law and Philosophy* (forthcoming, 2011).

Reus-Smit, Christian, *The Moral Purpose of the State* (Princeton: Princeton University Press, 1999).

Reydams, Luc, *Universal Jurisdiction: International and Municipal Legal Perspectives* (Oxford: Oxford University Press, 2003).

Roberts, Paul, and Lucy Carver, 'Penal Law and Global Justice'. Draft paper (2008), on file with the author.

Robertson, Geoffrey, *Crimes against Humanity* (London: Allen Lane, 1999).

Rodin, David, *War & Self-Defense* (Oxford: Clarendon Press, 2003).

—— 'Terrorism without Intention', *Ethics* 114 (2004), 752–71.

Roth, Kenneth, 'The Case for Universal Jurisdiction', *Foreign Affairs* 80/5 (2001), 150–4.

Rubin, Alfred P, *The Law of Piracy* (2nd edn, Irvington-on-Hudson: Transnational, 1998).

—— 'The International Criminal Court: Possibilities for Prosecutorial Abuse', *Law and Contemporary Problems* 64 (2001), 153–65.

Ryngaert, Cedric, *Jurisdiction in International Law* (Oxford: Oxford University Press, 2008).

Sabol, William J, and James P Lynch, 'Assessing the Effects of Mass Incarceration on Informal Social Control in Communities', *Criminology and Public Policy* 3/2 (2004), 267–94.

Safferling, Christoph, 'International Decisions: Public Prosecutor v. Djajic', *AJIL* 92 (1998), 528–32.

Sadat, Leila Nadya, 'Redefining Universal Jurisdiction', *New England L Rev* 35/2 (2001), 241–63.

Sammons, Anthony, 'The "Under-Theorization" of Universal Jurisdiction: Implications for Legitimacy on Trials of War Criminals by National Courts', *Berkeley J of International Law* 21 (2003), 111–43.

Schmitt, Michael N, and Jelena Pejic (eds), *International Law and Armed Conflict: Exploring the Faultlines—Essays in Honour of Yoram Dinstein* (Leiden: Martinus Nijhoff, 2007).

Sivakumaran, Sandesh, 'Courts of Armed Opposition Groups. Fair Trials or Summary Justice?', *J of International Crim Justice* 7/3 (2009), 489–513.

Schabas, William, 'Complementarity in Practice: Some Uncomplimentary Thoughts', *Crim Law Forum* 19 (2008), 5–33.

—— 'Genocide Trials and Gacaca Courts', *J of International Crim Justice* 3 (2005), 896–919.

Scharf, Michael P, 'The ICC's Jurisdiction over Nationals of Non-Party States: A Critique of the US Position', *Law and Contemporary Problems* 64/1 (2001), 67–117.

—— *Saddam on Trial: Understanding and Debating the Iraqi High Tribunal* (Durham, NC: Carolina Academic Press, 2006).

Scheffer, David, 'Opening Address at the Universal Jurisdiction Conference at the New England School of Law', *New England L Rev* 35/2 (2001), 233–40.

Scheffler, Samuel, *Boundaries and Allegiances: Problems of Justice and Responsibility in Liberal Thought* (Oxford: Oxford University Press, 2001).

—— 'Is Terrorism Morally Distinctive', *J of Political Philosophy* 14/1 (2006), 1–17.

Segev, Tom, *The Seventh Million: The Israelis and the Holocaust* (translated Haim Watzman, New York: Hill and Wang, 1993).

Semmelman, Jacques, 'Due Process, International Law, and Jurisdiction over Criminal Defendants Abducted Extraterritorially: The Ker-Frisbie Doctrine Reexamined', *Columbia J of Transnational Law* 30 (1992), 513–76.

Shachor-Landau, C, 'Extra-territorial Penal Jurisdiction and Extradition', *ICLQ* 29 (1980), 274–95.

Shane, S, 'China Inspired Interrogations at Guantánamo', *The New York Times*, 2 July 2008.

Shapiro, Scott, and Coleman, Jules L, *The Oxford Handbook of Jurisprudence and Philosophy of Law* (Oxford: Oxford University Press, 2002).

Simmons, Alan John, *The Lockean Theory of Rights, Studies in Moral, Political and Legal Philosophy* (Princeton: Princeton University Press, 1992).

Simpson, Gerry, 'The Guises of Sovereignty' in *The End of Westphalia* (ed Thakur and Sampford) (Tokyo: United Nations University Press, 2006).

—— *Law, War and Crime* (London: Polity Press, 2007).

Sissons, Miranda, and Bassin, Ari S, 'Was the Dujail Trial Fair?', *J of International Crim Justice* 5 (2007), 272–86.

Sloane, Robert D, 'The Expressive Capacity of International Punishment: The Limits of the National Law Analogy and the Potential of International Criminal Law', *Stanford J of International Law* 43 (2007), 39–94.

Smart, J J C, and Williams, Bernard, *Utilitarianism—For and Against* (London: Cambridge University Press, 1973).

Spector, Horacio, 'Value Pluralism and the Two Concepts of Rights', *San Diego L Rev* 46/4 (2009), 819–38.

Sponsler, Thomas H, 'The Universality Principle of Jurisdiction and the Threatened Trials of American Airmen', *Loyola L Rev* XI (1968–1969), 43–67.

Starkey, James G, 'Trials in Absentia', *St John's L Rev* 53 (1979), 721–45.

Stewart, Hamish, 'The Limits of the Harm Principle', *Crim Law and Philosophy* 4/1 (2010), 17–35.

Stewart, M A, *Law, Morality, and Rights* (Dordrecht: Reidel, 1983).

Steyn, Johan (Lord), 'Guantanamo Bay: The Legal Black Hole', *ICLQ* 53 (2004), 1–15.

Strawson, P F, *Freedom and Resentment, and Other Essays* (London: Methuen, 1974).

Sumner, L W, *The Moral Foundation of Rights* (Oxford: Clarendon Press, 1987).

Tallgren, Immi, 'The Sensibility and Sense of International Criminal Law', *European J of International Law* 13/3 (2002), 561–95.

Tamir, Yael, *Liberal Nationalism, Studies in Moral, Political, and Legal Philosophy* (Princeton: Princeton University Press, 1993).

Thieroff, Mark, and Edward A Amley Jr, 'Proceeding to Justice and Accountability in the Balkans: The International Criminal Tribunal for the Former Yugoslavia and Rule 61', *Yale J of International Law* 23 (1998), 231–74.

Thomson, Judith Jarvis, 'Self-Defense', *Philosophy & Public Affairs* 20 (1991), 283–310.

Tisdall, S, 'A Chance for Justice, but Will It Be Seized?', *The Guardian*, 19 October 2005.

Trahan, Jennifer, 'Military Commission Trials at Guantanamo Bay, Cuba: Do they Satisfy International and Constitutional Law?', *Fordham International LJ* 30 (2006–2007), 780–835.

Trechsel, Stefan, and Sarah J Summers, *Human Rights in Criminal Proceedings, Collected Courses of the Academy of European Law*, vol 12/3 (Oxford: Oxford University Press, 2005).

Tuck, Richard, *Natural Rights Theories: Their Origin and Development* (Cambridge: Cambridge University Press, 1979).

Uniacke, Suzanne, *Permissible Killing: The Self-Defence Justification of Homicide* (Cambridge: Cambridge University Press, 1994).

Van Schaack, Beth, 'The Definition of Crimes against Humanity: Resolving the Incoherence', *Columbia J of Transnational Law* 37 (1999), 787–850.

Vattel, Emmerich de, *Law of Nations; or, Principles of the Law of Nature, Applied to the Conduct and Affairs of Nations and Sovereigns* (trans Joseph Chitty) (reprint edn, New York: AMS Press, 1773; reprint 1982).

Vernon, Richard, 'What Is Crime against Humanity?', *J of Political Philosophy* 10/3 (2002), 231–49.

von Hirsch, Andrew, *Doing Justice: The Choice of Punishments* (New York: Hill and Wang, 1976).

—— *Censure and Sanctions* (Oxford: Clarendon Press, 1993).

—— and Andrew Ashworth, *Proportionate Sentencing: Exploring the Principles* (Oxford: Oxford University Press, 2005).

—— et al, *Criminal Deterrence and Sentence Severity: An Analysis of Recent Research* (Oxford: Hart, 1999).

Waldron, Jeremy, 'A Right to Do Wrong', *Ethics* 92 (1981), 21–39.

—— (ed), *Theories of Rights* (Oxford: Oxford University Press, 1984).

—— 'Terrorism and the Uses of Terror', *J of Ethics* 8 (2004), 5–35.

Walzer, Michael, *Just and Unjust Wars: A Moral Argument with Historical Illustrations* (3rd edn, New York: Basic Books, 2000).

Watson, Geoffrey R, 'Offenders Abroad: The Case for Nationality-Based Criminal Jurisdiction', *Yale J of International Law* 14 (1992), 41–84.

—— 'The Passive Personality Principle', *Texas International LJ* 28 (1993), 1–46.

Watts, Arthur and R Y Jennings, *Oppenheim's International Law*, vol 1, *Peace* (9th edn, Harlow: Longman, 1992).

Weill, Sharon, 'The Judicial Arm of the Occupation: The Israeli Military Courts in the Occupied Territories', *International Rev of the Red Cross* 89/866 (2007), 395–419.

Wellman, Carl, 'The Growth of Children's Rights', *Archiv für Rechts und Sozialphilosophie* 70/4 (1984), 441–53.

Wenar, Leif, 'The Nature of Rights', *Philosophy and Public Affairs* 33/3 (2005), 223–52.

Wendt, Alexander, *Social Theory of International Politics* (Cambridge: Cambridge University Press, 1999).

Wierda, Marieke, Habib Nassar, and Lynn Maalouf, 'Early Reflections on Local Perceptions, Legitimacy and Legacy of the Special Tribunal for Lebanon', *J of International Crim Justice* 5/5: 1065–81.

Wight, Martin, *Systems of States* (Swansea: Leicester University Press, 1977).

—— *International Theory: The Three Traditions* (London: Leicester University Press, 1991).

Williams, Sharon A, 'Nationality, Double Jeopardy, Prescription and the Death Sentence as Basis for Refusing Extradition', *International Rev of Penal Law* 62 (1991), 259–80.

Zaibert, Leo, *Punishment and Retribution* (Aldershot: Ashgate, 2006).

Zuckerman, Adrian A, 'Illegally-Obtained Evidence—Discretion as a Guardian of Legitimacy', *Current Legal Problems* 40 (1987), 55–70.

Index

The manufacturer's authorised representative in the EU for product
safety is Oxford University Press España S.A. of El Parque Empresarial
San Fernando de Henares, Avenida de Castilla, 2 - 28830 Madrid
(www.oup.es/en or product.safety@oup.com). OUP España S.A. also acts
as importer into Spain of products made by the manufacturer.
Printed and bound by CPI Group (UK) Ltd, Croydon, CR0 4YY
14/09/2026
02216307-0005